Why the Poor Pay More

Why the Poor Pay More

How to Stop
Predatory Lending

Edited by
GREGORY D. SQUIRES

Foreword by Clarence Page

PRAEGER

Westport, Connecticut
London

Library of Congress Cataloging-in-Publication Data

Why the poor pay more : how to stop predatory lending / edited by Gregory D. Squires ;
    foreword by Clarence Page.
        p.   cm.
    Includes bibliographical references and index.
    ISBN 0–275–98186–X (alk. paper)
    1. Discrimination in mortgage loans—United States.   2. Discrimination in consumer
    credit—United States.   I. Squires, Gregory D.
    HG2040.2.W49   2004
    322.7'43—dc22   2004011905

British Library Cataloguing in Publication Data is available.

Library of Congress Catalog Card Number: 2004011905
ISBN: 0–275–98186–X

First published in 2004

Praeger Publishers, 88 Post Road West, Westport, CT 06881
An imprint of Greenwood Publishing Group, Inc.
www.praeger.com

Printed in the United States of America

The paper used in this book complies with the
Permanent Paper Standard issued by the National
Information Standards Organization (Z39.48–1984).

10 9 8 7 6 5 4 3 2 1

Contents

Foreword: Loan Sharks in Pinstripes

Clarence Page

"The faults of the burglar," the playwright George Bernard Shaw once wrote, "are the qualities of the financier." Shaw's assessment, unfair to most major banking, aptly describes the less-scrupulous predators in the so-called subprime market who siphon money out of their unsuspecting customers' pockets like water through a hose.

Every year thousands of Americans take out home loans in good faith, only to have their faith in the American dream betrayed by practices that can best be called pinstriped loan-sharking. They find themselves paying excessive rates, far above the usual market rate in middle-class neighborhoods. A shortsighted desire for the fees that are generated by the loan moves some lenders to make loans based solely on a home owner's equity, even when it is obvious that the home owner will not be able to afford the payments.

The higher interest rates charged by lenders in the subprime market are intended to compensate lenders for taking a greater credit risk. But too many borrowers find themselves channeled unfairly into the subprime market. Borrowers with perfect credit can find themselves being charged interest rates three to six points higher than the market rates. No matter how good their credit may be, they are not offered a lower rate by some subprime lenders because there is no lower rate.

Many of those home owners find themselves subject to frequently high-pressure solicitations resulting in serial refinancing, a process called flipping. Some of those home owners eventually lose their homes for failure to keep up with the treadmill of excessive payments. Unscrupulous lending practices target the poor and the elderly, but are estimated to cost all Americans billions of dollars a year.

Predatory lending practices destroyed neighborhoods and accelerated white flight to suburbia in the late 1960s and early 1970s, when I was a young reporter covering housing issues in Chicago. In the wake of urban riots, President Lyndon B. Johnson signed the Fair Housing Act to help black home buyers acquire federally insured mortgages, from which they previously had been shut out by discriminatory federal policies. It did not take long for unscrupulous mortgage brokers to push FHA-backed mortgage loans, often on barely qualified buyers, then foreclose quickly when the home buyers fell behind in their payments, collect the full value from the FHA, and leave the home buyer homeless. Block after block of boarded-up houses with federal "No Trespassing" signs, most numerously in Detroit and Chicago, were the legacy of the federal government's best intentions cruelly exploited by mortgage hustlers.

Reforms cleaned up predatory lending, or so I thought. Unfortunately, the plague of predators is back, once again infecting the lives of families who are the most vulnerable to harsh shifts in financial winds. People who do not have many credit options are targeted, sometimes by small banks, sometimes by big banks working through subsidiaries. Sometimes all that the customer knows is that a check has arrived in the mail. Maybe it offers a couple thousand dollars. They cash the check, and soon more loan offers come—and more—often for bigger amounts of money. The money looks easy. The catch is high interest rates, repeated refinancing, costly fees, and high credit insurance. The predatory lender finances huge fees into loans, stripping thousands of dollars in hard-earned equity out of the property and racking up additional interest in the future. Loan officers at mortgage companies can earn big commissions and the house, once it is foreclosed upon, can be resold for a profit.

And here's the real scandal: it's legal. Mostly.

That's beginning to change. Many states have begun to enact their own anti-predatory lending laws, and anti-"preemption" resolutions have passed in Pittsburgh, Boston, Albuquerque, Philadelphia, New York, Bridgeport, Santa Fe, Providence, Washington, D.C., and Prince George's County, Maryland.

The new wave of predatory lending is beginning to stir a new debate on Capitol Hill. But with foreclosures soaring and thousands of predatory lending cases suspected, hitting communities across the country, more needs to be done.

As with most other neighborhood housing issues, the issue of predatory lending is closely interwoven with hot-button questions of race, economic class, the future of neighborhoods, and, in general, the ways in which we Americans want to organize the society that our children will inherit. This book offers a variety of expert perspectives, diagnoses, and prescriptions for the persistent problem of predatory lending. The goal of these authors is to expose the systemic flaws that have enabled today's sophisticated loan sharks to grab windfall profits and leave acres of broken dreams behind them.

For the sake of fairness and our country's future, I hope this book will lead to new reforms, effective reforms that will chase the feeding frenzy of predatory lenders back out to sea, this time for good.

1

The New Redlining

Gregory D. Squires

> It is clear that we need to focus a spotlight on predatory lenders whose sole purpose is to hijack the American dream from unsuspecting borrowers. We should leave no stone unturned to find and crack down on predatory lenders and Congress must pass the strongest legislation possible to end this pernicious practice.
>
> Senator Charles Schumer (D–NY)[1]

The American dream of owning a home has become an all-too-real nightmare for a growing number of families. Take the case of Florence McKnight, an 84-year-old Rochester widow who, while heavily sedated in a hospital bed, signed a $50,000 loan secured by her home for only $10,000 in new windows and other home repairs. The terms of the loan called for $72,000 in payments over 15 years, at which point she would still owe a $40,000 balloon payment. Her home is now in foreclosure.

And there is the case of Mason and Josie, an elderly African American couple with excellent credit and a primary source of income from Mason's veteran benefits. A broker convinced them to consolidate their 7 percent mortgage with some credit card debt. The first mortgage for $99,000 was at 8.4 percent, but the broker added a second mortgage for $17,000 at 13 percent. The initial loan financed almost $6,000 in broker and third-party fees, and both loans contained prepayment penalties for three and five years, respectively. In addition, both loans had balloon payments after 15 years. After making monthly payments of almost $950 for 15 years, they will face a payment for $93,000.

Other examples include a West Virginia widow who refinanced her mortgage seven times in 15 months, only to lose it in foreclosure. A disabled

Portland, Oregon, woman was charged more than 30 percent of the amount of her home loan due to credit life insurance and other financing fees that were added. A 68-year-old Chicago woman refinanced her loan three times in five years and found her monthly payments exceeded her income.[2]

Unfortunately, these are not isolated incidents. Predatory lending has emerged as the most salient public policy issue in financial services today. This book examines the rise of predatory lending practices and what is being done to combat them. If progress has been made to increase access to capital, including home mortgage loans, for racial minorities, low-income families, and economically distressed communities, that progress has always come with great struggle. And it appears there are few, if any, permanent victories. The emergence of predatory lending practices demonstrates that the struggle against redlining has not been won, but has simply taken some new turns.

After decades of combating redlining practices that starved many urban communities for credit and denied loans to racial minorities throughout metropolitan areas,[3] today a growing number of financial institutions are flooding these same markets with exploitative loan products that drain residents of their wealth. Such "reverse redlining" may be as problematic for minority families and older urban neighborhoods as has been the withdrawal of conventional financial services. Instead of contributing to home ownership and community development, predatory lending practices strip the equity home owners have struggled to build up, and deplete the wealth of those communities for the enrichment of distant financial services firms.

There are no precise quantitative estimates of the extent of predatory lending. But the growth of subprime lending (higher-cost loans to borrowers with blemishes on their credit records) in recent years, coupled with growing law enforcement activity in this area, clearly indicates a surge, if not a resurgence, of a range of exploitative practices with the economically most vulnerable populations most likely to be victimized. (Not all subprime loans are predatory, but virtually all predatory loans are subprime.) The Joint Center for Housing Studies at Harvard University[4] reported that mortgage companies specializing in subprime loans increased their share of home purchase mortgage loans from 1 percent to 13 percent between 1993 and 2000. *Business Week* reported that subprime loans accounted for 18 percent of all mortgage activity in early 2003.[5] Subprime loans are concentrated in neighborhoods with high unemployment rates and declining housing values.[6] Almost 20 percent of refinance loans to low-income borrowers were made by subprime lenders in 2002, compared with just over 7 percent for upper-income borrowers.[7] The Center for Community Change reported that African Americans are three times as likely as whites to finance their homes with subprime loans, and the racial disparity is larger at higher income levels.[8] The U.S. Department of Housing and Urban Development reported that residents of predominantly African American neighborhoods are five times as likely as those in white neighborhoods to receive subprime refinancing loans.[9]

The National Community Reinvestment Coalition found that even after controlling for credit scores and housing market variables, minority neighborhoods and neighborhoods with many elderly households were more likely to purchase or refinance homes with subprime loans.[10] Other econometric research has also revealed that race continues to be a factor in the distribution of subprime loans after other individual and neighborhood factors are taken into consideration.[11] The National Training and Information Center traced a surge in foreclosures in the Chicago metropolitan area to an increase in subprime lending. Between 1993 and 1998 home loan foreclosures doubled, while subprime lending grew from just over 3,000 to almost 51,000. Subprime lenders were responsible for 1.4 percent of foreclosures in 1993 and 35.7 percent in 1998.[12] Subsequent research on Chicago found that the rise in subprime lending between 1996 and 2001 was associated with a significant increase in the foreclosure rate in 2002, controlling for family income, unemployment rates, racial composition, owner occupancy rate, median property value, and other neighborhood characteristics.[13] According to William Apgar of the Joint Center for Housing Studies at Harvard, borrowers with subprime loans are eight times more likely to default than those with prime conventional loans.[14]

If most subprime loans serve the useful purpose of enabling high-risk borrowers to access credit for home purchase and refinance,[15] many of these loans do not serve the best interests of the borrowers. Fannie Mae and Freddie Mac have estimated that between 30 percent and 50 percent of those receiving subprime loans would, in fact, qualify for prime loans.[16] These borrowers are paying more than they should, given the level of risk they actually represent. A case study of Newark, New Jersey, found that the rise in subprime lending could not be explained in terms of borrower characteristics. In fact, among identically qualified borrowers, those taking out home improvement or refinancing loans in 1999 were 40 times more likely to be offered subprime loans than in 1993.[17] If subprime loans do benefit some consumers, those subjected to predatory practices are clearly not being served.

The distinction between subprime and predatory lending can be fuzzy. The National Community Reinvestment Coalition (NCRC) recently offered the following definitions to help clarify the differences. NCRC defined subprime lending in the following terms:

A subprime loan is a loan to a borrower with less than perfect credit. In order to compensate for the added risk associated with subprime loans, lending institutions charge higher interest rates. In contrast, a prime loan is a loan made to a creditworthy borrower at prevailing interest rates. Loans are classified as A, A–, B, C, and D loans. "A" loans are prime loans that are made at the going rate while A–loans are loans made at slightly higher interest rates to borrowers with only a few blemishes on their credit report. So-called B, C, and D loans are made to borrowers with significant imperfections in their credit history. "D" loans carry the highest interest rate because they are made to borrowers with the worst credit histories that include bankruptcy.[18]

Predatory loans are defined in the following terms:

A predatory loan is an unsuitable loan designed to exploit vulnerable and unsophisticated borrowers. Predatory loans are a subset of subprime loans. A predatory loan has one or more of the following features: 1) charges more in interest and fees than is required to cover the added risk of lending to borrowers with credit imperfections, 2) contains abusive terms and conditions that trap borrowers and lead to increased indebtedness, 3) does not take into account the borrower's ability to repay the loan, and 4) often violates fair lending laws by targeting women, minorities and communities of color.[19]

A variety of predatory practices have been identified. They include the following:

- Higher interest rates and fees than can be justified by the risk posed by the borrower.
- Balloon payments requiring borrowers to pay off the entire balance of a loan by making a substantial payment after a period of time during which they have been making regular monthly payments.
- Required single premium credit life insurance where the borrower must pay the entire annual premium at the beginning of the policy period rather than in monthly or quarterly payments; with this cost folded into the loan, the total cost, including interest payments, is higher throughout the life of the loan.
- Forced placed home insurance, where the lender requires the borrower to pay for a policy selected by the lender.
- High prepayment penalties, which trap borrowers in the loans.
- Fees for services that may or may not actually be provided.
- Loans based on the value of the property with no regard for the borrower's ability to make payments.
- Loan flipping, whereby lenders use deceptive and high-pressure tactics resulting in the frequent refinancing of loans with additional fees added each time.
- Negatively amortized loans and loans for more than the value of the home, which result in the borrower owing more money at the end of the loan period than when they started making payments.[20]

Targets of such practices are frequently older residents who have paid off their homes, particularly those who live in older urban neighborhoods with large minority populations. In other words, many of those families and neighborhoods that have long been underserved by traditional lenders find themselves victimized by what could be considered a form of reverse redlining. They are offered far more in the way of financial "services" than is in their financial interests. These practices perpetuate long-standing disinvestment of, and discrimination against, such communities and contribute to the uneven development of the nation's metropolitan areas.

SURGING INEQUALITY AND THE RISE OF A TWO-TIERED FINANCIAL SERVICES INDUSTRY

When Lester Thurow characterized the 1970s and 1980s as a time of surging inequality, he was also, perhaps unwittingly, accurately forecasting economic trends into the new millennium.[21] Income, wealth, and other key economic resources have become increasingly unequally distributed, with one outcome being heightened economic segregation of the nation's metropolitan areas. These developments have fueled unequal access to financial services and have prepared the ground for predatory lenders.

Various measures point in the same direction. Between 1967 and 2001 the share of income going to the top 5 percent of households grew from 17.5 percent to 22.4 percent. The share going to the lowest fifth dropped from 4.0 percent to 3.5 percent. In 1967 households in the top quintile received 10.9 times as much as those in the bottom quintile. This ratio grew to 14.3 in 2001.[22] Since the mid-1970s compensation for the top 100 CEOs went from $1.3 million, or 39 times the pay of an average worker, to $37.5 million, or more than 1,000 times the pay of the typical worker.[23]

Wealth has long been, and continues to be, even more unequally distributed than income. The share of wealth held by the top 5 percent increased from 56.1 percent in 1983 to 59.4 percent in 1998. This wealth disparity is the highest in the industrial world.[24] For most households, home equity is a major source of wealth. For half of all home owners more than 50 percent of their wealth is accounted for by the equity they have in their home.[25] Housing constitutes a more significant share of assets for racial minorities than for whites. Home equity accounts for two-thirds of assets held by blacks, compared to two-fifths for whites.[26] This reflects the lower share of home ownership among various racial groups—48.4 percent for blacks and 67.8 percent for whites in 2001—and disparities in the cost of home loans.[27] Biases in the nation's housing and home finance markets have cost the current generation of blacks approximately $82 billion, with the disparity in home equity between black and white averaging over $20,000.[28] And these were typical disparities for years before subprime and predatory lending took off in the mid-1990s.

Official poverty rates have declined during these years, but the concentration of the poor has increased. Between 1970 and 1990 the number of poor people residing in high-poverty neighborhoods, where the poverty rate exceeds 40 percent, rose from 1.9 million to 3.7 million. The share of poor people living in such neighborhoods went from 12.4 percent to 17.9 percent. The concentration of poverty is much greater for racial minorities, with 33.5 percent of the African American poor and 22.1 percent of the Hispanic poor, compared with just 6.3 percent of the white poor, residing in such areas.[29] During the 1990s the number of such tracts declined, as did the number of people residing in those neighborhoods. Despite the progress during the 1990s, the number of poverty tracts and the population of those neighborhoods were higher in 2000 than in either 1970 or 1980.[30] And the number of bankruptcies is up. Personal bankruptcies rose 15.2 percent for the 12 months ending in March 2002. The total number of 1.46 million bankruptcies was a record for any 12-month period.[31]

Not all communities are similarly affected by these developments. While suburban communities have become increasingly diverse in recent decades, with inner-ring suburbs in particular experiencing many of the problems long associated with inner cities,[32] in general, suburban communities have fared better than cities. Between 1970 and 2000 the suburban share of metropolitan populations increased from 55.1 percent to 62.2 percent.[33] A study of 92 large metropolitan areas found that three-quarters of the central cities lost private-sector employment market share to their suburbs in the mid-1990s,[34] while the rate of job growth reached 17.8 percent in the suburbs, compared with 8.5 percent in central cities between 1992 and 1997.[35] More significantly, per capita income for city residents dropped from 105 percent of suburban per capita income in 1960 to 84 percent by 1990.[36] Between 1970 and 1995 poverty rates in cities increased from 12.6 percent to just over 20 percent while rising slightly from 7 percent to 9 percent in the suburban rings.[37] From 1969 to 1998 the share of central-city families with low incomes grew from 21.9 percent to 25.5 percent while those with high incomes declined from 18.3 percent to 16.6 percent. For the suburbs those with low incomes accounted for 14.8 percent and 14.9 percent, while high-income families accounted for 26.5 percent and 25.8 percent during these years.[38] And while racial minorities moved to the suburbs in larger numbers during the 1990s, they continued to experience high levels of segregation, particularly in the case of African Americans in the nation's largest metropolitan areas.[39] Nationwide, levels of black–white segregation did diminish somewhat while Hispanic and Asian segregation increased. Still, the black–white index of dissimilarity (a measure of the distribution of two populations that indicates the percentage of either group that would have to move in order to achieve an even balance across the entire area) was .64 for African Americans, .51 for Hispanics, and .41 for Asians and Pacific Islanders.[40]

These numbers translate into very real quality-of-life barriers for a growing number of people, particularly in the nation's cities. Access to jobs is adversely affected for residents of communities most in need of employment. Health care is more difficult to obtain. The physical environment is more polluted. The cost of food and other consumer goods is higher. And financial services are less readily available.[41]

INEQUALITY AND THE RESTRUCTURING OF FINANCIAL SERVICES

Bank deregulation, in a climate of surging inequality, has fueled the emergence of a two-tiered banking system featuring predatory lending in a variety of markets.[42] The declining number of mainstream financial institutions in distressed neighborhoods, perhaps the most concrete manifestation of these changes, is both a cause and a consequence of the economic hardships those communities face. Between 1975 and 1995 the number of banking offices in low- and moderate-income areas declined by 21 percent while increasing by 29 percent overall.[43] That withdrawal has created opportunities for fringe institutions (e.g., check-cashing outlets, payday lenders, pawn shops, rent-to-own stores) to become prominent actors in those neighborhoods.[44] Between 1986 and 1997 the number of check-cashing businesses grew from 2,151 to 5,500.[45] A case study of Milwaukee, Wisconsin, found that in 1996 there were two banks for each check-cashing business in the city's economically distressed neighborhoods (as determined by the Milwaukee comptroller), compared to 10 banks for each check casher elsewhere. In predominantly African American neighborhoods there was one bank, compared with 15 in predominantly white areas, for each check-cashing business. For Hispanic neighborhoods there were two banks for each check casher, compared with eight banks in non-Hispanic communities. There was just over one bank per 10,000 households in African American areas, compared with six in Hispanic neighborhoods and almost eight banks per 10,000 households in white areas.[46]

Another cause and consequence of these developments is the large number of households with no bank accounts. Approximately 10 million households—that are disproportionately low-income, African American and Hispanic, young adults, and renters—do not have a bank account.[47] The primary reasons for not having such banking relationships are economic. The unbanked report that they have virtually no month-to-month financial savings to keep in an account. They also report that bank fees and minimum balances are too high and some are uncomfortable dealing with banks.[48]

However, there are many costs incurred by not having a conventional bank account. Such households often find themselves using check-cashing businesses to pay bills or cash paychecks, for which they are often charged 2 or 3 percent of the face value. This can add up to hundreds of dollars annually precisely for those who can least afford the costs. According to one Federal Reserve Bank report, a family with a $24,000 annual income using a check-cashing business will spend $400 in fees for services that would cost under $110 at a conventional bank.[49] Some households take out so-called payday loans, which are basically short-term (often two-week) cash advances on paychecks which frequently involve annual interest rates of 1,000 percent.[50] And these are not just one-time or occasional transactions. More than half of those who take out payday loans engage in seven or more transactions at one lender in a given year.[51] On the other hand, those with regular bank accounts are often offered a range of financial services, including credit counseling and lines of credit for various purposes (among them prime home mortgage loans) from their banks. Without that banking relationship, households are denied access to these services.[52]

In some cases, however, it is not that conventional lenders have left the central city. Rather, they may have closed their offices but then they invest or form partnerships with the check cashers, payday lenders, and other fringe bankers. For example, Wells Fargo, the nation's seventh largest lender at the time, arranged more than $700 million in loans between 1998 and 2002 to three large check-cashing chains: Ace Cash Express, EZ Corp., and Cash America. Mainstream financial institutions have created the opportunity for fringe institutions to enter the marketplace—often in partnership with the same institutions that have closed their own offices in the very same neighborhoods.

Ironically, some of the steps taken to increase access to credit for traditionally underserved communities have inadvertently created incentives for predatory lending. The Community Reinvestment Act of 1977, which banned redlining by federally chartered depository institutions (e.g., banks and savings institutions) and required them to serve their entire areas, including low- and moderate-income neighborhoods, along with the Fair Housing Act of 1968 prohibiting racial discrimination in home financing, and many other housing practices provided incentives for lenders to serve minority and low-income areas. FHA insurance and securitization of loans (whereby lenders sell loans to the secondary mortgage market, which in turn packages them into securities sold to investors) reduce the risk to lenders and increase capital available for mortgage lending. In turn, the federal government established affordable housing goals for the two major secondary mortgage market actors—Fannie Mae and Freddie Mac—whereby 50 percent of the mortgages they purchase must be for low- and moderate-income households.[53] Such acts have increased access to capital, but sometimes by predatory lenders.

It is precisely this environment, growing inequality and the restructuring of financial institutions, that has nurtured predatory lending in the home mortgage market. And bank deregulation, discussed below, portends more of the same in the near future. Again, it is not just marginal institutions that are involved. Wall Street has been a major player by securitizing subprime loans. Such involvement of investment banks in subprime lending grew from $18.5 billion in 1997 to $56 billion in 2000.[54]

With passage of the Financial Services Modernization Act of 1999, the consolidation and concentration of financial services that had been occurring for decades—often at the expense of already distressed neighborhoods—received the blessing of the federal government.[55] Between 1970 and 1997 the number of banks in the United States dropped from just under 20,000 to 9,100, primarily as a result of mergers of healthy institutions.[56] The 1999 act removed many post-Depression-era laws that had provided for greater separation of the worlds of banking, insurance, and securities than now exist. Subsequent to this "reform" it became far easier for financial service providers to enter into each of these lines of business. One consequence is that commercial banks and savings institutions, which formerly made the vast majority of mortgage loans, now make approximately one-third of all home loans as mortgage banking affiliates of depository institutions, independent mortgage banks, insurance companies and other institutions not regulated by federal financial regulatory agencies—including predatory lenders—have become a far more significant part of this market.[57]

A critical implication of deregulation is the declining influence of the Community Reinvestment Act. In conjunction with the 1968 federal Fair Housing Act and other fair lending initiatives, the CRA is credited with generating more than $1.7 trillion in new investment for low- and moderate-income neighborhoods and for increasing the share of loans going to economically distressed and minority markets.[58] Concentration and consolidation among financial institutions that had taken place for years—trends that were exacerbated by the 1999 act—reduced the impact of CRA by facilitating the entry into the mortgage market of many financial institutions that are not covered by that law. The share of mortgage loans subject to intensive review under the CRA dropped from 36.1 percent to 29.5 percent between 1993 and 2000.[59] Further evidence of the adverse impact of the 1999 act is the fact that the share of single-family home purchase loans to low- and moderate-income borrowers dropped from 29 percent in 2000 to 24.7 percent in 2001, after increasing steadily from 19 percent in 1993. Similarly, the share of loans going to African Americans dropped from 6.6 percent in 2000 to 4.8 percent in 2001 after climbing from 3.8 percent in 1993. For Hispanics the recent drop was from 6.9 percent to 6.2 percent after rising steadily from 4.0 percent at the beginning of this time frame.[60]

But the Financial Services Modernization Act of 1999 is not the last word on this debate. In many ways, community-based organizations, fair housing groups, and elected officials are responding to these developments and the predatory practices that have proliferated.

REACTIONS TO PREDATORY LENDING

Public officials, community organizations, and many lenders have begun to respond. Public officials, prodded by aggressive community organizing, have proposed many regulatory and legislative changes. During the 2001–2002 legislative year, five bills were introduced in Congress, 33 states considered new legislation, and 14 cities and counties debated local ordinances. One year later at least six states (North Carolina, New York, California, New Jersey, New Mexico, and Georgia) and three cities (New York, Los Angeles, and Oakland) enacted anti-predatory legislation.[61] As of the beginning of 2004 at least 25 states and 11 localities, along with District of Columbia, have passed laws addressing predatory lending.[62] These proposals call for limits on fees, prepayment penalties, and balloon payments; restrictions on practices leading to loan flipping; and prohibitions against loans that do not take into consideration borrowers' ability to repay. They provide for additional disclosures to consumers in the case of high-cost loans, credit counseling, and other consumer protections.[63]

In response to information provided and pressure exerted by the Association of Community Organizations for Reform Now (ACORN) and other consumer groups, the Federal Trade Commission (FTC) has taken enforcement actions against 19 lenders and brokers for predatory practices, and negotiated the largest consumer protection settlement in FTC history with Citigroup in 2002.[64] Citigroup agreed to pay $215 million to resolve charges against its subsidiary, The Associates, for various deceptive and abusive practices. The suit was aimed primarily at unnecessary credit insurance products that The Associates packed into many of its subprime loans.[65] In 2004 the Federal Reserve Board ordered Citigroup to pay $70 million for abusive lending practices. One practice was the conversion of personal loans to home equity loans without assessing borrowers' ability to repay, thus collecting short-term fees and subjecting borrowers to greater risk of default on the loans and loss of their homes. Citigroup was also cited for requiring a co-signer on loans to increase the sale of joint credit insurance when the borrowers in fact qualified for the loans on the basis of their own creditworthiness.[66]

The Office of the Comptroller of the Currency reached a $300 million settlement with Providian National Bank in California to compensate consumers hurt by its unfair and deceptive lending practices.[67] Despite the scope of the refunds and reductions in loan balances for the victims, some consumer groups maintained the settlement was inadequate, given the resources and extent of abusive practices on the part of the lender.[68] A month later Household International reached a $484 million agreement with a group of state attorneys general in which it agreed to many changes in its consumer loan practices. Household agreed to cap its fees and points, to provide more comprehensive disclosure of loan terms, to provide for an independent monitor to assure compliance with the agreement, and many other changes.[69] This was followed by a $72 million Foreclosure Avoidance Program that Household negotiated with ACORN, in which the company agreed to interest-rate reductions, waivers of unpaid late charges, loan principal reductions, and other initiatives to help families remain in their homes.[70]

The NCRC, more than 30 of its member organizations, and other nonprofit organizations have developed loan rescue programs in which they help victims of predatory lending to refinance those loans with lenders on more equitable terms that serve the financial interests of the borrowers. Such programs have been initiated in cities in every region of the country, including Atlanta, Baltimore, Cincinnati, Las Vegas, Milwaukee, and Omaha. Many lenders participate in these rescue programs and in related financial literacy programs to educate borrowers about financial services.[71]

Many lenders, often in partnership with community-based organizations, have launched educational and counseling programs to steer consumers away from predatory loans. One example is BorrowSmart in Richmond, Virginia. Financial service providers Wachovia Corporation and Saxon Capital joined with the fair housing group Housing Opportunities Made Equal to launch this counseling effort with several lenders and counseling agencies in that community. Consumers will be advised on the types of information they should obtain as well as what kinds of practices to be wary of in order to make them more knowledgeable borrowers.[72]

But progress cannot be assumed. Three federal financial regulatory agencies have issued opinions that federal laws preempt some state predatory lending laws for lenders they regulate. These include the Comptroller of the Currency, the National Credit Union Administration, and the Office of Thrift Supervision.[73] In communities where anti–predatory lending laws have been proposed, lobbyists for financial institutions have introduced state-level bills to preempt or nullify local ordinances or to weaken consumer protections. Legislation has also been introduced in Congress to preempt state efforts to combat predatory lending.[74] Preliminary research of the North Carolina anti–predatory lending law—the first statewide ban—suggested that such restrictions reduced the supply and increased the cost of credit to low-income borrowers.[75] Subsequent research, however, found that the law had the intended impact; there was a reduction in predatory loans but no change in access to or cost of credit for high-risk borrowers.[76] Debate continues over the impact of such legislative initiatives.[77] And the fight against redlining, in its traditional or "reverse" forms, remains an on-going struggle.

THE ROAD AHEAD

The following chapters elaborate on the origins, nature, and impact of predatory lending practices, how many have begun to respond, and current policy debates over future activity. Hopefully, these stories will inform and influence that debate.

The victims of predatory lending are not random. As John Taylor, Josh Silver, and David Berenbaum demonstrate in Chapter 2, "The Targets of Predatory and Discriminatory Lending: Who Are They and Where Do They Live?," exploitative practices are directed at racial minorities, the elderly, and in some communities Native Americans and female borrowers. The concentration of high-cost loans in these communities persists even after controlling for creditworthiness and a range of housing related factors.

Ira Goldstein vividly reveals many of the costs of predatory lending in Chapter 3, "The Economic Consequences of Predatory Lending: A Philadelphia Case Study." In Philadelphia, and no doubt most other cities, predatory lending has severe costs for households that are directly victimized and the neighborhoods where they live.

Chapter 4, "Predatory Lending Practices: Definition and Behavioral Implications," by Patricia A. McCoy, explains why victims do not behave as "rational actors" that traditional neoclassical market theory would predict in order to avoid abusive lenders. She demonstrates how the manipulative and fraudulent framing of choices (including the outright denial of information), coupled with high-pressure tactics, results in financially vulnerable households ultimately making bad decisions.

In Chapter 5, "Legal and Economic Inducements to Predatory Practices," Keith Ernst, Deborah N. Goldstein, and Christopher A. Richardson identify legal and economic forces that encourage predatory practices. They show how banking deregulation, coupled with securitization and other structural changes that reduce risk in credit markets, makes predatory lending predictable, if not virtually inevitable.

Many community organizations have launched intensive campaigns against predatory lending. They have culminated in new state and local laws with many others currently being debated, proposals for new federal regulations and laws, enforcement actions by financial service industry regulators, and private lawsuits. Some community groups have formed partnerships with lenders to help borrowers avoid predatory loans and find products for which they are qualified and from which they will benefit. In Chapter 6, "Community Organizing and Advocacy: Fighting Predatory Lending and Making a Difference," Maude Hurd and Lisa Donner, with

Camellia Phillips, assess the gains of those organizing efforts, focusing on the Household campaign described above, and identify directions for future campaigns.

Chapter 7, "Designing Federal Legislation That Works: Legal Remedies for Predatory Lending," reviews the legal protections that have been won and also notes their limitations. John P. Relman, Fred Rivera, Meera Trehan, and Shilpa S. Satoskar propose specific remedies to current loopholes that would make law enforcement efforts far more effective.

U.S. financial institutions have taken their predatory practices to Europe, Asia, Africa, and elsewhere. In Chapter 8, "Predatory Lending Goes Global: Consumer Protection in a Deregulation Network Economy," Matthew Lee examines the globalization of predatory lending in the absence of effective global regulation. He identifies some rudimentary oversight activities but demonstrates that far more scrutiny is required.

Chester Hartman examines recent developments in financial services industries and outlines directions for future initiatives in Chapter 9, "Predatoriness, and What We Can Do About It." As Hartman observes, there is no magic bullet. But actions on the part of lenders, regulators, elected officials, community organizations, and consumers can blunt the rise of predatory lending and increase the availability of fair and affordable credit to underserved communities. The Appendix which follows identifies some of the organizations that have already begun this effort.

The tools that have been used to combat redlining have always emerged in conflict. The Fair Housing Act was the product of a long civil rights movement and probably would not have been passed until several years later if it were not for the assassination of Martin Luther King Jr. in 1968.[78] Passage of the CRA followed years of demonstrations at bank offices, the homes of bank presidents, and elsewhere.[79] And recent fights against predatory lending reflect the maturation of several national coalitions of community advocacy and fair housing groups including ACORN, the National Community Reinvestment Coalition, the National Training and Information Center, the National Fair Housing Alliance, and others.[80] As Frederick Douglass famously stated in 1857:

> If there is no struggle, there is no progress.
> Those who profess to favor freedom and yet deprecate agitation
> Are men who want crops without plowing the ground.
> They want rain without thunder and lightening.
> They want the ocean without the awful roar of its waters.
> Power concedes nothing without a demand.
> It never did, and it never will.[81]

Home ownership remains the American dream, though for all too many it is a dream deferred. The predatory practices highlighted in this chapter and explored in the following pages constitute a major impediment. A question that remains unanswered is this: for how long will the dream be denied?

NOTES

1. National Community Reinvestment Coalition, *Anti Predatory Lending Toolkit* (Washington, D.C.: National Community Reinvestment Coalition, 2002), p. 5.

2. John LaFalce, "Open Forum: Predatory Lending 'Epidemic,'" *National Mortgage News* 24, no. 32 (April 24, 2000): 4; ACORN, "Separate and Unequal 2002: Predatory Lending in America," http://www.acorn.org/acorn10/predatory lending/plreports/SU2002/index.php, pp. 3, 4 (accessed December 26, 2002).

3. Katharine L. Bradbury, Karl E. Case, and Constance R. Dunham, "Geographic Patterns of Mortgage Lending in Boston, 1982–1987," *New England Economic Review* (September/October 1989): 3–30; Bill Dedman, "Blacks Turned Down for Home Loans from S&Ls Twice as Often as Whites," *Atlanta Journal/Constitution*, January 22, 1989; Bill Dedman, "The Color of Money," *Atlanta Journal/Constitution*, May 1–4, 1988; Alicia H. Munnell, Lynn E. Browned, James McEneaney, and Geoffrey M.B. Tootell, "Mortgage Lending in Boston: Interpreting HMDA Data," *American Economic Review* 86, no. 1 (1996): 25–53; Margery Austin Turner and Felicity Skidmore (eds.), *Mortgage Lending Discrimination: A Review of Existing Evidence* (Washington, D.C.: The Urban Institute, 1999); Gregory D. Squires and Sally O'Connor, *Color and Money: Politics and Prospects for Community Reinvestment in Urban America* (Albany: State University of New York Press, 2001).

4. Joint Center for Housing Studies of Harvard University, *The State of the Nation's Housing 2002* (Cambridge, Mass.: Joint Center for Housing Studies of Harvard University, 2002), p. 14.

5. Dean Foust. "Look Out Below, Lenders," *Business Week* (June 7, 2004): 118–19.

6. Anthony Pennington-Cross, "Subprime Lending in the Primary and Secondary Markets," *Journal of Housing Research* 13, no. 1 (2002): 31–50.

7. ACORN, "Separate and Unequal 2004: Predatory Lending in America," http://www.acorn.org/index.php?id=1994, p. 1 (accessed March 18, 2004).

8. Calvin Bradford, *Risk or Race? Racial Disparities and the Subprime Refinance Market* (Washington, D.C.: Center for Community Change, 2002), p. vii.

9. U.S. Department of Housing and Urban Development, *Unequal Burden: Income and Racial Disparities in Subprime Lending in America* (Washington, D.C.: U.S. Department of Housing and Urban Development, 2000).

10. National Community Reinvestment Coalition, *The Broken Credit System: Discrimination and Unequal Access to Affordable Loans by Race and Age* (Washington, D.C.: National Community Reinvestment Coalition, 2003).

11. Joint Center for Housing Studies of Harvard University, *Credit, Capital and Communities: The Implications of the Changing Mortgage Banking Industry for Community Based Organizations* (Cambridge, Mass.: Joint Center for Housing Studies of Harvard University, 2004).

12. National Training and Information Center, "Preying on Neighborhoods: Sub-

prime Mortgage Lending and Chicagoland Foreclosures," http://www.ntic-us.org/preying/preying.html (1999), p. 4.

13. Dan Immergluck and Geoff Smith, *Risky Business—An Econometric Analysis of the Relationship Between Subprime Lending and Neighborhood Foreclosures* (Chicago: The Woodstock Institute, 2004).

14. Peter T. Kilborn, "Easy Credit and Hard Times Bring a Flood of Foreclosures," *New York Times*, November 24, 2002.

15. Edward M. Gramlich, remarks at the Housing Bureau for Seniors Conference, Ann Arbor, Mich., January 18, 2002; Edward M. Gramlich, remarks at the Financial Services Roundtable Annual Housing Policy Meeting, Chicago, Ill., May 21, 2004.

16. Kathleen C. Engel and Patricia A. McCoy, "The CRA Implications of Predatory Lending," *Fordham Urban Law Journal* 29 (2002): 1578.

17. Kathe Newman and Elvin K. Wyly, "Geographies of Mortgage Market Segmentation: The Case of Essex County, New Jersey," *Housing Studies* 19, no. 1 (2004): 53–83.

18. National Community Reinvestment Coalition, *Anti Predatory Lending Toolkit*, p. 4.

19. Ibid.

20. ACORN, "Separate and Unequal 2002," p. 31.

21. Lester Thurow, "A Surge in Inequality," *Scientific American* 256, no. 5 (1987): 30–37.

22. Carmen DeNavas-Walt and Robert Cleveland, *Money Income in the United States: 2001*, U.S. Census Bureau, Current Population Reports, P60–218 (Washington, D.C.: Government Printing Office, 2002), pp. 19–21.

23. Paul Krugman, "For Richer," *New York Times Magazine* (October 20, 2002): 64.

24. Edward N. Wolff, "Recent Trends in Wealth Ownership, from 1983 to 1998," in Thomas M. Shapiro and Edward N. Wolff (eds.), *Assets for the Poor: The Benefits of Spreading Asset Ownership* (New York: Russell Sage Foundation, 2001), p. 40.

25. Joint Center for Housing Studies of Harvard University, *The State of the Nation's Housing 2002*, p. 7.

26. Melvin L. Oliver and Thomas M. Shapiro, *Black Wealth/White Wealth: A New Perspective on Racial Inequality* (New York: Routledge, 1995), p. 106.

27. Joint Center for Housing Studies of Harvard University, *The State of the Nation's Housing 2002*, p. 31.

28. Oliver and Shapiro, *Black Wealth/White Wealth*, pp. 151, 175; Thomas M. Shapiro, *The Hidden Cost of Being African American: How Wealth Perpetuates Inequality* (New York: Oxford University Press, 2004), pp. 108–9.

29. Paul Jargowsky, "Sprawl, Concentration of Poverty, and Urban Inequality," in Gregory D. Squires (ed.), *Urban Sprawl: Causes, Consequences and Policy Responses* (Washington, D.C.: Urban Institute Press, 2002), p. 42.

30. Paul Jargowsky, *Poverty and Place: Ghettos, Barrios, and the American City* (New York: Russell Sage Foundation, 1996), p. 30; Paul Jargowksy, *Stunning Progress, Hidden Problems: The Dramatic Decline of Concentrated Poverty in the 1990s* (Washington, D.C.: The Brookings Institution, 2003), pp. 4, 20.

31. Richard Newman, "American Consumers Increasingly Filing for Bankruptcy," *The Record* (Hackensack, N.J.), June 3, 2002, p. 22.

32. Myron Orfield, *American Metropolitics: Social Separation and Sprawl* (Washington, D.C.: Brookings Institution Press, 2002); Myron Orfield, *Metropolitics: A Regional Agenda for Community Stability* (Washington, D.C., and Cambridge, Mass.: Brookings Institution Press and Lincoln Institute of Land Policy, 1997).

33. U.S. Department of Housing and Urban Development, *The State of the Cities 2000* (Washington, D.C.: U.S. Department of Housing and Urban Development, 2000), p. 63.

34. John Brennan and Edward W. Hill, *Where Are the Jobs? Cities, Suburbs, and the Competition for Employment* (Washington, D.C.: The Brookings Institution, Center on Urban and Metropolitan Policy, 1999), p. 1.

35. U.S. Department of Housing and Urban Development, *The State of the Cities 2000*, pp. x, 10.

36. Henry G. Cisneros, "Interwoven Destinies: Cities and the Nation," in Henry G. Cisneros (ed.), *Interwoven Destinies: Cities and the Nation* (New York: W.W. Norton. 1993), p. 25.

37. U.S. Department of Housing and Urban Development, *The State of the Cities* (Washington, D.C.: U.S. Department of Housing and Urban Development, 1997), p. 32, exhibit 8.

38. U.S. Department of Housing and Urban Development, *The State of the Cities 2000*, p. 22.

39. Lewis Mumford Center, "Metropolitan Racial and Ethnic Change—Census 2000," http://www.albany.edu/mumford/census/ (accessed April 24, 2001).

40. John Iceland, Daniel H. Weinberg, and Erika Steinmetz, "Racial and Ethnic Residential Segregation in the United States: 1980–2000," paper presented at the annual meetings of the Population Association of America, Atlanta, Ga., May 9–11, 2002, tables 1, 3, 5.

41. Peter Dreier, John Mollenkopf, and Todd Swanstrom, *Place Matters: Metropolitics for the Twenty-first Century* (Lawrence: University Press of Kansas, 2001).

42. Joint Center for Housing Studies of Harvard University, *Credit, Capital and Communities*.

43. Robert B. Avery, Raphael W. Bostic, Paul S. Calem, and Glenn B. Canner, "Changes in the Distribution of Banking Offices," *Federal Reserve Bulletin* 83 (September 1997): 707–25.

44. John Caskey, *Fringe Banking: Check-Cashing Outlets, Pawnshops, and the Poor* (New York: Russell Sage Foundation, 1994); Engel and McCoy, "The CRA Implications of Predatory Lending," pp. 1582–83.

45. David Leonhardt, "Two Tier Marketing," *Business Week* (March 17, 1997): 84–86; Gregory D. Squires and Sally O'Connor, "Fringe Banking in Milwaukee: The Rise of Check-Cashing Businesses and the Emergence of a Two-Tiered Banking System," *Urban Affairs Review* 34, no. 1 (1998): 127–28.

46. Squires and O'Connor, "Fringe Banking in Milwaukee," pp. 131–32.

47. John Caskey, "Bringing Unbanked Households into the Banking System," http://www.brookings.edu/es/urban/capitalxchange/article10.htm, p. 1 (accessed January 21, 2002).

48. Ibid., p. 2.

49. Penny Lunt, "Banks Make Check-Cashing Work," *ABA Banking Journal* (December 1993): 51–52.

50. Michael Hudson, *Merchants of Misery: How Corporate America Profits from Poverty* (Monroe, Me.: Common Courage Press, 1996).

51. Community Reinvestment Association–North Carolina, Consumer Federation of America, Consumers Union, National Community Reinvestment Coalition, National Consumer Law Center, and U.S. Public Interest Research Group, letter to members of the 107th Congress, October 2, 2002.

52. ACORN, "Separate and Unequal 2002," p. 30.

53. Kathleen C. Engel and Patricia A. McCoy, "A Tale of Three Markets: The Law and Economics of Predatory Lending," *Texas Law Review* 80, no. 6 (2002): 1267–73.

54. ACORN, "Separate and Unequal 2002," pp. 29, 30.

55. Leadership Conference on Civil Rights, *Building Healthy Communities* (Washington, D.C.: Leadership Conference on Civil Rights, 2002), pp. 43–47.

56. Calvin Bradford and Gale Cincotta, "The Legacy, the Promise, and the Unfinished Agenda," in Gregory D. Squires (ed.), *From Redlining to Reinvestment: Community Responses to Urban Disinvestment* (Philadelphia: Temple University Press, 1992), p. 192; Laurence H. Meyer, remarks before the 1998 Community Reinvestment Conference of the Consumer Bankers Association, Arlington, Va., May 12, 1998.

57. Insurance Information Institute, *The Financial Services Fact Book* (New York: Insurance Information Institute, 2003), p. 29.

58. Joint Center for Housing Studies of Harvard University, *The 25th Anniversary of the Community Reinvestment Act: Access to Capital in an Evolving Financial Services System* (Cambridge, Mass.: Joint Center for Housing Studies of Harvard University, 2002); National Community Reinvestment Coalition, *CRA Commitments* (Washington, D.C.: National Community Reinvestment Coalition, 2001), p. 1; "Banking on Local Communities," *New York Times*, April 15, 2004, p. A-26.

59. Joint Center for Housing Studies of Harvard University, *The 25th Anniversary of the Community Reinvestment Act*, pp. iii, v.

60. National Community Reinvestment Coalition, *Home Loans to Minorities and Low- and Moderate-Income Borrowers Increase in 1990s, but Then Fall in 2001: A Review of National Data Trends from 1993 to 2001* (Washington, D.C.: National Community Reinvestment Coalition, 2002), pp. 5, 6.

61. Steven Kest, personal communication (May 13, 2003).

62. General Accounting Office, *Consumer Protection: Federal and State Agencies Face Challenges in Combating Predatory Lending* (Washington, D.C.: General Accounting Office, 2004), pp. 58–71.

63. National Community Reinvestment Coalition, *Anti Predatory Lending Toolkit*.

64. General Accounting Office, *Consumer Protection*, pp. 30–57; Steven Kest and Maude Hurd, "Fighting Predatory Lending from the Ground Up: An Issue of Economic Justice," in Gregory D. Squires (ed.), *Organizing Access to Capital: Advocacy and the Democratization of Financial Institutions* (Philadelphia: Temple University Press, 2003).

65. Federal Trade Commission, *Citigroup Settles FTC Charges Against the As-*

sociates: Record-Setting $215 Million for Subprime Lending Victims (Washington, D.C.: Federal Trade Commission, 2002).

66. "Fed Assesses Citigroup Unit $70 Million In Loan Abuse," *New York Times*, May 28, 2004, pp. C-1, C-2.

67. Edward M. Gramlich, remarks at the Texas Association of Bank Counsels Annual Convention, South Padre Island, Tex., October 9, 2003.

68. Anitha Reddy, "Lending Case to Cost Citigroup $215 Million," *Washington Post*, September 20, 2002.

69. Household International, news release (Prospect Heights, Ill.: Household International, October 11, 2002).

70. ACORN, "ACORN and Household Reach Settlement in Class Action Lawsuit," *ACORN News* (November 25, 2003).

71. Gramlich, remarks at Texas Association of Bank Counsels; National Community Reinvestment Coalition, *Anti Predatory Lending Toolkit*; Carla Wertheim, telephone interview (October 24, 2002).

72. Karen Lewis, "Smart Borrowing Group's Goal," *Richmond Times-Dispatch*, October 27, 2002.

73. General Accounting Office, *Consumer Protection*, pp. 68–71.

74. ACORN, "ACORN and Household Reach Settlement."

75. Gregory Elliehausen and Michel E. Staten, *An Update on North Carolina's High-Cost Mortgage Law* (Washington, D.C.: Credit Research Center, McDonough School of Business, Georgetown University, 2003); Gregory Elliehausen and Michael Staten, *The Regulation of Subprime Mortgage Products: An Analysis of North Carolina's Predatory Lending Law* (Washington, D.C.: Credit Research Center, McDonough School of Business, Georgetown University, 2002).

76. Roberto G. Quercia, Michael Stegman, and Walter R. Davis, *The Impact of North Carolina's Anti–Predatory Lending Law: A Descriptive Assessment* (Chapel Hill: Center for Community Capitalism, University of North Carolina, 2003).

77. Comptroller of the Currency, "OCC Working Paper: Economic Issues in Predatory Lending" (Washington D.C.: Comptroller of the Currency, 2003); "OCC Issues Final Rules on National Bank Preemption and Visitorial Powers; Includes Strong Standard to Keep Predatory Lending Out of National Banks," news release (Washington D.C.: Comptroller of the Currency, 2004).

78. Douglas S. Massey and Nancy Denton, *American Apartheid: Segregation and the Making of the Underclass* (Cambridge, Mass.: Harvard University Press, 1993), pp. 186–94.

79. Bradford and Cincotta, "The Legacy, the Promise, and the Unfinished Agenda"; Shel Trapp, *Dynamics of Organizing: Building Power by Developing the Human Spirit* (Chicago: Shel Trapp, 2004).

80. Gregory D. Squires (ed.), *Organizing Access to Capital: Advocacy and the Democratization of Financial Institutions* (Philadelphia: Temple University Press, 2003).

81. John W. Blassingame (ed.), *The Frederick Douglass Papers* (New Haven, Conn.: Yale University Press, 1985), p. 204.

REFERENCES

ACORN. "Separate and Unequal 2002: Predatory Lending in America." http://www.acron.org/acorn10/predatorylending/plreports/SU2002/index.php. Accessed December 26, 2002.

———. "Predatory Lending: Press Releases, Congress Considers Preempting All State and Local Laws on Predatory Lending." http://www.acorn.org/acorn10/ predatorylendng/plreleases/ccp.htm. Accessed January 29, 2003.

———. "ACORN and Household Reach Settlement in Class Action Lawsuit." *ACORN News* (November 25, 2003).

———. "Separate and Unequal 2004: Predatory Lending in America." http:// www.acorn.org/index.php?id=1994. Accessed March 18, 2004.

Avery, Robert B., Raphael W. Bostic, Paul S. Calem, and Glenn B. Canner. "Changes in the Distribution of Banking Offices." *Federal Reserve Bulletin* 83 (September 1997): 707–25.

"Banking on Local Communities." *New York Times*, April 15, 2004, p. A-26.

Blassingame, John W. (ed.). *The Frederick Douglass Papers*. New Haven, Conn.: Yale University Press, 1985.

Bradbury, Katharine L., Karl E. Case, and Constance R. Dunham. "Geographic Patterns of Mortgage Lending in Boston, 1982–1987." *New England Economic Review* (September/October 1989): 3–30.

Bradford, Calvin. *Risk or Race? Racial Disparities and the Subprime Refinance Market*. Washington, D.C.: Center for Community Change, 2002.

Bradford, Calvin, and Gale Cincotta. "The Legacy, the Promise, and the Unfinished Agenda." In Gregory D. Squires (ed.), *From Redlining to Reinvestment: Community Responses to Urban Disinvestment*. Philadelphia: Temple University Press, 1992.

Brennan, John, and Edward W. Hill. *Where Are the Jobs? Cities, Suburbs, and the Competition for Employment*. Washington, D.C.: Center on Urban & Metropolitan Policy, The Brookings Institution, 1999.

Caskey, John. *Fringe Banking: Check-Cashing Outlets, Pawnshops, and the Poor*. New York: Russell Sage Foundation, 1994.

———. "Bringing Unbanked Households into the Banking System." http://www.brookings.edu/es/urban/capitalxchange/article10.htm. Accessed January 21, 2002.

Cisneros, Henry G. "Interwoven Destinies: Cities and the Nation." In Henry G. Cisneros (ed.), *Interwoven Destinies: Cities and the Nation*. New York: W.W. Norton, 1993.

Community Reinvestment Association–North Carolina, Consumer Federation of America, Consumers Union, National Community Reinvestment Coalition, National Consumer Law Center, and U.S. Public Interest Research Group. Letter to members of the 107th Congress, October 2, 2002.

Comptroller of the Currency. "OCC Working Paper: Economic Issues in Predatory Lending." Washington D.C.: Comptroller of the Currency, 2003.

———. "OCC Issues Final Rules on National Bank Preemption and Visitorial Powers; Includes Strong Standard to Keep Predatory Lending out of National Banks." News release. Washington D.C.: Comptroller of the Currency, 2004.

DeNavas-Walt, Carmen, and Robert Cleveland. *Money Income in the United States: 2001*. U.S. Census Bureau, Current Population Reports, P60-218. Washington, D.C.: Government Printing Office, 2002.

Dedman, Bill. "The Color of Money." *Atlanta Journal/Constitution*, May 1–4, 1988.

———. "Blacks Turned Down for Home Loans from S&Ls Twice as Often as Whites." *Atlanta Journal/Constitution*, January 22, 1989.

Dreier, Peter, John Mollenkopf, and Todd Swanstrom. *Place Matters: Metropolitics for the Twenty-first Century*. Lawrence: University Press of Kansas, 2001.

Elliehausen, Gregory, and Michael E. Staten. *The Regulation of Subprime Mortgage Products: An Analysis of North Carolina's Predatory Lending Law*. Washington, D.C.: Credit Research Center, McDonough School of Business, Georgetown University, 2002.

———. *An Update on North Carolina's High-Cost Mortgage Law*. Washington, D.C.: Credit Research Center, McDonough School of Business, Georgetown University, 2003.

Engel, Kathleen C., and Patricia A. McCoy. "The CRA Implications of Predatory Lending." *Fordham Urban Law Journal* 29 (2002): 1571–1605.

———. "A Tale of Three Markets: The Law and Economics of Predatory Lending." *Texas Law Review* 80, no. 6 (2002): 1258–1381.

"Fed Assesses Citigroup Unit $70 Million in Loan Abuse." *New York Times*, May 28, 2004, pp. C-1, C-2.

Federal Trade Commission. *Citigroup Settles FTC Charges Against the Associates Record-Setting $215 Million for Subprime Lending Victims*. Washington, D.C.: Federal Trade Commission, 2002.

Foust, Dean. "Look Out Below, Lenders." *Business Week* (June 7, 2004): 118–119.

General Accounting Office. *Consumer Protection: Federal and State Agencies Face Challenges in Combating Predatory Lending*. Washington, D.C.: General Accounting Office, 2004.

Gramlich, Edward M. Remarks at the Housing Bureau for Seniors Conference, Ann Arbor, Mich., January 18, 2002.

———. Remarks at the Texas Association of Bank Counsels Annual Convention, South Padre Island, Tex., October 9, 2003.

———. Remarks at the Financial Services Roundtable Annual Housing Policy Meeting, Chicago, Ill., May 21, 2004.

Household International. "News Release." Prospect Heights, Ill.: Household International, October 11, 2002.

Hudson, Michael. *Merchants of Misery: How Corporate America Profits from Poverty*. Monroe, Me.: Common Courage Press, 1996.

Iceland, John, Daniel H. Weinberg, and Erika Steinmetz. "Racial and Ethnic Residential Segregation in the United States: 1980–2000." Paper presented at the annual meetings of the Population Association of America, Atlanta, May 9–11, 2002.

Immergluck, Dan, and Geoff Smith. *Risky Business—An Econometric Analysis of the Relationship Between Subprime Lending and Neighborhood Foreclosures*. Chicago: The Woodstock Institute, 2004.

Insurance Information Institute. *The Financial Services Fact Book*. New York: Insurance Information Institute, 2003.

Jargowsky, Paul. *Poverty and Place: Ghettos, Barrios, and the American City*. New York: Russell Sage Foundation, 1996.

———. "Sprawl, Concentration of Poverty, and Urban Inequality." In Gregory D. Squires (ed.)., *Urban Sprawl: Causes, Consequences and Policy Responses*. Washington, D.C.: The Urban Institute Press, 2002.

———. *Stunning Progress, Hidden Problems: The Dramatic Decline of Concentrated Poverty in the 1990s*. Washington, D.C.: The Brookings Institution, 2003.

Joint Center for Housing Studies of Harvard University. *The State of the Nation's Housing 2002*. Cambridge, Mass.: Joint Center for Housing Studies of Harvard University, 2002.

———. *The 25th Anniversary of the Community Reinvestment Act: Access to Capital in an Evolving Financial Services System*. Cambridge, Mass.: Joint Center for Housing Studies of Harvard University, 2002.

———. *Credit, Capital and Communities: The Implications of the Changing Mortgage Banking Industry for Community Based Organizations*. Cambridge, Mass.: Joint Center for Housing Studies of Harvard University, 2004.

Kest, Steven. Personal communication, May 13, 2003.

Kest, Steven, and Maud Hurd. "Fighting Predatory Lending from the Ground Up: An Issue of Economic Justice." In Gregory D. Squires (ed.), *Organizing Access to Capital: Advocacy and the Democratization of Financial Institutions*. Philadelphia: Temple University Press, 2003.

Kilborn, Peter T. "Easy Credit and Hard Times Bring a Flood of Foreclosures." *New York Times*, November 24, 2002.

Krugman, Paul. "For Richer." *New York Times Magazine* (October 20, 2002): 62–67, 76, 77, 141, 142.

LaFalce, John. "Open Forum: Predatory Lending 'Epidemic.' " *National Mortgage News* 24, no. 32 (April 24, 2000): 4.

Leadership Conference on Civil Rights. *Building Healthy Communities*. Washington, D.C.: Leadership Conference on Civil Rights, 2002.

Leonhardt, David. "Two Tier Marketing." *Business Week* (March 17, 1997): 82–90.

Lewis, Karen. "Smart Borrowing Group's Goal." *Richmond Times-Dispatch*, October 27, 2002.

Lewis Mumford Center. "Metropolitan Racial and Ethnic Change—Census 2000." http://www.albany.edu/mumford/census/. Accessed April 24, 2001.

Lunt, Penny. "Banks Make Check-Cashing Work." *ABA Banking Journal* (December 1993): 51–52.

Massey, Douglas S., and Nancy Denton. *American Apartheid: Segregation and the Making of the Underclass*. Cambridge, Mass.: Harvard University Press, 1993.

Meyer, Laurence H. Remarks before the 1998 Community Reinvestment Conference of the Consumer Bankers Association, Arlington, Va., May 12, 1998.

Munnell, Alicia H., Lynn E. Browned, James McEneaney, and Geoffrey M.B. Tootell. "Mortgage Lending in Boston: Interpreting HMDA Data." *American Economic Review* 86, no. 1 (1996): 25–53.

National Community Reinvestment Coalition. *CRA Commitments*. Washington, D.C.: National Community Reinvestment Coalition, 2001.

———. *Anti Predatory Lending Toolkit*. Washington, D.C.: National Community Reinvestment Coalition, 2002.

———. *Home Loans to Minorities and Low and Moderate-Income Borrowers Increase in 1990s, but Then Fall in 2001: A Review of National Data Trends from 1993 to 2001*. Washington, D.C.: National Community Reinvestment Coalition, 2002.

———. *The Broken Credit System: Discrimination and Unequal Access to Afford-

able Loans by Race and Age. Washington, D.C.: National Community Reinvestment Coalition, 2003.

National Training and Information Center. "Preying on Neighborhoods: Subprime Mortgage Lending and Chicagoland Foreclosures." http://www.ntic-us.org/preying/preying.html (1999).

Newman, Kathe, and Elvin K. Wyly. "Geographies of Mortgage Market Segmentation: The Case of Essex County, New Jersey." *Housing Studies* 19, no. 1 (2004): 53–83.

Newman, Richard. "American Consumers Increasingly Filing for Bankruptcy." *The Record* (Hackensack, N.J.), June 3, 2002, p. 22.

Oliver, Melvin L., and Thomas M. Shapiro. *Black Wealth/White Wealth: A New Perspective on Racial Inequality*. New York: Routledge, 1995.

———. *American Metropolitics: Social Separation and Sprawl*. Washington, D.C.: Brookings Institution Press, 2002.

Orfield, Myron. *Metropolitics: A Regional Agenda for Community Stability*. Washington, D.C., and Cambridge, Mass.: Brookings Institution Press and Lincoln Institute of Land Policy, 1997.

Pennington-Cross, Anthony. "Subprime Lending in the Primary and Secondary Markets." *Journal of Housing Research* 13, no. 1 (2002): 31–50.

Quercia, Roberto G., Michael Stegman, and Walter R. Davis. *The Impact of North Carolina's Anti–Predatory Lending Law: A Descriptive Assessment*. Chapel Hill: Center for Community Capitalism, University of North Carolina, 2003.

Reddy, Anitha. "Lending Case to Cost Citigroup $215 Million." *Washington Post*, September 20, 2002.

Shapiro, Thomas M., *The Hidden Cost of Being African American: How Wealth Perpetuates Inequality*. New York: Oxford University Press, 2004.

Squires, Gregory D. (ed.). *Organizing Access to Capital: Advocacy and the Democratization of Financial Institutions*. Philadelphia: Temple University Press, 2003.

Squires, Gregory D., and Sally O'Connor. "Fringe Banking in Milwaukee: The Rise of Check-Cashing Businesses and the Emergence of a Two-Tiered Banking System." *Urban Affairs Review* 34, no. 1 (1998): 126–49.

———. *Color and Money: Politics and Prospects for Community Reinvestment in Urban America*. Albany: State University of New York Press, 2001.

Thurow, Lester. "A Surge in Inequality." *Scientific American* 256, no. 5 (1987): 30–37.

Trapp, Shel. *Dynamics of Organizing: Building Power by Developing the Human Spirit*. Chicago: Shel Trapp, 2004.

Turner, Margery Austin, and Felicity Skidmore (eds.). *Mortgage Lending Discrimination: A Review of Existing Evidence*. Washington, D.C.: The Urban Institute, 1999.

U.S. Department of Housing and Urban Development. *The State of the Cities*. Washington, D.C.: U.S. Department of Housing and Urban Development, 1997.

———. *Unequal Burden: Income and Racial Disparities in Subprime Lending in America*. Washington, D.C.: U.S. Department of Housing and Urban Development, 2000.

————. *The State of the Cities 2000*. Washington, D.C.: U.S. Department of Housing and Urban Development, 2000.

Wertheim, Carla. Telephone interview, October 24, 2002.

Wolff, Edward N. "Recent Trends in Wealth Ownership, from 1983 to 1998." In Thomas M. Shapiro and Edward N. Wolff (eds.), *Assets for the Poor: The Benefits of Spreading Asset Ownership*. New York: Russell Sage Foundation, 2001.

2

The Targets of Predatory and Discriminatory Lending: Who Are They and Where Do They Live?

John Taylor, Josh Silver, and David Berenbaum

The credit system is broken, and discrimination is widespread in America. The National Community Reinvestment Coalition (NCRC) finds that minority and elderly communities receive a considerably higher level of high-cost subprime loans than is justified on the basis of credit risk of neighborhood residents. NCRC's conclusions are consistent with a substantial body of research on subprime lending that reveals disparities of lending that cannot be explained solely by differences in creditworthiness. Unscrupulous lenders target minorities, the elderly, women, and low- and moderate-income communities with high-cost loans. These lenders are seeking short-term maximization of profits, and do not consider that the long-term financial health of neighborhoods and of their own lending operations depend on residents successfully repaying their loans.

President Bush declared that his administration was committed to creating 5.5 million new minority home owners by 2010. The widespread evidence of price discrimination, however, threatens the possibility of creating sustainable and affordable home ownership opportunities for residents of traditionally underserved neighborhoods. Using the best available industry data on creditworthiness, NCRC uncovered a substantial amount of predatory lending involving rampant pricing discrimination and the targeting of minority and elderly communities.

Sadly, it is still the case in America that the lending marketplace is a dual marketplace, segmented by race and age. If a consumer lives in a predominantly minority community, he or she is much more likely to receive a high-cost and discriminatory loan than a similarly qualified borrower in a white community. At the same time, the elderly, who have often built up substantial amounts of equity and wealth in their homes, are much more likely to receive a high-cost refinance loan than a similarly qualified younger borrower. The disproportionate amount of subprime refinance lending in predominantly elderly neighborhoods imperils the stability of long-term wealth in communities and the possibilities of the elderly passing their wealth to the next generation.

Lending discrimination in the form of steering high-cost loans to minority and elderly borrowers qualified for market-rate loans results in equity stripping and has contributed to inequalities in wealth. According to the Federal Reserve Survey of Consumer Finances, the median value of financial assets was $38,500 for whites, but only $7,200 for minorities in 2001. Whites have more than five times the dollar amount of financial assets than minorities. Likewise, the median home value for whites was $130,000 and only $92,000 for minorities in 2001.[1]

Research findings confirm Americans' perceptions of bias in lending. In the winter of 2002, NCRC hired Republican pollster Frank Luntz and Democratic pollster Jennifer Laszlo Mizrahi to conduct a nationally representative poll of Americans' views of lending institutions. In the poll, fully 76 percent of Americans believed that steering creditworthy minorities and women to costly loan products was a significant problem. Unfortunately, this chapter verifies that these perceptions of discriminatory treatment are reality in too many instances.[2]

The single most utilized defense of lenders and their trade associations concerning bias is that credit scoring systems allow lenders to be colorblind in their loan decisions. Solid research, however, debunks that argument and clearly makes the case that traditionally underserved neighborhoods, regardless of the creditworthiness of their residents, receive a disproportionate number of high-cost subprime loans.

This chapter reviews NCRC's research and a large body of other research on subprime lending. It concludes by summarizing an NCRC econometric study that demonstrates widespread pricing discrimination, using the best industry data available on creditworthiness. While more research needs to be done, the burden of proof resides with those who assert that no discrimination exists in the lending marketplace.

TARGETING OF UNDERSERVED COMMUNITIES

In the spring of 2003, NCRC published a comprehensive study titled *America's Best and Worst Lenders*. The study is geared toward a wide audience consisting of policy makers, consumers, community groups, and lenders themselves. It ranks lenders on a series of community reinvestment and fair-lending indicators that show which lenders are making the most loans to traditionally underserved communities and which lenders are making the fewest loans to these communities in several metropolitan areas. The study provides context for the rankings through an overview of prime and subprime lending trends. Stakeholders should hold prime lenders particularly accountable in metropolitan areas in which the high-cost lenders are far ahead of their prime peers in reaching traditionally underserved communities.

We documented several troublesome trends. First, high-cost lenders had their greatest rates of penetration into minority neighborhoods in metropolitan areas that were the most segregated by race, after controlling for income levels and housing prices in 25 metropolitan areas. In other words, when holding critical housing market factors constant, the level of high-cost lending increases in minority communities solely as the level of race segregation in metropolitan areas increases. When fewer whites live in minority neighborhoods, high-cost lenders intensify their efforts to make loans in minority neighborhoods. Second, high-cost lenders make more of an effort than traditional prime lenders to issue loans in affordable metropolitan areas. Although traditional prime lenders make more loans in underserved neighborhoods as housing becomes more affordable in metropolitan areas, subprime lenders increase lending faster than their prime peers as housing becomes more affordable. Third, the disparities in prime and subprime lending are worse in refinance lending than home mortgage lending. Some pundits have lauded subprime lenders as making home ownership more available in underserved communities. But these pundits do not consider that high-cost lenders focus more of their attention on refinance lending in underserved communities. Predatory lenders, a subset of subprime lenders, are not interested in increasing home ownership, but are focused on making profits by stripping equity and wealth from home owners in underserved communities through high-cost refinance loans.

We found that in 2000, high-cost lenders had extraordinarily large shares of the refinance loan market in minority neighborhoods. When interest rates were relatively high, high-cost lenders found a niche by convincing borrowers to refinance in order to tap into their home equity for various types of expenses. By 2001, interest rates had dropped considerably, by a percentage point or more during parts of the year. High-cost lenders lost market share in minority tracts as refinancing for the purpose of lowering loan costs increased. However, the disparity in the market share of high-cost lenders between minority and white neighborhoods grew. Residents of white neighborhoods were refinancing for the purpose of lowering loan costs to a greater extent than residents of minority neighborhoods during 2001. At the same time, high-cost lenders stepped up their efforts to target residents of minority neighborhoods during low interest-rate years, as is revealed by increasing market share disparities.

Although high-cost market share dropped in minority tracts from 2000 to 2001, the disparity in the high-cost share between minority and white tracts increased for most of the 25 metropolitan areas in the study. For example, in Milwaukee during 2000, high-cost lenders had a 3.1 times greater market share in minority neighborhoods. They made 52.6 percent of the refinance loans in minority neighborhoods, which was three times the 16.9 percent of the loans high-cost lenders issued in white neighborhoods. By 2001, high-cost lenders in Milwaukee made 35.3 percent of the loans in minority neighborhoods, a whopping nine times greater than the 3.8 percent of the loans they issued in white neighborhoods.

In order to assess the relationship between high cost lending and race segregation, we used a widely accepted segregation index that had a scale of 0 to 100. A score of 100 indicates that a metropolitan area is hyper or "perfectly" segregated. A score of 0 indicates that a metropolitan area is perfectly integrated. If a score is 100, all the African Americans in a metropolitan area would need to move for the area to become integrated. If a score is 0, no African Americans would have to move in order for the metropolitan area to become integrated.

When the African American/white segregation index increases by 20 percentage points, the nonprime market share in refinance lending increases by seven percentage points, holding all other factors constant. In other words, the nonprime market share of refinance loans in minority tracts is nearly seven percentage points higher in the Detroit metropolitan area than the Washington, D.C., metropolitan area solely because the African American/white segregation index is 20 percentage points higher in Detroit (86 points) than Washington, D.C. (66 points). Reinforcing the finding that disparities are greater in refinance than in home mortgage lending, the nonprime market share in home mortgage lending is four percentage points higher in minority neighborhoods in Detroit than in Washington, D.C.

We also discovered disparities by income level of neighborhoods that indicate targeting by high-cost lenders. Regression analysis found that the high-cost market share of refinance lending in low- and moderate-income tracts increased in metropolitan areas in which housing costs were more affordable. Paradoxically, high-cost lenders intensified their refinance lending in low- and moderate-income tracts relative to prime lenders in those metropolitan areas that were more affordable.

High-cost lenders also targeted female borrowers, and the extent of the targeting intensified as the level of race segregation increased. We found that the difference between the high-cost and prime portions of loans for women was the greatest in Milwaukee, St. Louis, Cleveland, Detroit, and Minneapolis–St. Paul. In Milwaukee, for example, high-cost lenders issued a portion of loans to women that was 16.7 percentage points higher than the prime portion of loans during 2000, and 20.3 percentage points higher during 2001. After controlling for housing costs and income levels, the portion of high-cost loans to women climbed as the level of white and African American segregation increased across the 25 metropolitan areas.

NCRC's research has also revealed high-cost lending disparities in rural areas. In the late spring of 2002, NCRC issued a report on lending trends in Iowa. Subprime lenders among the top 50 lenders in Iowa significantly increased their market share in low- and moderate-income census tracts from 1995 to 1999, and captured an even larger share in 2000. In 1995, subprime lenders made 9.4 percent of the refinance loans in low- and moderate-income (LMI) tracts, and 2.6 percent of the loans in middle- and upper-income (MUI) tracts. Their market share in LMI tracts was 3.6 times greater than their market share in MUI tracts. By 1999, subprime lenders made more than 28 percent of the conventional refinance loans in LMI tracts. They made only 5.5 percent of the loans in MUI tracts. Subprime lenders' market share in LMI tracts was five times greater than their share in MUI tracts.

By 2000, the subprime lender market share in LMI census tracts had increased significantly. Subprime lenders made 43 percent of the refinance loans in LMI tracts in 2000, up from 28 percent in 1999. In a mere six years, the subprime share of refinance loans in LMI tracts increased from about 10 percent of all loans to more than 40 percent of all loans. It is unlikely that the creditworthiness of residents of LMI tracts would have deteriorated by such a huge amount as to justify a more than fourfold increase in subprime market share in refinance lending. Instead of dramatic differences in creditworthiness, a conscious strategy of targeting underserved neighborhoods is responsible for the surge of high-cost lender market share.

From the Midwest to Native American reservations, the phenomenon of targeting remains intense. During the spring and summer of 2003, the National American Indian Housing Council and NCRC conducted a survey and data analysis concerning the amount of high-cost and predatory lending on large Indian reservations across the country. In a survey of nearly 40 housing officials on Indian reservations, 70 percent of respondents indicated that predatory lending was a significant problem on their reservation, more than half believed that lenders discriminated on the basis of race, and 35 percent reported that they knew of someone experiencing a foreclosure due to predatory lending. NCRC's data analysis confirmed that the penetration of high-cost lenders was higher in states in which tribal officials were most likely to report widespread problems with predatory lending. In New Mexico, for example, Native Americans were six times more likely than whites to receive high-cost mortgage loans. Consistent with the data analysis, tribal officials in New Mexico were among the most likely to report a high level of predatory lending.

Targeting in New Mexico does not occur only on Indian reservations but also involves Hispanics in urban areas. In a report to the City of Santa Fe, NCRC found that subprime lenders increased their market share from 15 percent of all refinance loans issued to Hispanics in 1998 to 30 percent of loans made to Hispanics in 2000.

Despite a larger presence by subprime lenders in niche markets, overall lending to Hispanics decreased significantly in the city from 1994 through 2000. Hispanics received 31 percent of the home mortgage loans in the city in 1994, but only 21.7 percent in 2000. Although subprime lenders focus on underserved populations, the increased presence of subprime lenders in the city did not translate into increased share of mortgage loans for traditionally underserved borrowers through the 1990s. This contrasts sharply with rhetoric asserting that subprime lending has fueled the home mortgage boom among minorities in the 1990s.

LITERATURE REVIEW BOLSTERS NCRC'S FINDINGS OF DISCIMINATION

NCRC's findings are consistent with a body of research on subprime lending. A survey conducted by Freddie Mac analysts found that two-thirds of subprime borrowers were not satisfied with their loans, while three-quarters of prime borrowers believed they received fair rates and terms.[3] In previous years, Freddie Mac and Fannie Mae have often been quoted as stating that between a third and half of borrowers who receive subprime loans qualify for lower-cost loans.[4] Dan Immergluck, a professor at Grand Valley State University, was one of the first researchers to document the "hypersegmentation" of lending by race of neighborhood.[5] Like Immergluck, the Department of Housing and Urban Development found that after controlling for housing stock characteristics and the income level of the census tract, subprime lending increases as the minority level of the tract increases.[6] The Research Institute for Housing America, an offshoot of the Mortgage Bankers Association, released a controversial study in 2000 which concluded that minorities were more likely to receive loans from subprime institutions, even after controlling for the creditworthiness of the borrowers.[7]

Relatively few studies examine the relationship between the number of elderly residents of a neighborhood and the level of subprime lending, although anecdotal evidence suggests that abusive lenders target the elderly. In one study, the Southwest office of Consumers Union found that every increase of one percentage point in the proportion of people over 65 in a neighborhood increased subprime refinance lending by 1.3 percentage points. The Consumers Union examined neighborhoods in Dallas and Austin, and included demographic variables and a few underwriting variables, such as ratio of loan amount to income in its regression equations.[8] The AARP also conducted a national survey of elderly borrowers and found that older borrowers who were widowed, female, African American, and less educated were more likely to receive subprime loans than their married, male, white, and more educated counterparts. The survey also found that seniors receiving subprime loans were more likely to have been approached by brokers, to have refinanced two or more times in the past three years, and to be dissatisfied with their loans.[9]

Court cases also document targeting by race, age, and gender. In a relatively early case in 1996, the Department of Justice (DOJ) stated that Long

Beach Mortgage Company "directed its marketing efforts toward persons and neighborhoods, particularly minority neighborhoods, that Long Beach officials believed might be susceptible to the higher prices." DOJ found that African Americans, Latinos, women, and persons over the age of 55 were systematically charged higher prices. For example, African American females over the age of 55 were 2.6 times more likely than white males under 55 to be charged fees totaling 6 percent of the loan amount.[10]

In another prominent case, the attorney general of New York State documented that Delta Financial Corporation targeted minority census tracts in New York City that would be especially vulnerable to abusive lending because a high percentage of their residents lacked high school educations. Delta routinely charged fees of 10 percent or more of the loan amount.[11] Finally, the lawsuit against Capital City Mortgage Company in Washington, D.C., revealed that this lender made more than 90 percent of its high-cost and abusive loans to African American neighborhoods over 13-year period. The lender's foreclosure rate of 20 percent far exceeded the average foreclosure rate. During foreclosure sales, Capital City would buy back the foreclosed properties at discounted prices.[12]

Important research conducted by a Federal Reserve economist and two researchers from the Wharton School at the University of Pennsylvania revealed that high-cost lending surged in neighborhoods as the level of African Americans increased. Paul Calem of the Federal Reserve, and Kevin Gillen and Susan Wachter of the Wharton School used credit scoring data to conduct econometric analysis scrutinizing the influence of credit scores, demographic characteristics, and economic conditions on the level of subprime lending. Their study found that after controlling for creditworthiness and housing market conditions, the level of subprime refinance and home purchase loans increased in a statistically significant fashion as the proportion of African Americans increased on a census tract level in Philadelphia and Chicago.[13] NCRC was fortunate to acquire a database on creditworthiness similar to that used by Calem, Gillen, and Wachter. We now turn to an NCRC study in 10 metropolitan areas using creditworthiness data and confirming the conclusions of the Calem, Gillen, and Wachter study.

CONTROLLING FOR CREDITWORTHINESS: DISCRIMINATION JUMPS OUT

In December of 2003 NCRC released *The Broken Credit System: Discrimination and Unequal Access to Affordable Loans by Race and Age. Subprime Lending in Ten Large Metropolitan Areas*. The goal of the study was to determine the extent to which discrimination, rather than economic or credit factors, accounts for the rise of subprime lending. NCRC chose 10 metropolitan statistical areas (MSAs) from different parts of the United

States and conducted a statistical analysis in each. The MSAs selected were Atlanta, Baltimore, Cleveland, Detroit, Houston, Los Angeles, Milwaukee, New York, St. Louis, and Washington, D.C. These areas had different demographic and economic characteristics, which allowed NCRC to make credible and generalizable conclusions about the home lending patterns across large metropolitan areas. A multivariate regression approach controlled for demographic and risk factors.

Variables for the analysis belonged to three categories: home lending, credit scoring, and demographics. We used 2001 Home Mortgage Disclosure Act (HMDA) data for home lending, 1999 credit scoring data, and 1990 census tract demographic information. We obtained the 1999 credit scoring data on a one-time basis from one of the three large credit bureaus. We chose 2001 HMDA data, not 1999 data, because we believed that the distribution of credit scores on a census tract level did not vary significantly over a three-year period. We ran regression equations using 1999 and 2000 home loan data to confirm the hypothesis. The results were similar over the years. Also, 2001 was a year of lower interest rates. We wanted to see if minority neighborhoods were benefiting from lower interest rates as measured by a decrease in the statistical significance of race of neighborhood on the level of subprime lending. We would have preferred to use 2000 census tract data, but the HMDA data will not use 2000 census data until the 2003 release in the summer of 2004. The 2001 HMDA data used 1990 census tract boundaries. We believe the results will be similar to HMDA data using 2000 census tract boundaries, and are engaged in follow-up research to confirm this.

We used a list of subprime lending specialists developed by the Department of Housing and Urban Development (HUD) to characterize loans as subprime. Since HMDA data do not have information on the annual percentage rate (APR) or other loan terms and conditions, HUD developed its list by complementing data analysis with interviews of lending institutions and a literature search. As an additional step, HUD called the lenders on its list and asked them if they considered themselves subprime and manufactured home specialists. Generally speaking, a lender was included on the list if more than 50 percent of the loans in its portfolio were subprime or for manufactured homes. HUD itself admits that the list is incomplete, but it is widely used by researchers and is currently the best available information on subprime lending until pricing information becomes available in the 2004 HMDA data released in the summer of 2005.

The regression equations included the following variables:

Home lending variables (dependent variables)
- The percent of home purchase loans in a census tract that were subprime
- The percent of refinance loans in a census tract that were subprime

Demographic variables
- The percent of residents in a census tract who were African American
- The percent of residents in a census tract who were Hispanic
- The percent of residents in a census tract who were over 65 years old

A dummy variable showing the median age of houses in a census tract
- 0 when the median age of housing was between 20 and 0 years (built between 1970 and 1990)
- 1 when the median age of housing was between 50 and 21 years (built between 1940 and 1969)
- 2 when the median age of housing was 51 years or older (built before 1940).

Income variable. 1989 median household income in a census tract.

A housing turnover variable. This variable was a ratio of all home purchase loans made in 2001 divided by owner-occupied units in 1990. The research literature indicated that a higher housing turnover (as revealed by larger values of this variable) suggests a more vibrant market and faster home value appreciation. This should make a census tract more attractive to prime lenders and thus decrease the proportion of subprime lending.

A "capitalization" variable, which was a ratio of gross median rent divided by median housing value. The literature suggests that owner-occupied units appreciate more slowly in neighborhoods where the median rent is higher relative to the median housing value (higher ratio values for this variable). Therefore, prime lenders may find neighborhoods with higher values for the capitalization variable less attractive, meaning that the portion of subprime loans will be higher in these neighborhoods.

Credit scoring variables involved the percentage of neighborhood residents lacking credit scores and the cumulative percentage of neighborhood residents in very high, high, and moderate credit risk categories added together.

The credit risk scores used in our report measured the likelihood of future delinquencies and foreclosures. The database had a credit score range from 0 to 1,000, with lower scores indicating lower risk or chance of borrower delinquency. The scores were divided into five equal categories or quintiles of risk; the specific categories were very low, low, moderate, high, and very high risk. For each census tract, the database contains the number and percentage of neighborhood residents in each of the five risk categories, and the number and percentage of neighborhood residents with no credit scores.

As expected, the number of subprime loans increased as the number of neighborhood residents in higher credit risk categories increased. Also, the number of subprime loans increased, as expected, due to housing market conditions. Older median age of the housing stock, higher capitalization values, and low levels of housing turnover increased subprime lending in a neighborhood. After controlling for risk and housing market conditions, however, the race and age composition of the neighborhood had an independent and strong effect, increasing the amount of high-cost subprime lending. In particular, the following were true.

- The level of refinance subprime lending increased as the portion of African Americans in a neighborhood increased in 9 of the 10 metropolitan areas. In the case of home purchase subprime lending, the African American composition of a neighborhood boosted lending in six metropolitan areas.

- The percentage of African Americans in a census tract had the strongest impact on subprime refinance lending in Houston, Milwaukee, and Detroit. Even after holding income, creditworthiness, and housing market factors constant, going from an all-white to an all–African American neighborhood (100 percent of the census tract residents are African American) increased the proportion of subprime loans by 41 percentage points in Houston. For example, if 10 percent of the refinance loans in the white neighborhood were subprime, then 51 percent of the loans in an African American neighborhood in Houston would be subprime. The proportion of subprime refinance loans increased by 29, 26, and 20 percentage points in Milwaukee, Detroit, and Cleveland, respectively, from an all-white to an all–African American neighborhood.

- Solely because the percentage of the African American population increased, the amount of subprime home purchase lending surged in Cleveland, Milwaukee, and Detroit. From an all-white to an all–African American neighborhood in Cleveland, the portion of subprime home purchase loans climbed 24 percentage points. The portion of subprime purchase loans similarly rose by 18 and 17 percentage points in Milwaukee and Detroit, respectively, in African American neighborhoods compared to white neighborhoods.

- The impact of the age of borrowers was strong in refinance lending. In seven metropolitan areas, the proportion of subprime refinance lending increased when the number of residents over 65 increased in a neighborhood.

- Neighborhoods with elderly populations experienced the greatest increases in subprime refinance lending in St. Louis, Atlanta, and Houston. Even after holding income, creditworthiness, and housing market factors constant, the proportion of subprime refinance lending surged 31 percentage points in St. Louis from a neighborhood with none of its residents over 65 to all of its residents over 65. Likewise, the increases were 27 and 25 percentage points in Atlanta and Houston, respectively. Although neighborhoods with such extreme age distributions (none or all residents over 65) are unusual, the regression analysis highlights and isolates the impacts of age on the level of subprime lending. Indeed, the level of subprime lending is likely to be considerably higher in neighborhoods with large concentrations of senior citizens.

- The findings for Hispanics were inconsistent. The amount of subprime lending increased as the number of Hispanic neighborhood residents increased in only a subset of MSAs. The proportion of Hispanics in a census tract had the strongest impact in the Detroit and Houston MSAs for refinance lending. In Detroit, for example, going from an all-white to an all-Hispanic neighborhood would lead to a 12.8 percentage point increase in the proportion of subprime refinance lending.

- The level of subprime lending increased in a statistically significant fashion in the great majority of metropolitan areas as the percentage of neighborhood residents with no credit scores increased. Subprime refinance and home purchase lending climbed in nine and seven metropolitan areas, respectively, as the portion of neighborhood residents without credit scores increased. This is a significant issue for recent immigrants and other unbanked populations, many of whom are creditworthy for loans at prevailing interest rates, but receive high-cost loans simply because they lack conventional credit histories.

CONCLUSION

For years, researchers have documented that high-cost lenders target minorities, women, the elderly, and low- and moderate-income borrowers and communities. In response to this evidence, the lending industry maintained that traditionally underserved populations were not as creditworthy as white, male, and relatively affluent borrowers. Lenders, therefore, were providing a valuable service; they were extending high-cost loans to a subset of risky borrowers who would not receive loans otherwise. The overwhelming evidence, however, indicates that the industry argument is incorrect. After controlling for creditworthiness and housing market characteristics, traditionally underserved populations receive a disproportionate amount of high-cost loans. In other words, widespread pricing discrimination strips equity and wealth from minority and elderly borrowers and neighborhoods.

Subprime lending has not driven the increase in home ownership among minorities during the last several years. Instead, subprime lenders specialize in refinance lending and a subset of subprime lenders are predatory, making refinance loans in order to strip equity from homeowners in underserved communities.

Three main actors are responsible for the discrimination. First and foremost are the abusive lenders, who prey on unsuspecting and vulnerable consumers and strip equity from their homes. Second are the traditional prime lenders, whose retreat from traditionally underserved neighborhoods leaves a vacuum that abusive lenders eagerly fill with their high-cost and discriminatory loans. It is inexcusable that high-cost lenders increase their lending faster than prime lenders as housing becomes more affordable in metropolitan areas. High-cost lenders realize that a profit is to be made when economic conditions become favorable, but many prime lenders still need to learn the lesson that profits can be made in underserved communities when lending is responsible and nondiscriminatory. Third are the federal regulatory agencies, because their lax enforcement of the nation's fair lending and anti-discrimination laws enable abusive lenders.

The need for continued organizing and advocacy in general, and for strengthening the Community Reinvestment Act (CRA) in particular, is clear.[14] Congress must bolster CRA and the fair lending laws in order to significantly reduce the amount of discrimination and wealth stripping that victimize minorities, women, the elderly, and low- and moderate-income borrowers and communities. Congress must pass a comprehensive anti-predatory law outlawing usurious practices that strip equity from American homeowners. Our findings must serve as a wake-up call to lawmakers and regulators to pass strong anti-discrimination laws and implement rigorous regulations.

NOTES

1. Ana M. Aizcorbe, Arthur B. Kennickell, and Kevin B. Moore, "Recent Changes in U.S. Family Finances: Evidence from the 1998 and 2001 Survey of Consumer Finances," *Federal Reserve Bulletin* (January 2003).

2. Frank Luntz and Jennifer Laszlo Mizrahi, Poll conducted January 21 to February 13, 2002. Overall poll of 1,258 adults, margin of error ±3.3 percent. Available from NCRC.

3. Marsha J. Courchane, Brian J. Surette, and Peter M. Zorn, "Subprime Borrowers: Mortgage Transitions and Outcomes," prepared for Credit Research Center, Subprime Lending Symposium, McLean, Va., 2002.

4. "Fannie Mae Vows More Minority Lending," *Washington Post*, March 16, 2000, p. E01. See also Freddie Mac Web page, http://www.freddiemac.com/corpo rate/reports/moseley/chap5.htm.

5. Dan Immergluck, *Two Steps Back: The Dual Mortgage Market, Predatory Lending, and the Undoing of Community Development* (Chicago: Woodstock Institute, 1999).

6. Randall M. Scheessele, *Black and White Disparities in Subprime Mortgage Refinance Lending* (Washington, D.C.: Office of Policy Development and Research, U.S. Department of Housing and Urban Development, 2002).

7. Anthony Pennington-Cross, Anthony Yezer, and Joseph Nichols, *Credit Risk and Mortgage Lending: Who Uses Subprime and Why?* Working paper no. 00-03 (Washington, D.C.: Research Institute for Housing America, September 2000).

8. Consumers Union, "Elderly in the Subprime Market," www.consumers union.org. (October 2002).

9. Neal Walters and Sharon Hermanson, "Older Subprime Refinance Mortgage Borrowers," AARP Public Policy Institute, Data Digest no. 74 (July 2002), http://www.aarp.org/ppi.

10. Department of Justice complaint against Long Beach Mortgage Company; see also press release of September 5, 1996.

11. Complaint by New York State attorney general against Delta Funding, in the U.S. District Court, Eastern District of New York, August 19, 1999.

12. Amicus brief of the United States in support of plaintiffs, *Clyde Hargraves et al. v. Capital City Mortgage*, filed in the U.S. District Court for the District of Columbia, undated. See also Judge Joyce Hens Green, memorandum and order, in *Clyde Hargraves v. Capital City Mortgage*, September 2000.

13. Paul S. Calem, Kevin Gillen, and Susan Wachter, "The Neighborhood Distribution of Subprime Mortgage Lending," pcalem@frb.gov (October 30, 2002).

14. Gregory D. Squires (ed.), *Organizing Access to Capital: Advocacy and the Democratization of Financial Institutions* (Philadelphia: Temple University Press, 2003).

3

The Economic Consequences of Predatory Lending: A Philadelphia Case Study

Ira Goldstein

Predatory lending is a problem that has grabbed the national spotlight. Legislatures at the federal and state levels, as well as local governments around the country, have made numerous attempts to understand and address the problem. And while predatory lending is a national problem, it is experienced at the most local level: in neighborhoods and by households that have long struggled to obtain appropriate and sufficient access to credit. The following pages examine the nature, extent, and consequences of predatory lending in Philadelphia, an older industrial city with a large minority population that typifies the urban communities where predatory lending has been particularly problematic.

This chapter is an effort to systematically define and measure the nature and extent of predatory lending in one city, the City of Philadelphia. Our findings and conclusions derive from a set of interviews conducted with persons in every sector that touches the lending process—from the borrower to the securitizer, and everyone in between—and also rely upon a quantitative analysis of actual properties and their respective sale and mortgage histories. Compared with the growing body of literature singularly showing growth in the rates of subprime lending to various demographic sub-groups,[1] this effort represents a different and complementary way to understand the predatory lending problem.

Our quantitative data and interviews show that subprime loans are making credit available in communities where credit likely historically has not been—and likely still is not—as readily available. Loans that are made are often for amounts exceeding the value of the underlying property (i.e., collateral) and at levels beyond what the borrowers want, need, or can afford. In general we find that (1) subprime loans are more prevalent in lower-income communities; (2) because subprime loans, rather than those in the prime market, disproportionately are made in lower-income communities, the economic benefits of the government-sponsored enterprises (GSEs) are not as commonly achieved; (3) patterns of financing suggest an erosion of home equity over a relatively short period of time; (4) mortgage foreclosures are disproportionately higher in communities with lower and moderate housing values; (5) subprime loans in communities with lower and moderate housing values go into foreclosure very quickly (i.e., within two years of origination), suggesting that initial underwriting was not properly done. The chapter closes with a consideration of how both lenders and consumers experience subprime market activity.

PREDATORY LENDING DEFINED

Others in this volume have taken great care to develop workable definitions of the term "predatory lending." For purposes of this chapter, I will define and operationalize predatory lending as having three sets of essential characteristics related to (1) the terms and consequences of the loan; (2) the manner in which the individual came to obtain the loan; (3) the imbalance of information, experience, and thus power inherent in the transaction. The quantitative analysis focuses on the second feature of the definition, while the interview results illustrate the other features.

The Terms and Consequences of the Loan

As most who have studied this problem have noted, predatory loans generally carry interest rates and fees that cannot be justified by the characteristics of the borrower or collateral.[2] Fees that have no reasonable justification get packed into these transactions which, because they drive up the level of indebtedness unnecessarily, also strip equity and enhance the riskiness of the transaction *over and above the risk that would otherwise have been presented by the borrower*. The sample HUD-1 settlement sheet (Figure 3.1), obtained from a housing counseling agency assisting victims of predatory lending in Philadelphia, details a transaction in which the terms and other circumstances of the loan typify many of the loans one might consider predatory—at least along this dimension of the definition.

The Manner in Which the Individual Came to Obtain the Loan

Target marketing within mainstream commerce is a generally accepted practice. The notion is that you increase the efficiency of the market by going more directly to the market that will want or need the product. This is qualitatively different from the sort of targeting employed by those who practice predatory lending.[3]

The purchase of the typical consumer good is neither dangerous nor potentially financially ruinous. Generally speaking, such a purchase represents a small proportion of the purchaser's assets and is more or less suitable to the purchaser. However, as a matter of public policy, I have generally operated under the principle that it is not acceptable to target market a consumer group when the products are not suitable (e.g., marketing campaigns for cigarettes that are attractive to children) or attempt to exploit a vulnerability (e.g., high-alcohol-content beer targeted to African Americans).[4] The marketing of predatory loans is easily analogous to marketing cigarettes to children or high-alcohol-content beer to African Americans.

And although there is established public policy in the securities industry (e.g., the "suitability"—overall appropriateness of an investment, considering factors such as their age, experience, and tolerance of risk and loss— has bearing on investors who are solicited), there is no such standard within the world of residential lending. Interviews with lenders and mortgage brokers reveal the manner by which they find customers.[5] One broker, for example, reported going to a Web site that allows the user to enter characteristics such as age, sex, income, likelihood of home ownership, likelihood of living alone, and zip code; for pennies a name, he obtains a list that can be used to market by mail or telephone.[6] Another broker reported searching the public records for people who held mortgages with a previously active finance company. It was his logic and strategy that anyone who had a loan with this particular company could easily be talked into a loan with another, similar entity.

The Imbalance of Information

A review of the documents for loans arguably considered predatory and interviews with attorneys who represent borrowers suggest that the transactions make no economic sense. Moreover, were the borrowers to have had full and accurate information, they would never have entered into the transactions.

Interviews with borrowers, lenders, attorneys representing both lenders and borrowers, and settlement agents reveal that this lack of information is perhaps the defining character of the transactions. When settlement is made on a predatory loan, the borrower is the least experienced, least informed, and most at-risk in the transaction. Borrowers report loan settlements around the kitchen tables taking little more than a few minutes. Settlement agents readily admit that borrowers, although signing numerous documents, generally have no idea what they are getting into.

Specifically, borrowers often report having no knowledge that the loan they got was secured by their home and that should they be unable to pay, they could lose their home. They also report thinking they had one loan when they had two. Borrowers report thinking, albeit incorrectly in Penn-

Figure 3.1
Manner in Which the Individual Comes to "Own" a Predatory Loan

7.25% "Discount Points" ($4,642) ▶

!lement Statement — U.S. [illegible] of Housing and Urban Develo[illegible] (Page 2 of 2)
ional Form for
nsactions without Sellers

e and Address of Borrower:	Name and Address of Lender:
erty Location (If different than above)	Settlement Agent: ● Lender ( ) Other
	Place of Settlement: SAME AS ABOVE
Number:	Settlement Date: 09/13/2001

SETTLEMENT CHARGES	
ITEMS PAYABLE IN CONNECTION WITH LOAN:	
Loan Origination Fee ("Closing Costs"): %	
Loan Discount Fee ("Points"): 7.25 %	4,642.06
Appraisal Fee To: IRES	280.00
Credit Report To:	
Inspection Fee To:	
Mortgage Insurance Application Fee To:	
Mortgage Broker Fee To:	
Document Preparation Fee	
Application Fee %	
Flood Certification	
ITEMS REQUIRED BY LENDER TO BE PAID IN ADVANCE:	
Invest From To @ $ Per Day	
Mortgage Insurance Premium For Months To	
Hazard Insurance Premium For Year(s) To	
RESERVES DEPOSITED WITH LENDER:	
Hazard Insurance Months @ $ Per Month	
Mortgage Insurance Months @ $ Per Month	
City Property Taxes Months @ $ Per Month	
County Property Taxes Months @ $ Per Month	
Annual Assessments Months @ $ Per Month	
Months @ $ Per Month	
Months @ $ Per Month	
Months @ $ Per Month	
TITLE CHARGES	
Settlement Or Closing Fee ("Escrow Fee") To:	
Abstract Or Title Search To:	
Title Examination To:	
Title Insurance Binder To:	
Document Preparation To:	
Notary Fees To:	
Attorney's Fees To: (Includes Above Item Numbers)	
Title Insurance To: IRES (Includes Above Item Numbers)	618.75
Lender's Coverage $	
Owner's Coverage $	
GOVERNMENT RECORDING AND TRANSFER CHARGES:	
Recording Fees: Mortgage/Deed of Trust $ 43.50 Release $	43.50
City/County Tax/Stamps: $	
State Tax/Stamps $	0.00
ADDITIONAL SETTLEMENT CHARGES:	
Survey To:	
Pest Inspection To:	
Architectural/Engineering Services To:	
Building Permit To:	
TOTAL SETTLEMENT CHARGES (Enter On Line 1602)	5,584.31

M. DISBURSEMENT TO OTHERS	
1501. AMERICAN APPLIANCE	282.00
1502. CHASE MORTGAGE	49,581.15
1503. FINGERHUT	1,480.00
1504. HOME DEPOT	1,068.00
1505. M WARD	170.00
1506. UNVL BK NATIONAL	408.00
1507. CADWICKS	368.00
1508. LERNER	355.00
1509. VICTORIA	253.00
1510. CREDIT LIFE INSURANCE	2,458.05
1511. CREDIT DISABILITY INSURANCE	1,928.71
1512.	
1513.	
1514.	
1515.	
1520. TOTAL DISBURSED (Enter On Line 1603)	58,351.91
N. NET SETTLEMENT	
1600. LOAN AMOUNT RL= Initial Advance (includes line 1400) CE= Principal Loan Amount	$64,028.39
1601. Plus Cash/Check From Borrower	
1602. Minus Total Settlement Charges (Line 1400)	$5,584.31
1603. Minus Total Disbursement To Others (Line 1520)	$58,351.91
1604. Equals Disbursement To Borrower (After Expiration Of Any Applicable Rescission Period Required By Law)	$92.17

ower's Signature — Borrower's Signature

Date:

er:

Loan features: mandatory arbitration; inflated appraisal; excessive debt: income; prepayment penalty; rate increased; payment increased over previous loan.

Some of the borrower's disbursements: Chase Mortgage $49,518.15; Fingerhut $1,480; Montgomery Ward $170; American Appliance $282; Home Depot $1,068; Credit Life $2,458; Credit Disability $1,928.

Figure 3.1 (continued)

SECONDARY MORTGAGE LOAN
This agreement is subject to the provisions of the Secondary Mortgage Loan Act
REVOLVING LOAN FIXED RATE AGREEMENT (Page 1 of 5)

LENDER (called "We", "Us", "Our")

BORROWERS (called "You", "Your")   LOAN NO:

ON PORTION OF AVERAGE DAILY BALANCE	MONTHLY PERIODIC RATE	ANNUAL PERCENTAGE RATE:	CREDIT LIMIT	DATE OF LOAN	APPLICATION FEE/ FINANCE CHARGE
.01 AND OVER	1.666 % =	19.989 %	15000	09/13/01	$ 450.00
	=		INITIAL ANNUAL FEE 50.00	SUBSEQUENT ANNUAL FEE 50.00	
		%			

In this Agreement, "you", "your" and "Borrower" mean the customer(s) who signs this Agreement. "We", "us", and "our" refer to Lender. This Agreement covers the terms and conditions of your Home Equity Credit Line Revolving Loan Account. We want you to understand how your Home Equity Credit Line Revolving Loan Account works. Read this carefully, ask us any questions, and if you agree to be bound by this Agreement, sign below. If more than one person signs, each will be responsible for repaying all sums advanced under this Agreement.

Your Home Equity Credit Line is a revolving line of credit extended to you and secured as described below. You can obtain funds from your Home Equity Credit Line Revolving Loan Account (up to your credit limit) directly from us or by using the special checks we supply to you. You may pay your total unpaid balance at any time or in installments.

YOU ARE GIVING US A SECURITY INTEREST IN THE REAL ESTATE LOCATED AT THE ABOVE ADDRESS.

REQUIRED INSURANCE. You must obtain insurance for term of loan covering security for this loan as indicated by the word "YES" below, naming us as Loss Payee:

    Title Insurance on real estate security.
    Fire and extended coverage insurance on real estate security.

    You may obtain any required insurance from anyone you choose.

NOTICE: SEE THE FOLLOWING PAGES FOR ADDITIONAL PROVISIONS AND IMPORTANT INFORMATION REGARDING YOUR RIGHTS TO DISPUTE BILLING ERRORS.

09-01-00
F PHL

PA057451

KP07124EB1J95RLA8DDDPA057451C**PASCHAL   *   CUSTOMER COPY

This second loan was originated at the same time as the initial loan to cover the other "usual" fees—beyond the points—associated with that first loan.

sylvania and many other states, that the broker they hired represented their interest. Brokers in the Commonwealth of Pennsylvania do not have a fiduciary obligation to their customers, and while some act as though they do, many do not. Where the borrower already has a wide-angle view of the credit markets, as many higher-income borrowers do, this may not present a serious problem. However, where the borrower's view of the credit market is limited, the broker can arrange a transaction that produces a nice return for his/her efforts but no real benefit for the borrower. To the extent that borrowers—especially lower-income borrowers—either do not read relevant documents or lack the capacity to understand them, brokers can easily take advantage of the borrower's constricted view of the mortgage market.[7]

Finally, unlike the prime mortgage market, subprime lenders generally operate under a veil of secrecy when it comes to pricing, thus intentionally placing the borrower at a disadvantage. White states:

In contrast, subprime mortgage rates at the retail level are secret. No newspaper's real estate section will list current subprime mortgage rates. The rate tables used by wholesale subprime lenders are made available only to brokers and are sometimes regarded as trade secrets.[8]

And so, taken together, the terms—and—consequences the method by which the borrower comes to get the loan—and the imbalance of information create the conditions within which the predatory loan is made.

PHILADELPHIA: PAST AND PRESENT

Philadelphia has experienced a steady and substantial decline in population since its peak of over 2.1 million in 1950 to just over 1.5 million in 2000. Were it not for net natural increases in population and a small increase due to net international migration between 1990 and 2000, net domestic migration would have taken the population down by more than 260,000 people in that period.[9]

The housing stock, built largely prior to the peak population period,[10] has in many areas been abandoned and devalued. Between 1990 and 2000, while there were areas of the city where residential rents and property values appreciated strongly (e.g., the residential downtown), average values fell by 5.9 percent and rents by 6.1 percent (net of inflation). During the 1990s, Philadelphia demolished more than 1,000 buildings a year, but could not keep pace with its abandonment problem; the city is in many ways a "blight machine." Although there are recent signs that Philadelphia's residential property market is strengthening, it is still struggling with more than 26,000 vacant residential buildings, 2,500 vacant industrial buildings and 31,000 vacant lots.[11]

In contrast to the City of Philadelphia, the population of the Philadelphia region is actually growing, albeit slowly. It is not only growing slowly but it is consuming land for residential development at a disproportionate rate. Data from the American Housing Survey suggest that average new home lot sizes in the Philadelphia region are increasing. Between 1985 and 1999, the percent of homes situated on lots between one-half and one acre in size more than doubled, from 11.9 percent to 25.9 percent.[12] As a result of the thinning growth pattern, since 1969 the Philadelphia region has lost about one-third of its agricultural land, mostly in the far reaches of the suburban counties.[13]

And while Philadelphia remains the core of the region, its role as a central organizing economic force has diminished. Total full- and part-time employment dropped from 1.05 million in 1970 to 792,000 in 2000,[14] and one ZIP code in Montgomery County, Pennsylvania—King of Prussia, the home of the King of Prussia Mall—has at least as many retail jobs as the entirety of downtown Philadelphia.[15] Manufacturing, once the economic locus of Philadelphia's strength, has declined consistently and significantly (e.g., the percentage of the region's manufacturing jobs in the city of Philadelphia declined from over 77 percent at the turn of the twentieth century to just over 50 percent in 1950 to the current figure of under 20 percent). Between 1970 and 2000 alone, employment in the manufacturing sector fell from nearly 242,000 to 58,000.[16]

Racially, Philadelphia's African American and Latino populations have grown steadily. Today, African Americans constitute 43.2 percent of all Philadelphians, and Latinos, 8.5 percent. Yet Philadelphia remains a highly segregated city (with an Index of Dissimilarity score of 76.4 for African Americans). The Philadelphia region, although showing some small signs of improvement, remains the twelfth most segregated region (having more than 1 million residents in 1980) in the country, with a D value of 72.0.[17]

Philadelphia's banking community has historically invested more heavily in certain communities, leaving the others to rely upon smaller banking institutions and other outlets for housing capital.[18] Patterns of lending that avoided areas of racial concentration many decades ago can be found to impact racial segregation patterns for many years into the future.[19] Without several significant Community Reinvestment Act (CRA) settlements and special programs like the Philadelphia Mortgage Plan (and its successor, the Delaware Valley Mortgage Plan), many of Philadelphia's lower-income and minority communities would have been without reasonable access to the city's mainstream financial institutions. Founded in 1975 in response to community-based charges of redlining and disinvestment, the Delaware Valley Mortgage Plan has provided nearly 28,000 loans totaling $763 million—the vast majority of which are in the City of Philadelphia. As much as that sounds, it is important to recognize that in a typical year, more than

15,000 loans are made for the purchase of homes or refinance of mortgages in Philadelphia.[20] So the Delaware Valley Mortgage Plan has clearly been a help, but it hasn't fundamentally altered access to credit for the majority of Philadelphia's lower-income people and places.

Lending in Lower-Income Areas of Philadelphia

Data from the 2001 (HMDA) reports for the City of Philadelphia reveal that 14 percent of all home purchase mortgage loans were originated by subprime lenders, as were 24 percent of refinances.[21] The proportions of prime and subprime vary dramatically by the average income level in census tracts. Specifically, as incomes increase, so does the percent of loans that are prime. In low-income tracts (i.e., those with income below 50 percent of the Metropolitan Statistical Area [MSA] average), the percent of home purchase mortgage loans that are subprime is 21.0 percent; in moderate-income areas (i.e., those with incomes between 50 percent and 79 percent of the MSA average), the percent of home purchase mortgage loans that are subprime is 21.2 percent; in middle-income areas (i.e., those with incomes between 80 percent and 119 percent of the MSA average), the percent of home purchase mortgage loans that are subprime is 11.1 percent; in high-income areas (i.e., those with incomes greater than 120 percent of the MSA average), the percent of home purchase mortgage loans that are subprime is 5.4 percent (see Figure 3.2).[22]

Subprime activity in Philadelphia is generally more prevalent among mortgage refinances. And, as with home purchase mortgage loans, the shares of prime and subprime vary by income level of census tracts such that lower-income areas have higher rates of subprime lending. In low-income tracts, the percent of refinance mortgages that are subprime is 46.6 percent; in moderate-income areas, the percent of refinance mortgages that are subprime is 28.1 percent; in middle-income areas, the percent of refinance mortgages that are subprime is 17.8 percent; in high-income areas, the percent of refinance mortgages that are subprime is 10.8 percent.

The presence of subprime loans in and of itself does not necessarily mean that borrowers are getting a less appropriate product. To the extent that differences in credit, income, and collateral justify the subprime loans, they are entirely appropriate. On the other hand, to the extent that there are not such differences, subprime loans are disadvantageous.[23]

HMDA data show that the array of institutions most active in the lower- and moderate- income communities is substantially different from those in the middle- and higher-income places (see Appendix 3.1). The substantial market penetration of subprime lenders into lower- and moderate-income communities represents a double-edged sword. While lenders are making credit available, they are doing so at a price. Richard Williams, Reynold Nesiba, and Eileen McConnell said it well:

Figure 3.2
Percent of Loans That Are Subprime by Census Tract Income Level:
Philadelphia, 2001

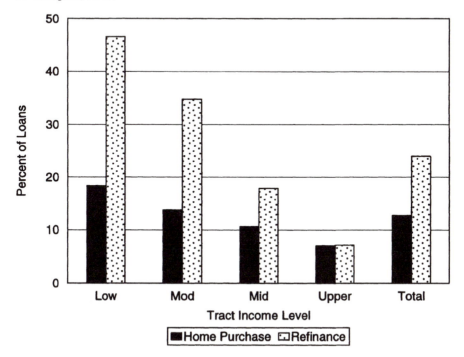

As classical economic theory would predict, a deregulated marketplace has made it possible for low income and minority groups to get credit like never before. This has helped them to achieve record rates of home ownership and to also get loans for any number of other purposes. But, as sociological network theories suggest, the new lenders are quite unlike the old ones. As a result, the gains made by underserved markets have come in very different ways than those made by the rest of American society. For better or for worse, as the old inequalities have slowly diminished, new inequalities have replaced them.[24]

Extent of GSE Benefit in Lower-Income Communities

When Fannie Mae Corporation (and later Freddie Mac) were established, Congress had several intentions, among which was to create liquidity in the home mortgage market. Beyond that, the congressional intention was to provide for standardization and, along with that, market efficiencies that would translate into advantageous pricing for borrowers. Generally, subprime loans are not purchased by the nation's GSEs. The logical inference, then, is that communities of lower income tend not to have the economic advantages afforded by the GSEs to higher-income communities. Kenneth

Figure 3.3
Percent of Conventional Loans Purchased by GSEs: Philadelphia, 2001

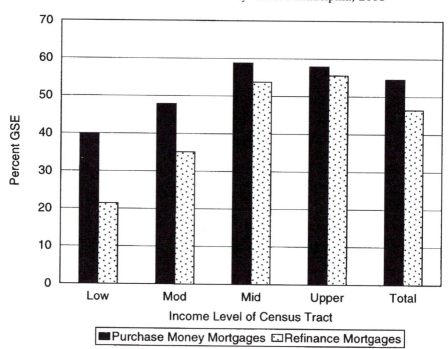

Temkin, Jennifer Johnson, and Diana Levy[25] and Brent Ambrose, Thomas Thibodeau, and Kenneth Temkin[26] suggest that were the GSEs to get more actively involved in the market, the price differential (rates, points and fees) between prime and subprime rates that borrowers with subprime credit pay would be reduced.[27]

In Philadelphia, the percentage of home purchase mortgage loans purchased by GSEs in low-income areas is 39.9 percent; in moderate-income areas, it is 47.8 percent; in middle-income areas, 58.8 percent; in high-income areas, 57.9 percent. The percentage of home purchase mortgage loans purchased by "others" (i.e., neither a GSE, commercial bank, savings bank or savings institution, or life insurance company or affiliate institution) in low-income areas is 42.0 percent; in moderate-income areas, it is 33.2 percent; in middle-income areas, 29.1 percent; in high-income areas, 27.8 percent (see Figures 3.3 and 3.4).

GSEs purchase 21.4 percent of refinance mortgages in low-income areas; 35.1 percent in moderate-income areas; 53.8 percent in middle-income areas; 55.6 percent in high-income areas. The percent of refinance mortgages purchased by "others" in low-income areas is 55.5 percent; 43.1 per-

Figure 3.4
Percent of GSE Mortgage Purchases by Census Tract Income Level:
Philadelphia, 2002

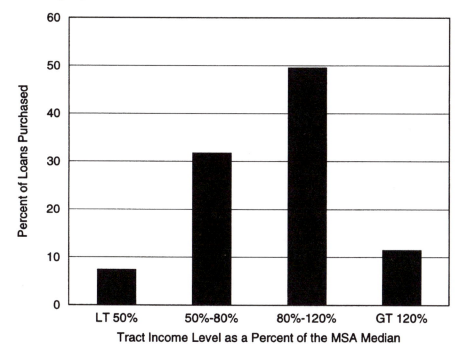

cent in moderate-income areas; 27.8 percent in middle-income areas; 28.3 percent in high-income areas.[28]

One important question that remains is whether the price paid by borrowers with subprime loans is commensurate with the risk they present, and whether that risk exceeds the reward to both the borrower and the community.

Patterns of Lending in Philadelphia: When Lending Erodes Equity

In order to comprehend the totality of loan transactions on a property, I selected a random sample of 2,289 properties in the city of Philadelphia. Those properties are representative of the entirety of the city.[29]

Among those properties, 24.6 percent had a refinance mortgage in the recorded mortgage history. Seven percent of the sample properties had a Sheriff Sale recorded; the likelihood of a Sheriff Sale is higher in lower-priced areas. The percent of properties in low-priced areas with a history including a Sheriff Sale is 13.6 percent; in moderate-priced areas, 10.5 percent; in middle-priced areas, 4.3 percent; in high-priced areas, 2.1 percent.[30]

In Philadelphia, the Board of Revision of Taxes is responsible for assessing the value of all property. It typically estimates a property's market value on the basis of comparable properties in the area and then applies a ratio to determine the assessed value of the property for tax purposes. That ratio is approximately one-third. It is acknowledged locally that properties are not evaluated at their true and complete market value; there is something known locally as the "implicit discount." If we use a ratio of 5.0—far in excess of the 3.3 that the ratio of market to assessed value should be—we can determine a conservative estimate of a home's value. Then, by comparing that value with the principal amount due, we can determine whether homes have mortgages in excess of their value.[31]

Overall, regardless of the number of liens existing against a property, approximately 18 percent of homes have loans exceeding five times the assessed value. This figure is, however, not uniform across the city. In low-priced areas, 12.5 percent of properties have loans exceeding five times the estimated value; in moderately-priced areas, 23 percent have such excessive loans; in middle-priced areas, 16.7 percent have excessive loans; in high-priced areas, 13.4 percent have excessive loans.[32]

If we look only at homes with two or more liens (attempting to capture the phenomena of a refinance in excess of the home's value), the percentages of loans exceeding value are substantially different. In low-priced areas, 50 percent of properties have excessive loans; in moderately priced areas, 50.9 percent; in middle-priced areas, 23.1 percent; in high-priced areas, 15.8 percent. Under either scenario, it appears that homes in lower and moderately priced areas are more likely to have principal balances in excess of the home's value.

In terms of mortgage refinances, approximately 21 percent of all properties in the sample had a mortgage refinance in their history with the current owner and had complete information on the first and most recent mortgages. Among those properties, 61.1 percent had the first mortgage with a prime lender; among those same properties, 52.1 percent had a second/subsequent loan with a prime lender.[33]

Repeated mortgage refinances on a home may suggest loss of equity. One distinct (and measurable) pattern is when the property owner has multiple small loans that are ultimately rolled into a larger loan. If we focus on owners with multiple small loans refinanced into a large loan after 1993 (a watershed year for the securitization of subprime loans),[34] we observe that in lower-value areas, refinances suggesting equity loss are more prevalent.[35] Owing to sample size concerns, I have collapsed low- and moderate-priced areas into one group ("low/mod"). In low/mod areas, 20.4 percent of homes manifest this pattern; in middle-priced areas, 16.3 percent; in high-priced areas, 12.8 percent.

One can always argue that the refinance and consolidation of various forms of debt into a mortgage advantages the borrower by making the interest paid tax-deductible. However there is research to suggest that at lower income levels, people are less likely to itemize their deductions and thus are not reaping such benefits.[36] Further, it is not uncommon to find people who have rolled small, short-term unsecured debt into home mortgages. This may lower monthly payments, but it raises long-term debt and removes equity from the home. It also makes the impact of any (even minor) household financial stressor far more serious because the loss of a home, rather than the repossession of household goods, hangs in the balance.

Among those properties that started out with a prime loan and had that loan refinanced, 66.6 percent refinanced into a prime loan; 27.9 percent refinanced into a subprime loan; 5.6 percent refinanced with a lender that could not readily be identified as either prime or subprime (i.e., these lenders did both sorts of lending).[37] Among those properties that started with a subprime loan and refinanced, 29.0 percent ended up with a prime lender; 66.7 percent ended up with a subprime lender; and 4.3 percent ended up with a lender that did both sorts of lending.

The refinance pattern is very different, depending upon the value of homes in the surrounding area. For example, the likelihood of a prime-to-subprime refinance in a lower-price area (34.8 percent) is substantially higher than in higher-price areas (12.5 percent). The refinance pattern reflecting "credit repair" (subprime to prime loan refinances) is far more prevalent in higher-value areas (42.9 percent) than in lower-value areas (20.7 percent) (see Figures 3.5 and 3.6).

Foreclosures in Philadelphia

Legally, a foreclosure is defined as follows:

The process by which a mortgagor of real property or personal property, or other owner of property subject to a lien, is deprived of his interest therein. A proceeding in equity whereby a mortgagee either takes title to or forces the sale of the mortgagor's property in satisfaction of a debt.[38]

At the most basic level, a foreclosure generally means that an individual has stopped making payments on a mortgage (voluntarily or involuntarily) and, unless those payments begin—or, in the case of Philadelphia, the Commonwealth intervenes—a bankruptcy is successfully filed or some other extraordinary event occurs, the individual is going to lose his or her home.[39] Whether the foreclosure results from an abusive lending practice or an individual's abuse of his or her own credit, the result is the same. For the individual, the loss is personally devastating. Loss as well is experienced by

Figure 3.5
Refinance Patterns of Loans by Census Tract Housing Values

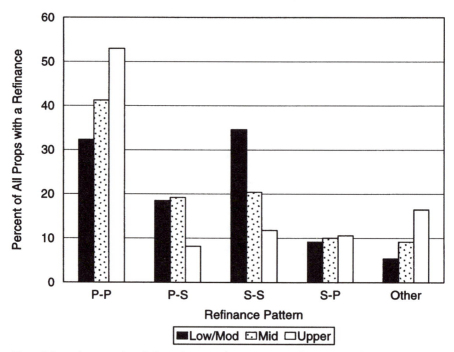

Note: P-P = prime to prime; P-S = prime to subprime; S-S = subprime to subprime; S-P = subprime to prime; Other = refinance involves a lender that cannot be identified as either prime or subprime.

the lender and the investor. And unless the vitality of the property market within which the property is located is strong, it foreshadows another long-term vacant property and thus community loss.

A random sample of 770 mortgage foreclosures filed in Philadelphia between 2000 and 2002 was selected from a database of all foreclosures filed during that period.[40] In Philadelphia, a foreclosure action must be filed with the court, and it is the prothonotary (who serves as the clerk of the courts) who is the official responsible for accepting these filings. Foreclosures, however, are not necessarily filed in the name of the originating lender. These filings are typically in the name of whatever entity is servicing the loan at the time of the foreclosure; they can also be filed in the name of the trust into which a loan has been sold or even the attorney who filed the foreclosure action. Since any issues related to the underwriting or origination of the loan need to be attributed back to that original lender, each of the sampled foreclosures was looked up in a database of public record filings

Figure 3.6
Likelihood of a Specified Refinance Pattern by Area Housing Value

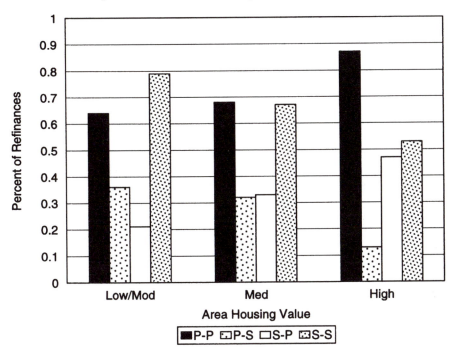

Note: P-P = prime to prime; P-S = prime to subprime; S-P = subprime to prime; S-S = subprime to subprime.

which allowed, in most cases, identification of the original lender and the date that the loan in foreclosure was made.[41] (See Appendix 3.2 for a sample of the data used to identify the lender responsible for originating the loan in foreclosure.)

Of all foreclosed loans, 6.2 percent occurred in areas with average housing values under $25,000; 48.9 percent in areas with homes valued between $25,000 and $49,999; 41.3 percent in areas with homes valued between $50,000 and $99,999; 3.6 percent in areas with homes valued at $100,000 and over.[42]

The average period of time between origination and foreclosure in low-priced areas was 2.4 years (median = 2.0 years); in moderate-priced areas, 3.1 years (median = 2.6 years); in middle-priced areas, 3.4 years (median = 2.9 years); in high-priced areas, 4.9 years (median = 3.7 years).

Among loans in foreclosure originated by prime lenders, 6.8 percent were in low-priced areas; 40.7 percent were in moderate-priced areas; 45.8 percent were in middle-priced areas; 6.8 percent were in high-priced areas. Among loans in foreclosure originated by subprime lenders, 6.5 percent were in low-priced areas; 51.4 percent were in moderate-priced areas; 39.5 percent were in moderate-priced areas; 2.6 percent were in high-priced areas.

On average, the period of time between origination and foreclosure for prime loans was 5.9 years (median = 5.0 years); for subprime loans, 2.9 years (median = 2.5 years). Of all foreclosure filings, 33.9 percent occurred within two years of loan origination; 49.9 percent occurred between two and five years of origination; 16.1 percent occurred after five years. Among foreclosure filings by prime lenders, 6.5 percent occurred within two years; among foreclosure filings by subprime lenders, 37.8 percent occurred within two years.[43]

In low-priced areas, the average principal amount due exceeds the average estimated value of the homes in foreclosure (i.e., average principal is 1.4 times average estimated value); in moderate-priced areas, it is slightly less than the average estimated value of homes in foreclosure; in middle-priced areas, it is approximately 82 percent of the average estimated value of homes in foreclosure; in high-priced areas, it is 74.3 percent. Among loans in foreclosure originated by prime lenders, the average principal amount is 84 percent of the average value of homes in foreclosure; among loans in foreclosure originated by subprime lenders, it is 90.1 percent.[44] Because a higher percentage of loans originated in higher-priced areas tend to be prime and those loans take longer to go to foreclosure, some of the difference in average time to foreclosure by area housing price may be explained simply by the different market penetration of prime and subprime lenders. What that does not explain, though, is how so many homes have principal amounts due exceeding average home values. That can be explained by only two things: (1) drops in home prices since mortgages were originated; (2) loans initially made in excess of the home's value.[45] Data on housing prices in Philadelphia suggest that prices in lower-value areas tended to be relatively stable over the 1990s and recently have experienced somewhat of a rise.

In short, the data on foreclosures in Philadelphia suggest a few basic facts: (1) foreclosures overall disproportionately occur not in the lowest-priced areas, but in areas of slightly higher values; (2) loans in foreclosure that were originated by subprime lenders are, more than loans originated by prime lenders, clustered in the lower (but not lowest) value areas; (3) subprime loans go into foreclosure much faster than prime loans; (4) properties in foreclosure that have subprime loans have substantially higher loan amounts in relation to estimated property values—in some instances exceeding the property value.

The Sheriff Sale is one possible conclusion of a mortgage foreclosure; others include curing the mortgage, entering into a forbearance agreement, obtaining assistance from the Commonwealth of Pennsylvania's Homeowners' Emergency Mortgage Assistance Program, and giving up the deed

Figure 3.7
Comparison of Distribution of Owner-Occupied Properties, Foreclosures, and
Sheriff Sales

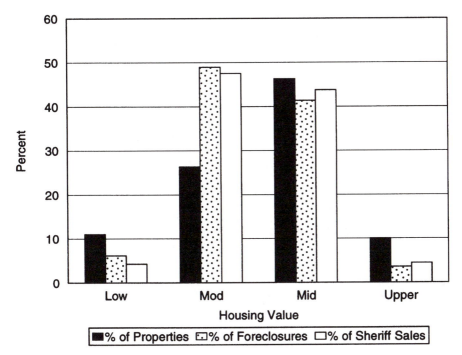

in lieu of foreclosure.[46] Data describing the monthly number of homes actually sold at Sheriff Sale between the second half of 1996 and the first half of 2002 depict a radical rise in Philadelphia. In 1996, the monthly average sold was 104; by the first half of 2002, it was 239.

The distribution of properties sold at Sheriff Sale between 2000 and 2003 (first half of the calendar year) reveals a disproportionality most notable in the moderately priced areas (see Figure 3.7). That is, there are many more homes sold at Sheriff Sale than one would expect from the number of owner-occupied properties and foreclosure actions filed.

Quantifying the Impact of a Sheriff Sale on Housing Prices

The listing of a home for auction by the Sheriff of a jurisdiction is undoubtedly a traumatic event for the person or family residing in the home. And our interviews with members of the lending industry suggest that Sheriff Sales generally cost lenders money. But what happens to a community when homes are put up for auction in this manner? There is little if any research to date that speaks to this issue. At best in Philadelphia there is a

Figure 3.8
2000 Median Home Value by Tract

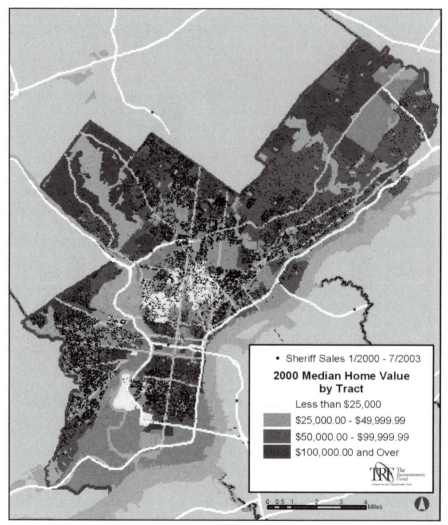

study that quantifies the impact of a vacant property on surrounding values.[47]

However, as is shown in Figure 3.8, there are entire communities devastated by foreclosure filings and Sheriff Sales.

Using data from the Philadelphia Board of Revision of Taxes regarding residential sales between 1996 and 2003, I attempted to quantify this impact. A simple regression model was built to predict median sale price in 2003 using median price in 1996, percent of homes listed for Sheriff Sale

Table 3.1
Regression Results Showing the Effects of Clustered Sheriff Sale Activity on Local Housing Prices

Variable	Unstandardized	Standardized	Sig.	Adj. R²
Median Price, 1996	1.676	.720	.000	
Percent of Listings Sold	382.035	.039	NS	.654
Moderate Sales per 1,000 Units	−28832.857	−.184	.000	
High Sales per 1,000 Units	−34563.603	−.136	.000	.678

that were actually sold, and the rate of Sheriff Sales per 1,000 owner-occupied housing units in 2000. Sheriff Sales included all listings between 2000 and 2003 inclusive.

The results of a straightforward regression model (Table 3.1) suggest the following, holding constant other factors:

- Home prices at the end of the period were higher in areas where homes were of higher value at the beginning of the period.

- Home prices were substantially lower where Sheriff Sales per 1,000 owner-occupied units were moderate or high, as opposed to areas where they were less frequent. Specifically, holding constant other factors, the average tract price was lower by nearly $29,999 where Sheriff Sales per 1,000 owner-occupied units were between 18.14 and 46.62 (the 50th through 90th percentile), and by some $34,563 in areas where sales per 1,000 owner-occupied units exceeded 46.62.

- Although not statistically significant, the impact of the indicator of the percent of listings that were sold suggests that property values tended to be higher where listings were being sold with greater frequency. Intuitively, this makes sense, because in areas with more substantial value, Sheriff Sales constitute an opportunity to obtain a property of significant value for a discount. Areas with lower values are generally associated with homes listed for Sheriff Sale that, if not sold, remain vacant and thus impact negatively on surrounding values.

In short, while this analysis is not definitive, it is suggestive that where Sheriff Sales occur in great numbers, there are substantial and significant decreases of local property values.

WHAT THE CONSUMERS AND PRACTITIONERS SAY

The processes and outcomes that are described in this research are more than just the consequences of a series of economically rational (or irrational) decisions. They are processes that impact individuals, families, and communities in a most tangible way. Purely economic logic may suggest that the underlying transaction(s) should never have taken place.[48] But in the context of what people bring to the transaction, they are understandable.

Interviews with both brokers and borrowers affirm what we know of a historical pattern that minority group members and lower-income individuals, as well as individuals residing in minority and lower-priced areas, typically have not had complete access to mainstream financial institutions. Unilaterally, interviewees in the lending industry acknowledge a history of restricted capital access in lower-priced areas (and especially in areas that are home to members of minority groups). This absence of mainstream mortgage money left a void that was filled by consumer discount and finance companies that made loans in small amounts (albeit commensurate with need) but with very high interest rates. One interviewee, a former owner of a finance company quite active in the Philadelphia market, reported that his institution was more lenient than the mainstream banks, which simply would not lend money in the communities in which he operated. Another interviewee, an attorney who conducts closings primarily for subprime lenders, noted that in many of the lower- and moderate-income African American communities of Philadelphia there are no (or few) bank branches. Once outside the city limits, bank branches are plentiful.[49]

With changes in the legal environment and the concomitant evolution of the lending industry, the consumer discount and finance companies were largely replaced by the bigger subprime lenders that were willing to make loans in the areas of more modest means.[50] But those loans were in amounts far in excess of what people needed—or wanted. People were frequently talked into paying off items in transactions that simply made no financial sense.

Lower-income people are more likely to suffer from a lack of savings and sufficient income to maintain their homes.[51] Such individuals have historically used their homes as credit cards because savings generally are not as plentiful as they are for individuals of greater means. One consequence of the use of the home in this way is creation of a data artifact that is used to identify individuals who may be solicited for various financial products. Brokers and those who sell credit information report that some brokers target people with a history of borrowing from finance companies—which is more frequent among lower-income individuals—and actively solicit them for subprime debt-consolidation/refinance loans. Brokers and those who sell credit information additionally report that credit scores help target those whose alternatives may be limited.[52]

Our interviews and the literature suggest that lower-income individuals are less likely to be able to fully comprehend the totality of the transactions—with all of its complexities.[53] First, most borrowers interviewed had no knowledge of the fees associated with their loans. We did not interview a single borrower who knew about the fees that he or she paid for their loan; some had a general idea about the interest rate for their loan. Most also had an idea of what they were supposed to be paying monthly, since that was the focus of discussion between them and the loan officer/broker. One interviewee, a 48-year-old African American female, upon being asked about whether the lender discussed the costs associated with her loan, responded, "What do you mean 'costs'?" More than one interviewee didn't realize that borrowing money meant that there would be a lien against their home. The current collection of disclosure documents does not add much to the understanding of the process. In the words of an African American mortgage broker interviewee, "They don't mean shit."

Second, borrowers didn't always understand other aspects of their loans. For example, a 67-year-old African American male interviewee stated that he understood he had one loan that wasn't very advantageous to him; he did not know that there was a second loan, with a higher interest rate, that covered just the fees of his first loan—and costs associated with making the second loan. Another interviewee, a 71-year-old African American female, stated that she thought she had just one loan, only to find out that there was a second loan representing the costs associated with a forced-placed property insurance policy. The loan was for more than $3,000, covered one year, and excluded the contents of her home; and she already had a policy. (See Appendix 3.5 for a copy of this interviewee's property history.)

And to the extent that lower-income individuals deal with institutions that deliver product through wholesale channels (i.e., brokers), since those brokers report typically dealing with as few as three to five lenders, the lower-income individual is not seeing the benefit of the totality of the market.[54]

Mortgage brokers remain a troubling part of the transaction—especially for individuals of more modest means. Interviewees representative of the title and appraisal businesses report many more problematic transactions when brokers are involved. One representative of a title company stated quite clearly that he preferred to deal with retail lenders so that brokers were not involved.

Brokers in Pennsylvania have a very low threshold for licensure and have no fiduciary responsibility to the borrower.[55] Although they typically view the borrower as their customer, in the final analysis the brokers can just as easily arrange deals that benefit them more than the borrower. Brokers report a range of behavior in this regard, with some stating that they do whatever is quickest and easiest;[56] others report shopping a borrower's application around and finding the best deal. In fact, the NAMB Model Mortgage Loan Origination Agreement states:

Section 1. Nature of Relationship

In connection with this mortgage loan we are acting as an independent contractor and not as your agent. We will enter into separate independent contractor agreements with various lenders. While we seek to assist you in meeting your financial needs, we do not distribute the products of all lenders or investors in the market and cannot guarantee the lowest price or best terms available in the market.[57]

For most borrowers, the legal distinction between "agent" and "independent contractor" is meaningless. They think the broker is working for them.[58]

Structurally, there may in fact be a market problem in finding ways to deliver small loans. While reports vary, brokers report actual costs per transaction in excess of $1,000—accordingly, individuals needing smaller amounts of money are likely to have to pay more (as a percentage) than individuals needing larger amounts of money. The alternative, as has been reported by borrowers and others, is that small needs for money are converted into larger loans than the borrower would otherwise require.

CONCLUSIONS

One can argue about the exact percentage of transactions that have predatory lending characteristics in Philadelphia or other places. What is without dispute, though, is that it is clearly a problem requiring our attention and that foreclosures and resultant community damage are on the rise.

There is a dearth of financially responsible product effectively pursuing markets in the lower- and moderately priced areas of Philadelphia. Accordingly, persons who reside in these areas historically have resorted to a set of lenders and loan products that, unlike those that have routinized and brought economic efficiency to the higher-priced areas, tend to be less routine and more expensive, and end up producing severe financial distress for the borrower far more frequently. These effects touch not only the persons who have experienced the loss, but their neighbors as well.[59] Estimates of the impact of a mortgage foreclosure on surrounding values can be as much as 20 percent. Our own interviews with attorneys who handle mortgage foreclosures suggest that the extended time period between foreclosure and Sheriff Sale and then after the sale adversely impacts the property itself as well as those around the vacated property. Some other research suggests that the foreclosure, independent of other factors, can even speed the process of racial transition.[60] And so, lower- and moderate-income areas, already strained by the array of products and financial actors available to them, are placed under added social and economic pressure.

In recognition of the elevated likelihood of predatory lending on the lower-income communities and residents of Philadelphia, the city created two loan products—PHIL Plus and Mini Phil.[61] These are designed to make credit available to people with less than perfect credit, in amounts not exceeding need, and at reasonable rates. To facilitate the participation of mainstream financial institutions, the city used funds from its neighborhood municipal blight bond to create a reserve fund for lenders that participate. A fund was also created to refinance people who had fallen victim to abusive lending practices, the Home Equity Loan Preservation Program. That loan fund is administered by a housing counseling association, ACORN, and The Reinvestment Fund.

Almost all who have studied this issue, regardless of political orientation, conclude that in order to make the financing experience of lower-income people and people residing in lower-priced communities more transparent and less exploitative than it is now, three things must happen: (1) vigorous law enforcement to protect consumers from fraudulent and other illegal acts; (2) creation/delivery of good product to supplant that which is problematic; (3) education of consumers. All of these have their role. Yet it is without doubt that the number of foreclosures in the pipeline threatens the very life not only of the poorest of communities but also of those at the next rung up.[62] Law enforcement, reasonable product, and education must therefore be targeted to those places under financial stress before the tidal wave of foreclosures threatens their very existence.

Finally, the question of price versus risk needs to be broadened. The analysis must not include only the risk of default[63] or prepayment against the price of capital, but also the individual costs to the homeowner who loses a home and the social costs that ensue when homes in a community are foreclosed and sit vacant, acting as a blighting influence on the neighbors.[64]

APPENDIX 3.1: LENDERS ACTIVE IN PHILADELPHIA HOUSING SUBMARKETS

The most active subprime lenders for conventional refinance mortgages are:

Upper Income	Lower/Moderate Income
Greenpoint Mortgage	Delta Funding
Aegis Mortgage	American Business Financial
First Union National Bank	Option One Mortgage
Decision One Mortgage	Beneficial Corporation
Travelers Bank & Trust, FSB	Conseco Finance—tied with Household Bank, FSB[65]

The most active prime lenders for conventional refinance mortgages are:

Upper Income	Lower/Moderate Income
GMAC Mortgage	First Union NB
Wells Fargo Home Mortgage	PNC Bank NA
Chase Manhattan Mortgage	Police & Fire CU

Washington Mutual Bank, FA   Key Bank USA, NA
PNC Bank NA   GMAC Mortgage

The most active subprime lenders for conventional home purchase mortgage loans are:

Upper Income   **Lower/Moderate Income**

Greenpoint Mortgage Funding   Option One Mortgage Corp.
Chase Manhattan Bank USA, NA   Greenpoint Mortgage Funding
Equity One, Inc.   Equity One, Inc.
Option One Mortgage Corp.   First Franklin Financial Corp.
Aegis Mortgage Corp.   Superior Bank FSB

The most active prime lenders for conventional home purchase mortgage loans are:

Upper Income   **Lower/Moderate Income**

Sovereign Bank   Sovereign Bank
Chase Manhattan Mortgage   Countrywide Home Loans
Wells Fargo Home Mortgage   First Union Mortgage Corp.
Cendant Mortgage   Beneficial Savings Bank
GMAC Mortgage   Mellon Bank, NA

APPENDIX 3.2: LEADING LENDERS AMONG PROPERTIES IN FORECLOSURE

Leading lenders among loans going quickly to foreclosure (i.e., within two years of origination)

Lender	Percent of All Foreclosures Within Two Years
Equicredit	16.9%
Option One	12.8%
Delta Funding	7.4%
New Century	5.4%
Ameriquest	4.1%

Leading lenders among loans going to foreclosure in census tracts with median value under $25,000

Lender	Percent of All Foreclosures in Areas With Median Value <$25,000
Equicredit	17.4%
Ameriquest	8.7%
New Century	8.7%

Delta Funding	6.5%
United Companies	6.5%

Leading lenders among loans going to foreclosure in census tracts with median value between $25,000 and $49,999

Lender	Percent of All Foreclosures in Areas with Median Value >$25,000 and <$50,000
Equicredit	13.5%
Option One	6.3%
Delta Funding	4.9%
United Companies	4.7%
Advanta	3.3%
Money Store	3.3%

APPENDIX 3.3 SAMPLE DATA USED TO IDENTIFY THE LENDER ORIGINATING THE LOAN IN FORECLOSURE

Data from the foreclosure filing stated that the process was initiated by Manufacturers and Traders Trust Company on October 17, 2002. The principal balance of the loan at that time was $33,501. Although redacted to protect personal privacy, these data show that the mortgage in foreclosure was originated by another mortgage company in January 1998.

Property Detail Report

For Property Located At
MUSGRAVE ST, PHILADELPHIA PA

RealQuest.com

Owner Information:

Owner Name:

Mailing Address: **MUSGRAVE ST, PHILADELPHIA PA 19119**

Phone Number: Vesting Codes: / /

Location Information:

Legal Description:

County:	**PHILADELPHIA, PA**	APN:	
Census Tract/Block:	**252.00 / 6**	Alternate APN:	
Township-Range-Sect:		Subdivision:	
Legal Book/Page:		Map Reference:	/
Legal Lot:		Tract #:	
Legal Block:		School District:	**1**
Market Area:	**17-D7**	Munic/Township:	**PHILADELPHIA**

Owner Transfer Information:

Recording/Sale Date:	/	Document Number:	
Sale Price:		Deed Type:	

Last Market Sale Information:

Recording/Sale Date:	1998 / (1997	1st Mtg Amount/Type:	**$34,350 / CONV**
Sale Price:	**$45,800**	1st Mtg Int. Rate/Type:	/
Sale Type:		2nd Mtg Amoun/Type:	**$13,740 / PRIVATE PARTY**
Document Number:		2nd Mtg Int. Rate/Type:	/
Deed Type:	**DEED (REG)**	Price Per SqFt:	**$39.35**
Transfer Doc Number:		Multi/Split Sale:	
New Construction:			
Title Company:			
Lender:			
Seller Name:			

Prior Sale Information:

Prior Rec/Sale Date:	1950 /	Prior Lender:	
Prior Sale Price:		Prior 1st Mtg Amt/Type:	/
Prior Doc Number:		Prior 1st Mtg Rate/Type:	/
Prior Deed Type:	**DEED (REG)**		

Property Characteristics:

Gross Area:		Parking Type:	**BASEMENT**	Construct Type:	
Living Area:	**1,164**	Garage Area:		Heat Type:	
Tot Adj Area:		Garage Capacity:		Exterior wall:	**MASONRY**
Above Grade:		Parking Spaces:		Porch Type:	
Total Rooms:		Basement Area:		Patio Type:	
Bedrooms:		Finish Bsmnt Area:		Pool:	
Bath(F/H):	/	Basement Type:		Air Conditioning:	
Year Built / Eff:	/	Roof Type:		Style:	
Fireplace:		Foundation:		Quality:	
# of Stories:	**2.00**	Roof Material:		Condition:	**AVERAGE**
Other Improvements:					

Site Information:

Zoning:		Acres:	**0.02**	County Use:	**RES-ROW WITH BASEMENT GARAGE**
Flood Zone:	**X**	Lot Area:	**870**	State Use:	
Flood Panel:		Lot Width/Depth:	**14 x 60**	Res/Comm Units:	**1 /**
Flood Panel Date:		Site Influence:		Sewer Type:	
Land Use:	**TOWNHOUSE/ROWHOUSE**			Water Type:	

Tax Information:

Assessed Value:	**$12,640**	Assessed Year:	**2004**	Property Tax:	**$1,044.57**
Land Value:	**$1,127**	Improve %:	**091%**	Tax Area:	
Improvement Value:	**$11,513**	Tax Exemption:		Tax Year:	**2004**
Total Taxable Value:					

Transaction History Report
For Property Located At
MUSGRAVE ST, PHILADELPHIA PA

RealQuest.com

TRANSACTION HISTORY

History Record #:	**1**		
Mortgage Recording Date:	**05/24/2002**	Mortgage Loan Type:	**CNV**
Mortgage Document No:		Mortgage Rate Type:	**FIXED**
Lender:	**PENNSYLVANIA HSNG FIN AGCY**	Mortgage Term:	
Loan Amount:	**$1,000**	Mortgage Rate:	**9**

History Record #:	**2**		
Mortgage Recording Date:	**03/01/2002**	Mortgage Loan Type:	**CNV**
Mortgage Document No:		Mortgage Rate Type:	**FIXED**
Lender:	**PENNSYLVANIA HSNG FIN AGCY**	Mortgage Term:	
Loan Amount:	**$13,000**	Mortgage Rate:	**9**

History Record #:	**3**		
Sale Recording Date:	**1998**	Sale Price:	**$45,800**
Sale Date:	**1997**	Sale Price Type:	
Recording Document No:		Multi/Split Sale:	
Document Type:	**DEED (REG)**	Other Document No:	
Title Company:			
Grantor:			
Grantee:			
Mortgage Recording Date:	**1998**	Mortgage Loan Type:	**CNV**
Mortgage Document No:		Mortgage Rate Type:	
Lender:	**GREENTREE MTG**	Mortgage Term:	**30 YEARS**
Loan Amount:	**$34,350**	Mortgage Rate:	
Mortgage Recording Date:	**1998**	Mortgage Loan Type:	**PP**
Mortgage Document No:		Mortgage Rate Type:	
Lender:		Mortgage Term:	**20 YEARS**
Loan Amount:	**$13,740**	Mortgage Rate:	
Mortgage Recording Date:	**1998**	Mortgage Loan Type:	**CNV**
Mortgage Document No:		Mortgage Rate Type:	
Lender:		Mortgage Term:	
Loan Amount:	**$6,870**	Mortgage Rate:	

History Record #:	**4**		
Sale Recording Date:	**07/01/1950**	Sale Price:	
Sale Date:		Sale Price Type:	
Recording Document No:		Multi/Split Sale:	
Document Type:	**DEED (REG)**	Other Document No:	
Title Company:			
Grantor:			
Grantee:			

APPENDIX 3.4: FORBEARANCE AGREEMENT AND ACCOMPANYING DEED IN LIEU OF FORECLOSURE

FORBEARANCE AGREEMENT

THIS FORBEARANCE AGREEMENT is made this ____ day of December, 2002, by and between   Mortgage.Services, Inc. (   ), a Pennsylvania corporation with an office at .
        Pennsylvania   , an individual with an address Michener Avenue, Philadelphia, Pennsylvania

BACKGROUND

A.   On October 31, 2001,   made a certain loan, advance and extension of credit to or for the benefit of .   (the "Borrower") in the original principal amount of $53,000.00 (the "Loan") pursuant to the terms and subject to the conditions of that certain promissory note dated October 31, 2001 in the original principal amount of $53,000.00 (the "Note") executed and delivered by the Borrower to

B.   In consideration of the Loan and as collateral security for the debts, liabilities and obligations of the Borrower to   as set forth in the Note (the "Obligations"),   granted, mortgaged and pledged to ABMS a continuing first lien on and security interest in that certain parcel of real property and the improvements thereon located at   Michener Avenue, City of Philadelphia, County of Philadelphia , Commonwealth of Pennsylvania (the "Property"), pursuant to the terms and subject to the conditions of that certain mortgage dated October 31, 2001 (the "Mortgage") executed and delivered by   to

C.   The Borrower is sometimes referred to herein as the "Obligor".

D.   The Note and the Mortgage, together with all other instruments, agreements and documents delivered in connection therewith are sometimes hereinafter collectively referred to as the "Loan Documents".

E.   The Obligor is in default under the Obligation to   by reason, inter alia, of (i) the failure to make timely payments as required under the Loan Documents, and (ii) the acknowledgment of the inability to cure the past due Obligation (the "Existing Defaults").

F.   The Obligor's Existing Defaults under the Obligation constitute an event of default under the Note and the Loan Documents. As a result of the Existing Defaults,   is permitted to exercise various rights and remedies arising under the Loan Documents.

G.   The Obligor has offered to deliver to   for the Property a Deed in Lieu of Mortgage Foreclosure which is to be held but not filed or recorded by provided that (i) the Obligor is in compliance with the obligations under the terms of this Forbearance Agreement, and (ii) this Forbearance has not terminated.

payments, $1,986.96, late charges of $298.03, unpaid fees of $6.00 and the Forbearance Fee of $500.00, shall be assessed to the Obligors as a Miscellaneous Fee. This Miscellaneous Fee of $2,790.99 must be paid in full by the Obligor as set forth in the following Paragraph.

VI. Forbearance Payments by Obligors.

The Obligor shall make the following payments to   , each of which, to be deemed timely and properly made, must be in good U.S. funds, and must be <u>received</u> by   on or before its due date:

      a. $500.00 upon the execution of this Forbearance Agreement.

      b.   On or before February 5, 2003, the Obligor shall commence the regular monthly payments under the Loan Documents in the amount of $496.74.

      c.   In addition to the regular monthly payment due, as well as any repayment of the Miscellaneous Fee described above, the Obligor shall pay   one-half (1/2) of any and all income tax refunds received, from both federal and state taxing authorities, within ten (10) days of receipt of such refund.

VII. Terminating Events.

For the purposes of this Agreement, a "Terminating Event" shall mean any one of the following:

      a.   The failure of the Obligor to comply with any warranty, covenant, condition, requirement, provision or agreement with which the Obligor is required to comply under the terms of this Agreement, the Loan Documents and all related instruments, agreements and documents referenced herein or therein.

      b.   Any representation, warranty or statement made by the Obligor in any financial statement or other document furnished or to be furnished to   in connection with this Agreement or the Loan Documents that is false or misleading in any respect.

      c.   The occurrence of any other event of default as defined in any of the Loan Documents or any of the instruments, agreements or documents executed in connection herewith or therewith.

      d.   The failure of the Obligor to remit any payment when due, whether under this Agreement or any Loan Document.

DEED IN LIEU OF FORECLOSURE

This Deed is made on December ___, 2002,

    BETWEEN   , unmarried, whose address is   Michener Avenue, Philadelphia, Pennsylvania 19150, referred to as the **Grantor,**

    AND

                    Company, whose address is   Boulevard, PA 19004, referred to as the **Grantee;**

WITNESSETH :

In consideration of One Dollar ($1.00), in hand paid, the receipt and sufficiency of which are hereby acknowledged, the Grantor does hereby grant and convey to the Grantee, in lieu of foreclosure, all that property that consists of the land and all the improvements, buildings and structures on the land at   Michener Avenue in the City of Philadelphia, County of Philadelphia and the Commonwealth of Pennsylvania. The legal description is attached as **Exhibit "A"**.

This Deed is intended to constitute a Deed in Lieu of Foreclosure and is under and subject to the provisions of that certain Mortgage dated October 31, 2001, in the original amount of $53,000.00 given to   Services, Inc. and recorded in the Office of the Recorder of Deeds for Philadelphia County in Mortgage Book _____, Page _____ &c. (the "Mortgage"), Grantee being a wholly-owned subsidiary and assignee of   Services, Inc. The execution, delivery and recording of this Deed shall not constitute a merger of all or any part or portion of the Mortgage or any rights of the mortgagee or the Grantee under the Mortgage, all of which are expressly reserved.

TOGETHER with all and singular the buildings and improvements, ways, streets, alleys, driveways, passages, waters, water-courses, rights, liberties, privileges, hereditaments and appurtenances, whatsoever belonging to the granted premises, or in any wise appertaining, and the reversions and remainders, rents, issues, and profits thereof; and all the estate, right, title, interest, property, claim and demand whatsoever of the said Grantor, as well at law as in equity, of, in, and to the same.

TO HAVE AND TO HOLD the said lot or piece of ground above described, with the buildings and improvements thereon erected, hereditaments and premises hereby granted, or mentioned and intended so to be, with the appurtenances, unto the Grantee, its successors, and assigns, to and for the only proper use and behoove of the Grantee, its successors and assigns forever.

APPENDIX 3.5: PROPERTY HISTORY OF INTERVIEWEE WHO HAD A SECOND LOAN ABOUT WHICH SHE WAS UNAWARE

The loan the property owner reports she did not realize she had was the 2/12/1997 loan from American Mortgage Reduction, for $2,815.

```
02/22/2001                     Property Detail              Copyright
04:14 pm                         RED Base              First American RES
------------------------------------------------------------------------

------------------------------ Location --------------------------------

Mun  :16                         HAGERT ST              Carrier
Map                          PHILADELPHIA, PA           Route : C031
Prcl                            PHILADELPHIA            Census: 0168.006
TaxId:

------------------------------ Ownership Data --------------------------

Current Owner:
Mail Address :      HAGERT ST PHILADELPHIA PA
Phone        :

------------------------------ Tax Data --------------------------------

Bldg/Subdiv  :
Land Use: O30, Row (3 or more), 2 Stories, Masonry
Land Assm:    $1,203   Lot Size: 152' x 112'   Style  : Unknown
Totl Assm:    $4,960   Lot Area: 17,156 sqft   Units  :     1
Exmp Assm:             Bld Area: 1,357 sq ft   Zoning :
YearlyTax: $410        Stories : 2.0           Corner : No
CrossSts :
------------------------------ Recording History -----------------------
                      Rec Dt/  Book/ Grantee/Mortgagee
 Type    Amount      Stlmt Dt  Page  Address


Sale $7,500          10/01/1980 0
                                0
Mort $8,064          08/26/1987       MID PENN CONS DISC CO

Mort $5,676          02/19/1988       ALL STATE DISC BLDRS INC

Mort $7,063          03/29/1988       MID PENN NATL BK

Mort $6,840          06/15/1990       MID PENN CONS DISC CO

Mort $5,128          07/16/1992       MID PENN CONS DISC CO

Mort $7,680          03/31/1993       SECOND NATL MTGE CO

Mort $17,233         12/16/1993       COMMERCIAL CREDIT PLAN CONS DISC CO

Mort $19,062         01/24/1994       COMMERCIAL CREDIT CORP

Mort $24,503         03/21/1995       COMMERCIAL CREDIT CORP

Mort $29,250         12/15/1995       INDUSTRY MTGE CO

Mort $3,828          11/26/1996       PHILA GAS HEATING CO

Mort $35,250         02/12/1997       AMERICAN MTGE REDUCTION INC

Mort $2,815          02/12/1997       AMERICAN MTGE REDUCTION INC

Mort $2,880          10/27/1999       NORWEST FINANCIAL CONS DISC CO
end.

------------------------------ Description -----------------------------
```

NOTES

Research on Philadelphia reported in this chapter was supported by a grant from the Ford Foundation.

1. See, for example, Calvin Bradford, *Risk or Race? Racial Disparities and the Subprime Refinance Market* (Washington, D.C.: Center for Community Change, 2002); ACORN, "Separate and Unequal 2002: Predatory Lending in America," http://www.acorn.org/acorn10/predatorylending/plreports/SU2002/index.php (2002); Glen B. Canner, Wayne Passmore, and Elizabeth Laderman, "The Role of Specialized Lenders in Extending Mortgage Credit to Lower-Income and Minority Homebuyers," *Federal Reserve Bulletin* 85, no. 11 (1999): 709–26.

2. For example, in the conventional prime market, "points" are of basically two types: (1) origination—essentially fees charged by the lender to the borrower to make the transaction; (2) discount—fees charged up front to discount (or reduce) the interest rate. In the subprime predatory market there is no such distinction, and points are simply fees charged by lenders to borrowers.

3. As Carr and Kolluri state, "Predatory lenders use target marketing not to meet the needs of their customers, but rather to identify households most vulnerable to the lenders' aggressive or fraudulent behavior." James H. Carr and Lopa Kolluri, *Predatory Lending: An Overview* (Washington, D.C.: Fannie Mae Foundation, 2001), p. 33.

4. See for example, Federal Trade Commission, "Self-Regulation in the Alcohol Industry: A Review of Industry Efforts to Avoid Promoting Alcohol to Underage Consumers," http://ftc.gov/reports/alcohol/alcoholreport.htm (September 1999).

5. NASD Rule 2310 states:

NASD Conduct Rule 2310
2310. Recommendations to Customers (Suitability)

(a) In recommending to a customer the purchase, sale or exchange of any security, a member shall have reasonable grounds for believing that the recommendation is suitable for such customer upon the basis of the facts, if any, disclosed by such customer as to his other security holdings and as to his financial situation and needs.

(b) Prior to the execution of a transaction recommended to a non-institutional customer, other than transactions with customers where investments are limited to money market mutual funds, a member shall make reasonable efforts to obtain information concerning:

(1) the customer's financial status;
(2) the customer's tax status;
(3) the customer's investment objectives; and
(4) such other information used or considered to be reasonable by such member or registered representative in making recommendations to the customer.

6. See for example, www.usadata.com.

7. Courchane, Surette, and Zorn state, "We find that subprime borrowers are less knowledgeable about the mortgage process, are less likely to search for the best mortgage rates, and are less likely to be offered a choice among alternative mortgage terms and instruments, *possibly making them more vulnerable to unfavorable*

mortgage terms" (emphasis added). Marsha J. Courchane, Brian Surette, and Peter Zorn, "Subprime Borrowers: Mortgage Transitions and Outcomes," *Journal of Real Estate Finance and Economics* 29, no. 4 (2004).

8. Alan White, "Risk-Based Mortgage Pricing—Present and Future Research," paper presented at the John Marshall Law School, 2003, p. 8.

9. *County Population Estimates for July 1, 1999 and Demographic Components of Population Change: April 1, 1990 to July 1, 1999*, U.S. Census report CO-99-4 (Washington, D.C.: U.S. Census Bureau, 1999).

10. Census data indicate that approximately 58 percent of the city's 660,000 housing units were built prior to 1950. In the 1990s, rental housing construction outpaced owner-occupied housing more than two to one. Much of that construction has been subsidized by some form of public housing funding.

11. The Reinvestment Fund, "Choices: A Report on the State of the Region's Housing Market," http://www.trfund.com/about/publications/bookpdf (2001); City of Philadelphia, "Neighborhood Transformation Initiative (NTI): Why It's Needed Now," www.phila.gov/mayor/jfs/mayorsnit/pdfs/nti_rationale.pdf (2001).

12. The Reinvestment Fund, "Choices."

13. Metropolitan Philadelphia Policy Center, "Fight or Flight: Metropolitan Philadelphia and Its Future," http://www.metropolicy.org/pdfs/Flight-all%20pages.pdf (2001).

14. Putting Philadelphia's decline in the context of its surrounding counties, Montgomery County experienced a growth in employment over the same time period from 328,000 to 600,000; Delaware County grew from 196,000 to 278,000; Chester County grew from 114,000 to 285,000; Bucks County grew from 140,000 to 325,000. Delaware Valley Regional Planning Commission (DVRPC), *Regional Economic Information System (REIS) Employment, 1970–2000*, Regional Data Bulletin no. 74 (2002), www.dvrpc.org. The New Jersey counties which comprise part of the Philadelphia region also experienced increases in employment over the same time period.

15. The Reinvestment Fund, analysis of U.S. Department of Commerce ZIP code business pattern data for 1998.

16. DVRPC, *Regional Economic Information System (REIS) Employment.*

17. The Index of Dissimilarity (D) is a widely used measure of segregation. The D value measures the percentage of a specific racial group that would need to move from its current residential location to another in order to achieve racial uniformity across the entire area. In the case of Philadelphia, the calculated D value implies that 76.4 percent of African Americans would need to move in order to achieve uniformity in racial composition across the city. See http://www.census.gov/hhes/www/housing/resseg/app_b.html for an explanation of a number of the more commonly used measures of segregation.

18. Carolyn Adams, David Bartelt, David Elesh, Ira Goldstein, Nancy Kleniewski, and William Yancey, *Philadelphia: Neighborhoods, Division, and Conflict in a Postindustrial City* (Philadelphia: Temple University Press, 1991).

19. David Bartelt, "Redlines and Breadlines: Depression Recovery and the Structure of Urban Space," unpublished manuscript (1984); Ira J. Goldstein, "The Wrong Side of the Tracts: A Study of Residential Segregation in Philadelphia, 1930–1980," Ph.D. dissertation, Temple University, 1985.

20. Data on GSE activity for 2002 indicate that Fannie Mae purchased loans with principal balances totaling $1.8 billion and Freddie Mac purchased an addi-

tional $703 million. Thus more than twenty-five years of cumulative activity of the Delaware Valley Mortgage Plan is exceeded by a single year's activity of a GSE.

21. HMDA data for this report were obtained through subscription to PCI Services, *CRA Wiz*. HMDA reporting of lenders as prime and subprime is based on Randall M. Scheessele, "HUD Subprime and Manufactured Home Lenders List," http://www.huduser.org/datasets/manu.html (2001).

22. The median family income for the Philadelphia–New Jersey MSA in 1999, as reported in the 2000 census, is $58,395.

23. Barr points out that lower-income people often do not have well-established credit histories; thus their profiles generally make them difficult to underwrite and subject to "alternative financial services." Michael Barr, "Banking the Poor," *Yale Journal on Regulation* 21 (2004), http://www.law.umich.edu/centersandprograms/olin/papers/Fall%202003/barr.pdf. Carr and Kolluri, *Predatory Lending*, report survey results indicating that anywhere from 35 percent to 50 percent of individuals with subprime loans could have qualified for prime loans.

24. Richard Williams, Reynold Nesiba, and Eileen McConnell, "The Changing Face of Inequality in Home Mortgage Lending," Working paper 2000-11 (University of Notre Dame, Department of Sociology, 2001; revised July 2001).

25. Kenneth Temkin, Jennifer E.H. Johnson, and Diane Levy, "Subprime Markets, the Role of GSEs, and Risk-Based Pricing," prepared for the Office of Policy Development and Research, U.S. Department of Housing and Urban Development, www.huduser.org (2002).

26. Brent W. Ambrose, Thomas Thibodeau, and Kenneth Temkin, "An Analysis of the Effects of the GSE Affordable Goals on Low- and Moderate-Income Families," prepared for the Office of Policy Development and Research, U.S. Department of Housing and Urban Development, hwww.huduser.org (2002).

27. Freddie Mac suggests that adoption of its automated underwriting could help move borrowers with subprime loans into the prime market saving them up to $100 million annually. Freddie Mac, "Automated Underwriting," www.freddiemac.com/corporate/reports (1996).

28. According to one commenter, the absolute accuracy of GSE activity derived from HMDA data may be questioned. Data from the GSE public access database for single-family purchase mortgages in 2002 reveal that 7.4 percent of all GSE purchases were in the lowest-income areas, 31.5 percent were in moderate-income areas, 49.3 percent were in middle-income areas, and 11.8 percent were in the highest-income areas.

29. 7.7 percent of properties are in low-priced areas; 35.0 percent are in moderate-priced areas; 46.7 percent are in middle-priced areas; 10.0 percent are in high-priced areas. These figures are sufficiently comparable for us to believe the random sample produced a result representative of the City of Philadelphia.

30. Low-priced areas are defined as those with median housing values reported in the census (2000) under $25,000; moderate-priced areas have median values between $25,000 and $49,999; middle-priced areas have values between $50,000 and $99,999; high-priced areas have median values of $100,000 or more.

31. The principal amount could exceed the estimated market value for a number of reasons—as noted previously. First and most obviously, values could have fallen since the loan was obtained. Second, there could have been an appraisal that was greater than the true value.

32. Research has shown that one of the most consistent predictors of foreclosure is the loan-to-value ratio (see Quercia and Stegman). Specifically, properties with a higher loan-to-value ratio are more likely to go into foreclosure. Where the loan exceeds a reasonable property value, one must question the veracity of the appraisal. An important question then becomes why this would be so prominent in lower- and moderate-value areas. Roberto G. Quercia and Michael A. Stegman, "Residential Mortgage Default: A Review of the Literature," *Journal of Housing Research* 3, no. 2 (1992): 341–79.

33. When analyzing lenders that are HMDA reporters, we are able to use the HUD list of reputed subprime lenders. However, for this analysis (and the analysis of mortgage foreclosures), there were a large number of lenders that are not (or were not) HMDA reporters, and therefore we needed to augment that list to include the other lenders. The process involved review of a lender's advertising, Web site, corporate filings, and, where possible, descriptions of loans within a pool of mortgages. Additionally, we conferred with subject matter experts who could confirm our designation and/or provide supplemental information for lenders we were otherwise unable to locate.

34. See, for example, U.S. Department of Housing and Urban Development and U.S. Department of the Treasury, *Curbing Predatory Home Mortgage Lending* (Washington, D.C.: U.S. Department of Housing and Urban Development and U.S. Department of the Treasury, 2000).

35. The sample for this analysis includes only properties having three or more liens with the current owner.

36. See, for example, Edward L. Glaeser and Jess M. Shapiro, "The Benefits of the Home Mortgage Interest Deduction," working paper W9284 (Washington, D.C.: National Bureau of Economic Research, 2002).

37. Examples of these lenders include, but are not limited to, GMAC, Cendant, and Bank of America, FSB.

38. Henry Campbell Black, *Black's Law Dictionary* (St. Paul, Minn.: West Publishing, 1990).

39. Preliminary data suggest that among properties in foreclosure, the median time elapsed between the original purchase of the property and the foreclosure filing is just under seven years.

40. Counting mortgage foreclosures may represent a conservative estimate of those who lose their homes, because often people refinance only to find that their taxes and insurance are no longer being escrowed by the lender/servicer. At this time, there are approximately 75,000 residential properties in the City of Philadelphia with tax delinquencies—some of these are likely a result of a disadvantageous mortgage refinance.

41. To date, most research on this topic has simply coded the "plaintiff" as a prime or subprime entity. See Debbie Gruenstein and Chris Herbert, *Analyzing Trends in Subprime Originations and Foreclosures: A Case Study of the Boston Metro Area* (Cambridge, Mass.: Abt Associates, 2000); Debbie Gruenstein and Chris Herbert, *Analyzing Trends in Subprime Originations and Foreclosures: A Case Study of the Atlanta Metro Area* (Cambridge, Mass.: Abt Associates, 2000); Kimberly Burnett, Chris Herbert, and Bulbul Kaul, *Subprime Originations and Foreclosures in New York State: A Case Study of Nassau, Suffolk, and Westchester Counties* (Cambridge, Mass.: Abt Associates, 2002); U.S. Department of Housing and Urban Development and U.S. Department of the Treasury, *Curbing Predatory Home Mortgage Lending*.

42. Census data for Philadelphia indicate that 11.0 percent of homes are valued under $25,000; 26.3 percent are valued between $25,000 and $49,999; 46.2 percent are valued between $50,000 and $99,999; 16.5 percent are valued at $100,000 and over.

43. Although the methodology differed somewhat, and we were able to trace back to the originating lender in most cases, these results do not vary markedly from those reported in Harold L. Bunce, Debbie Gruenstein, Christopher Herbert, and Randall M. Scheessele, *Subprime Foreclosures: The Smoking Gun of Predatory Lending?* (Washington, D.C.: U.S. Department of Housing and Urban Development, 2001).

44. One would expect that for a loan amortizing over a thirty-year period, approximately 2 percent of the principal amount would be paid at the end of two years and approximately 5 percent would be paid at the end of five years.

45. One interviewee, a licensed appraiser in the City of Philadelphia, reports that lenders try and "direct the value of the appraisal." Appraisers are then confronted with the conflict of remaining true to their estimate of the value of the property or altering the value to match what the broker/lender is seeking.

46. The phrase "cure a mortgage" means that the default status of an individual's mortgage is being corrected through some mutual agreement between the borrower and the lender. See http://www.phfa.org/programs/hemap for a full description of the Homeowner's Emergency Mortgage Assistance Program. A forbearance agreement is entered into between a borrower and a lender. It typically comes about when the borrower is unable to meet the mortgage obligation. Under such an agreement, the lender will typically agree not to foreclose and give the borrower temporary relief from the obligation; in return, the borrower agrees to pay all that is due as well as any interest that may accrue during the term of the agreement. Appendix 3.4 presents a particularly egregious use of the forbearance agreement: the lender not only requires the borrower to pay a fee, but also to agree to sign a deed in lieu of foreclosure, which the lender holds in case the borrower again goes into default. The result of signing this deed in lieu of foreclosure is that the borrower then loses all rights to contest any future foreclosure action. In December 2003, the U.S. attorney for the Eastern District of Pennsylvania reached agreement with the lender to stop this practice and to provide relief to those who had been adversely impacted. See http://www.usdoj.gov/usao/pae/News/Pr/2003/dec/jointa.html.

47. Temple University Center for Public Policy and Eastern Philadelphia Organizing Project, "Blight Free Philadelphia: A Public–Private Strategy to Create and Enhance Neighborhood Value," report prepared for Research for Democracy (2001), http://www.temple.edu/cpp/content/reports/Blight_Free_Phila_Pt1.pdf (2002).

48. One interviewee securitized loans for one of the largest securities firms in the world. Upon showing him a sample property history that displays a set of loans culminating in one that far exceeds the value of the collateral property, he suggested that the property owner should just "give up the keys" and subject the lender to the loss that it deserves for making that irrational loan. While that sort of "ruthless put" (defaulting on the loan immediately when the mortgage balance exceeds the property value) would indeed make purely economic sense, the problem is that the home owner was more than seventy-five years old and had no place to go while

exercising that abstract economic option. See Chester Foster and Robert van Order, "FHA Terminations: A Prelude to Rational Mortgage Pricing." *AREUEA Journal* 13, no. 3 (1985): 273–91; Kerry D. Vandell, "How Ruthless Is Mortgage Default? A Review and Synthesis of the Evidence," *Journal of Housing Research* 6, no. 2 (1995): 245–63.

49. While the presence of branches is generally considered an important factor in the extent to which people in a community avail themselves of traditional banking services, there is evidence to suggest that other factors, such as convenience, impact the extent to which people utilize those services. See Barr, "Banking the Poor"; or John P. Caskey, *Fringe Banking: Check-Cashing Outlets, Pawnshops, and the Poor* (New York: Russell Sage Foundation, 1994).

50. See, for example, Cathy Lesser Mansfield, "The Road to Subprime 'HEL' Was Paved with Good Congressional Intentions: Usury Deregulation and the Subprime Home Equity Market," *South Carolina Law Review* 51, no. 3 (2000): 473–587.

51. Data from the 1998 Survey of Consumer Finances, as reported by Catherine Montalto to the Consumer Federation of America and the National Credit Union Foundation, demonstrate that households with no or little net asset value were disproportionately low-income: "Householders with households with low net assets were younger, less educated, less likely to be White NonHispanic, less likely to be married, and less likely to own their homes, compared to the total population of householders." Catherine P. Montalto, "Wealth-Poor Households in the U.S.," report prepared for the Consumer Federation of America and National Credit Union Foundation (2002), p. 2.

52. Although it was not a brokered transaction, one interviewee reports that she was referred to one of the nation's largest subprime lenders over the telephone by a person attempting to collect a delinquent credit card bill.

53. See Alan White and Cathy Lesser Mansfield, "Literacy and Contract," *Stanford Law and Policy Review* 13, no. 2 (2002): 233–66; and Courchane, Surette, and Zorn, "Subprime Borrowers."

54. See, for example, Susan Woodward, "Consumer Confusion in the Mortgage Market," Sand Hill Econometrics (2003), www.sandhill.econ.com/mortgage/.

55. Although most states have some sort of licensure or registration, most do not require registration of employee originators, nor do most have a continuing education requirement. National Association of Mortgage Brokers, "Model State Statute Initiative: Licensing, Pre-licensure Education and Continuing Education Requirements for All Originators," http://www.namb.org/government_affairs/state_li censing/model_state_statute.pdf (2002).

56. One broker, a former official of the mortgage broker trade association, stated during an interview that one practice brokers use involves getting customers started with an especially disadvantageous loan product that is easily refinanced in the not-too-distant future.

57. National Association of Mortgage Brokers, "Model State Statute Initiative."

58. The confusion experienced by borrowers is certainly reasonable, given the dual roles—and allegiances—of mortgage brokers. In a deposition of mortgage broker Jules Clearfield by Irv Ackelsberg, Esq. (plaintiff attorney), in the case *Priscilla Fountain v. United Companies Lending Corporation*, the following was recorded:

By Mr. Ackelsberg:

Q. Mr. Clearfield, I do have some other questions of a general nature but—

A. Before we get to that, you know, there's one point I wanted to bring up when you were hassling me about customers and you got me confused who my customers were.

Q. Mr. Clearfield, it certainly wasn't—there was no intent to be hassling or meddling.

A. You were hassling me. You kept who are your customers. And I just want to bring out the contractors, I consider them my clients. The customer who gets the loan, I consider them my customers. I just want to separate the two.

Q. Well, now you have me completely confused. What's the difference between your client and your customer?

A. The clients are people I have dealt with up through the years that I went along with to service them and help them in their field just like a doctor or an attorney has clients. They would be my clients. The customers would be the people who needed the money who are actually the lending sources who needed the money to do whatever purpose it was; whether it was financing, home improvement. They're the customers.

Civil Action 96-8095 in the U.S. District Court for the Eastern District of Pennsylvania.

59. See, for example, James H. Carr and Jenny Schuetz, *Financial Services in Distressed Communities: Framing the Issue, Finding Solutions* (Washington, D.C.: Fannie Mae Foundation, 2001).

60. Vern Baxter and Mickey Lauria, "Residential Mortgage Foreclosure and Neighborhood Change," *Housing Policy Debate* 11, no. 3 (2000): 675–99.

61. PHIL is an acronym for Philadelphia Home Improvement Loan. See www.phila.gov/mayor/jfs/mayorsnti/news/releases/releases_2.html.

62. A matter of local public policy concern involves the city's decision not to write-down municipal tax liens on properties sold at Sheriff Sales. One interviewee, an attorney who handles literally thousands of mortgage foreclosures annually, stated that the city solicitor of Philadelphia refuses to write-down tax liens at all, so lenders walk away from the properties (especially where the amount owed exceeds the value of the property—which he estimated to be true in more than 90 percent of the cases he handles). These properties, in his experience, stay vacant for extended periods and become obvious blighting influences on the neighborhood.

63. The source of risk is important to appreciate. Borrowers who were interviewed often report that the amount of money they were seeking was far less than what they ultimately borrowed. If they had borrowed what they needed, they would not be in financial distress. The larger loan amount (induced by the loan officer or broker) made the transaction unaffordable, and thus riskier than it would otherwise have been. Borrowing a phrase from the medical world, this may be considered "iatrogenic risk." Hudson states that lenders will "milk as much money as possible out of customers who can't afford it. It's a high wire act: When the game's played well, the lenders squeeze customers to the limit." Michael Hudson (ed.), *Merchants of Misery: How Corporate America Profits from Poverty* (Monroe, Me.: Common Courage Press, 1996), p. 16.

64. One study that begins to address the question of the impact of vacant property on a community was completed in Philadelphia by Research for Democracy, a collaboration between Temple University and the Eastern Philadelphia Organizing

Project (2001). This study estimates that the impact of an abandoned home on the surrounding property values is approximately $6,720. While we cannot draw an exact parallel between abandoned property and Sheriff Sales, this study offers some insight into how significant the impact may be of a home that ends up being offered at a Sheriff Sale and for which there is no buyer.

65. With the merger of Beneficial and Household, Household would have the largest market share with over 4 percent of all originations.

REFERENCES

Adams, Carolyn, David Bartelt, David Elesh, Ira Goldstein, Nancy Kleniewski, and William Yancey. *Philadelphia: Neighborhoods, Division, and Conflict in a Postindustrial City*. Philadelphia: Temple University Press, 1991.

Ambrose, Brent W., Thomas Thibodeau, and Kenneth Temkin. "An Analysis of the Effects of the GSE Affordable Goals on Low- and Moderate-Income Families." Prepared for the Office of Policy Development and Research, U.S. Department of Housing and Urban Development, 2002. www.huduser.org.

Barr, Michael. "Banking the Poor." *Yale Journal on Regulation* 21 (2004). http:// www.law.umich.edu / centersandprograms / olin / papers /Fall%202003/barr. pdf.

Bartelt, David, "Redlines and Breadlines: Depression Recovery and the Structure of Urban Space." Unpublished manuscript, 1984.

Baxter, Vern, and Mickey Lauria. "Residential Mortgage Foreclosure and Neighborhood Change." *Housing Policy Debate* 11, no. 3 (2002): 675–99.

Black, Henry Campbell. *Black's Law Dictionary*. St. Paul, Minn.: West Publishing, 1990.

Bradford, Calvin. *Risk or Race? Racial Disparities and the Subprime Refinance Market*. Washington, D.C.: Center for Community Change, 2002.

Bunce, Harold L., Debbie Gruenstein, Christopher Herbert, and Randall M. Scheessele. *Subprime Foreclosures: The Smoking Gun of Predatory Lending?* Washington, D.C.: U.S. Department of Housing and Urban Development, 2001.

Burnett, Kimberly, Chris Herbert, and Bulbul Kaul. *Subprime Originations and Foreclosures in New York State: A Case Study of Nassau, Suffolk, and Westchester Counties*. Cambridge, Mass.: Abt Associates, 2002.

Canner, Glen B., Wayne Passmore, and Elizabeth Laderman. "The Role of Specialized Lenders in Extending Mortgage Credit to Lower-Income and Minority Homebuyers." *Federal Reserve Bulletin*, 85, no. 11 (1999): 709–26.

Carr, James H., and Lopa Kolluri. *Predatory Lending: An Overview*. Washington, D.C.: Fannie Mae Foundation, 2001.

Carr, James H., and Jenny Schuetz. *Financial Services in Distressed Communities: Framing the Issue, Finding Solutions*. Washington, D.C.: Fannie Mae Foundation, 2001.

Carroll, Thomas M., Terrence M. Clauretie, and Helen R. Neill. "Effect of Foreclosure Status on Residential Selling Price: Comment." *Journal of Real Estate Research* 13, no. 1 (1997): 95–102.

Caskey, John P. *Fringe Banking: Check-Cashing Outlets, Pawnshops, and the Poor*. New York: Russell Sage Foundation, 1994.

City of Philadelphia. "Neighborhood Transformation Initiative (NTI): Why It's Needed Now." www.phila.gov/mayor/jfs/mayorsnit/pdfs/nti_rationale.pdf (2001).

Courchane, Marsha J., Brian Surette, and Peter Zorn. "Subprime Borrowers: Mortgage Transitions and Outcomes." *Journal of Real Estate Finance and Economics* (2003).

Cutts, Amy Crews, and Robert A. van Order. "On the Economics of Subprime Lending." www.freddiemac.com/corporate/reports/ (2003).

Delaware Valley Regional Planning Commission. *Regional Economic Information System (REIS) Employment, 1970–2000.* Regional Data Bulletin no. 74 (2002). www.dvrpc.org.

Federal Trade Commission. "Self-Regulation in the Alcohol Industry: A Review of Industry Efforts to Avoid Promoting Alcohol to Underage Consumers." http://ftc.gov/reports/alcohol/alcoholreport.htm (1999).

Fishbein, Allen, and Harold Bunce. *Subprime Market Growth and Predatory Lending.* Washington, D.C.: U.S. Department of Housing and Urban Development, 2001.

Forgey, F.A., R.C. Rutherford, and M.L. van Buskirk. "Effect of Foreclosure Status on Residential Selling Price." *Journal of Real Estate Research* 9, no. 3 (1994): 313–18.

Foster, Chester, and Robert van Order. "FHA Terminations: A Prelude to Rational Mortgage Pricing." *AREUEA Journal* 13, no. 3 (1985): 273–91.

Freddie Mac. "Automated Underwriting: Making Mortgage Lending Simpler and Fairer for America's Families." www.freddiemac.com/corporate/reports (1996).

Glaeser, Edward L., and Jess M. Shapiro. "The Benefits of the Home Mortgage Interest Deduction." Working paper W9284. Washington, D.C.: National Bureau of Economic Research, 2002.

Goldstein, Ira J. 1985. "The Wrong Side of the Tracts: A Study of Residential Segregation in Philadelphia, 1930–1980." Ph.D. dissertation, Temple University.

Gruenstein, Debbie, and Chris Herbert. 2000. *Analyzing Trends in Subprime Originations and Foreclosures: A Case Study of the Boston Metro Area.* Cambridge, Mass.: Abt Associates, 2000.

Gruenstein, Debbie, and Chris Herbert. *Analyzing Trends in Subprime Originations and Foreclosures: A Case Study of the Atlanta Metro Area.* Cambridge, Mass.: Abt Associates, 2000.

Hudson, Michael (ed.). *Merchants of Misery: How Corporate America Profits from Poverty.* Monroe, Me.: Common Courage Press, 1996.

Listokin, David, and Elvin K. Wyly. "Making New Mortgage Markets: Case Studies of Institutions, Home Buyers, and Communities." *Housing Policy Debate* 11, no. 3 (2000): 575–644.

Mansfield, Cathy Lesser. "The Road to Subprime 'HEL' Was Paved with Good Congressional Intentions: Usury Deregulation and the Subprime Home Equity Market." *South Carolina Law Review* 51, no. 3 (2000): 473–587.

Metropolitan Philadelphia Policy Center. "Fight or Flight: Metropolitan Philadelphia and Its Future." http://www.metropolicy.org/pdfs/Flight-all%20pages.pdf (2001).

Montalto, Catherine P. "Wealth-Poor Households in the U.S." Report prepared for the Consumer Federation of America and National Credit Union Foundation, 2002.

Mortgage Bankers Association of America. National Delinquency Survey. 2003. Data as of December 31, 2002, for 4th quarter 2002.

National Association of Mortgage Brokers. "Model State Statute Initiative: Licensing, Pre-licensure Education and Continuing Education Requirements for All Originators." http://www.namb.org/government_affairs/state_licensing/model_state_statute.pdf (2002).

Pennington-Cross, Anthony. "Subprime and Prime Mortgages: Loss Distributions." Working paper 03-1. Washington, D.C.: Office of Federal Housing Enterprise Oversight, 2003.

Quercia, Roberto G., and Michael A. Stegman. "Residential Mortgage Default: A Review of the Literature." *Journal of Housing Research* 3, no. 2 (1992): 341–79.

The Reinvestment Fund. "Choices: A Report on the State of the Region's Housing Market." http://www.trfund.com/about/publications/bookpdf (2001).

Scheessele, Randall M. "HUD Subprime and Manufactured Home Lender List." Machine readable data file downloadable from http://www.huduser.org/datasets/manu.html (2001).

Squires, Gregory D. (ed.). *From Redlining to Reinvestment: Community Responses to Urban Disinvestment.* Philadelphia: Temple University Press, 1992.

Temkin, Kenneth, Jennifer E.H. Johnson, and Diane Levy. "Subprime Markets, the Role of GSEs, and Risk-Based Pricing." Prepared for the Office of Policy Development and Research, U.S. Department of Housing and Urban Development, www.huduser.org.

Temple University Center for Public Policy and Eastern Philadelphia Organizing Project. "Blight Free Philadelphia: A Public–Private Strategy to Create and Enhance Neighborhood Value." Report prepared for Research for Democracy. 2001. http://www.temple.edu/cpp/content/reports/Blight_Free_Phila_Pt1.pdf.

U.S. Department of Commerce, Bureau of the Census. "U.S. Census of Population and Housing, Summary File 3," 2000. Machine readable data file.

U.S. Department of Commerce, Bureau of the Census. "Racial and Ethnic Residential Segregation in the United States: 1980–2000." http://www.census.gov/hhes/www/housing/resseg/pdf (2002).

U.S. Department of Housing and Urban Development and U.S. Department of the Treasury. *Curbing Predatory Home Mortgage Lending.* Washington, D.C.: U.S. Department of Housing and Urban Development and U.S. Department of the Treasury, 2000.

Vandell, Kerry D. "How Ruthless Is Mortgage Default? A Review and Synthesis of the Evidence." *Journal of Housing Research* 6, no. 2 (1995): 245–63.

White, Alan. "Risk-Based Mortgage Pricing—Present and Future Research." Paper presented at the John Marshall Law School, 2003.

White, Alan, and Cathy Lesser Mansfield. "Literacy and Contract." *Stanford Law and Policy Review* 13, no. 2 (2002): 233–66.

Williams, Richard, Reynold Nesiba, and Eileen McConnell. "The Changing Face of Inequality in Home Mortgage Lending." Working paper 2000-11. University of Notre Dame, Department of Sociology, 2001 (revised July 2001).

Woodward, Susan E. "Consumer Confusion in the Mortgage Market." Sand Hill Econometrics, 2003. http://www.sandhillecon.com/mortgage/.

4

Predatory Lending Practices: Definition and Behavioral Implications

Patricia A. McCoy

To the dispassionate observer, predatory lending presents a conundrum. Its victims are home owners who are wedded to staying in their homes. Many of them, particularly the elderly, have minuscule mortgages or own their homes free and clear. Nevertheless, they sign seemingly irrational loan contracts that are structured to result in financial ruin in the form of impaired credit, bankruptcy, or foreclosure.

Understanding why this happens has key public policy implications for the debate over predatory lending. Are affected borrowers to be viewed as rational economic actors who maximize expected utility when signing loan contracts that later are disputed? Or, rather, do predatory lenders induce suboptimal decisions by exploiting anomalies in consumer behavior through marketing?

New insights from behavioral economics indicate the latter. As prologue, this chapter analyzes the pathologies underlying predatory lending in the home mortgage market. The remainder of the chapter discusses evidence from behavioral economics and the implications of that evidence, both for understanding borrowers' choices and for redressing predatory lending. Specifically, I posit that predatory lenders exploit the behavioral principle of framing effects to manipulate home owners' otherwise strong aversion to losing their homes to foreclosure. Through clever marketing, distraction, and an often legal lack of transparency concerning the true risks involved, predatory lenders are able to divert the focus of home owners from the fear of losing their homes to other fears, many of which are often conducive to less destructive solutions.

PREDATORY LENDING DESCRIBED

In the popular press, predatory mortgage lending is generally described as a catalog of abusive practices, which are often racially discriminatory and targeted at naïve individuals, and may result in bankruptcy, foreclosure, and ultimate poverty. As the opening chapter by Gregory Squires suggests, the breadth of these practices is limited only by the ingenuity of disreputable brokers, lenders, and servicers.

In thinking about predatory practices and their underlying pathologies, five basic problems emerge. The following five problems form a syndrome of abusive loan terms or practices that define predatory lending:

1. Loans structured to result in seriously disproportionate net harm to borrowers
2. Rent-seeking
3. Loans involving fraud or deception
4. Other forms of lack of transparency in loans that are not actionable as fraud
5. Provisions requiring borrowers to waive meaningful legal redress

Predatory loans crop up primarily in the subprime market, which offers high-cost loans designed for borrowers who do not qualify for conventional prime loans, due to poor credit, low income, or unconventional underwriting profiles.[1] Not all subprime loans, however, are predatory. Conversely, it is possible, although rare, for prime loans to be predatory. Because most predatory loans are subprime, this chapter focuses on the predatory sector of the subprime market.

Loans Structured to Cause Seriously Disproportionate Net Harm to Borrowers

The subprime mortgage industry relaxes numerous conventional underwriting standards in order to lend to less creditworthy customers. Many of the newly relaxed standards benefit lenders and borrowers alike. Examples include legitimate risk-based subprime loans to trustworthy borrowers with credit blemishes or scant credit histories, and loans with reduced down payment requirements or higher loan-to-value ratios.[2]

In some segments of the subprime loan industry, however, lenders override conventional lending norms by structuring loans to inflict seriously disproportionate net harm on borrowers. When the harm outweighs the benefit of loans to borrowers and society at large, such practices are predatory. One of the most compelling examples involves violations of the norm that no mortgage shall be made to a home owner who lacks the ability to repay, a practice known as asset-based lending.[3] All too often, these loans force borrowers into bankruptcy or foreclosure.[4]

Victims of asset-based lending frequently default, which can lead to another predatory lending phenomenon, "loan flipping." Loan flipping occurs when lenders persuade home owners to refinance their mortgages at short, repeated intervals, as often as three or four times a year. Since the borrowers are cash-poor, with each refinancing the lenders tack prepayment penalties and refinancing fees onto the original principal. Thus, with each refinancing the borrowers' principal increases. In the meantime, the lenders offer the borrowers temporary relief in the form of refinance loans with longer maturity dates, negative amortization,[5] or balloon payments, all of which can reduce borrowers' monthly payments.[6] In the end, however, the borrowers owe higher total principal and interest to the lenders and have lost the equity in their homes. To make matters worse, as the borrowers' loan-to-value ratios rise and their credit scores fall, their ability to refinance with legitimate lenders dwindles. Eventually the borrowers lose all of their equity and can find themselves facing foreclosure. Predatory lenders ensure this vicious cycle by making loans that borrowers cannot repay in the first place.

Other examples of loans that result in seriously disproportionate net harm to borrowers include loans that shift unsecured debt into mortgages for the purpose of stripping equity, loans where lenders insist on financing higher principal amounts than customers desire, and loans that refinance subsidized mortgages (such as no-interest Habitat for Humanity loans) at higher interest rates for no economic reason.[7] Similarly, net harm results when lenders steer prime-eligible customers to high-cost subprime loans that are designed for customers with lower credit scores.[8] Steering is driven by yield-spread premiums, which are side payments by lenders to mortgage brokers to reward them for getting borrowers to agree to higher interest rates than the lenders were originally willing to accept.[9] Even when borrowers realize that they are paying yield-spread premiums, they do not understand why, or that their interest rates are higher as a result.

Harmful Rent-Seeking

Subprime loans involve higher interest rates and fees. High costs are not problematic per se. However, when subprime lenders use market power to charge rates and fees that exceed competitive levels, they extract harmful rents from borrowers. Such rent-seeking is another common marker of predatory lending.

Subprime loans to riskier borrowers entail higher costs that lenders have to recoup. This is because subprime loans historically have had higher rates of delinquency, default, and foreclosure than prime loans.[10] Thus, the market demands higher interest rates to compensate for the added risk.[11] In addition, higher interest rates, either alone or with prepayment penalties, are said to compensate the ultimate holders of the loans (whether those holders are lenders themselves or secondary market investors)[12] for any added prepayment risk that might arise if subprime loans were prepaid at a faster rate than prime mortgages, as the industry asserts is the case.[13]

Origination costs and servicing costs of subprime loans are higher because subprime loans require greater scrutiny of income and credit history and have lower approval rates.[14] At the same time, subprime mortgages are smaller on average than their prime counterparts. This smaller average loan size makes fixed origination costs for subprime loans higher than for prime loans when expressed as a percentage of the principal.[15] Subprime servicing costs are higher as well because credit-impaired borrowers have higher default rates than prime borrowers and require greater vigilance by servicing agents.[16]

Nevertheless, for certain high-cost loans, an added component of the price consists of rent-seeking. For example, when lenders steer prime-eligible borrowers to high-cost loans, their purpose is to extract rents. Similarly, when lenders charge fees and interest that exceed risk-adjusted rates, they are engaged in rent-seeking.[17] Other forms of rent-seeking are more blatant, including fees for services never rendered, surcharges on government recording fees, and duplicative charges.[18] Credit life insurance and its cousins represent other pricing abuses. These abuses include excessive premium charges relative to actual loss payouts, single-premium payments for insurance that extends beyond the life of the loan, policies issued to borrowers who do not qualify for insurance for reasons such as advanced age, and insurance policies written on total indebtedness, not on repayment of principal.[19]

Fraud or Deceptive Practices

In its most blatant form, predatory lending involves the age-old problem of fraud. All of the deceptive practices in this category violate existing laws, such as state fraud statutes, state consumer-protection laws, state fiduciary duties, or federal disclosure statutes such as the Truth in Lending Act (TILA)[20] and the Real Estate Settlement Procedures Act (RESPA).[21]

Loan fraud comes in countless varieties and springs up, Hydra-like, in new forms. Nevertheless, loan fraud can be classified into two types. The first type is deception aimed at borrowers.[22] Among the most notorious deceptions are fraudulent disclosures, failures to disclose information required by law, bait-and-switch tactics, and loans made in collusion with home-repair scams. Lenders reportedly have financed fees without borrowers' knowledge, secretly conveyed title to borrowers' property, and deliberately concealed liens on borrowers' homes. Some lenders and brokers mislead borrowers into thinking that they must purchase credit life insurance in order to obtain a loan. Others falsely state that they are affiliated with a federal agency such as the Veterans Administration or the Federal Housing

Administration, giving borrowers a false sense of the lenders' legitimacy. Brokers regularly dupe borrowers into believing that they are acting in the borrowers' best interests when their true financial loyalties are to the lenders. Brokers and lenders alike may lure borrowers to closing by promising to finance needed home repairs or to refinance loans later on at lower rates.

The second type of fraud is aimed at capital sources, such as secondary-market purchasers of loans, federal loan guarantors, and even loan originators themselves. Such fraud typically takes the form of falsified loan applications or inflated real estate appraisals.[23] An unsuspecting borrower may be induced to sign a blank loan application that the mortgage broker or lender then falsifies to paint a bright financial picture of the borrower so the loan can qualify for resale on the secondary market. Similarly, unethical lenders may order inflated appraisals to win federal loan guarantees. Unethical mortgage brokers may do the same to secure loans with higher principal, thus generating higher fees. In most cases, the borrowers are not aware that this type of fraud is going on.

Other Forms of Lack of Transparency That Are Not Actionable as Fraud

Mortgages can lack transparency even when they are devoid of fraud. Such loans involve misleading omissions that are not currently prohibited by law.

In most mortgages, TILA or RESPA requires the disclosure of certain loan terms or costs. Both laws have the purpose of supplying consumers with standardized cost information about mortgages in order to aid comparison-shopping. TILA does so by requiring lenders to disclose the finance charge and the annual percentage rate (APR). The finance charge is supposed to measure the total cost of credit in dollars, including interest payments, points, origination fees, and private mortgage insurance. The APR provides a different yardstick of the total cost of credit by translating the lump-sum finance charge into an effective interest rate per year.[24]

RESPA seeks to inform consumers about the closing costs of mortgages. Under RESPA, lenders must provide loan applicants with two different disclosure statements. The good-faith estimate of settlement costs (GFE), provided three days after application, gives an itemized estimate of the closing costs. Later, at the closing, lenders must provide HUD-1 settlement statements itemizing the final closing costs that borrowers must pay.[25]

Both RESPA and TILA have loopholes that hinder effective disclosure. Under TILA, significant costs are excluded from the finance charge and APR. As a result, the reported total cost of credit is artificially deflated. Such exclusions include fees for credit reports, appraisals, inspections by lenders, flood certification, document preparation, title searches, and title insurance, as well as notary fees, recording fees, and government taxes.[26]

RESPA has flaws in timing and enforcement. Lenders do not have to provide GFEs until three days after the date of application, when borrowers are already psychologically committed to the loans and have already paid their application fees. Furthermore, lenders are not liable for erroneous GFEs, which means that the mandated cost estimates can bear little relationship to actual costs. As a result, GFEs are not useful for comparison-shopping.[27] Similarly, while borrowers may request their HUD-1 settlement statements the day before closing, lenders need not inform them of that right.[28] Furthermore, as with the GFE, there is no requirement that HUD-1 statements be accurate.[29] These deficiencies in the federal disclosure laws create opportunities for lenders to exploit borrowers.

Other pricing practices impede transparency. In the prime-mortgage industry, points generally are accompanied by a reduction in the interest rate.[30] This trade-off gives borrowers the option of paying a fixed sum up front in points in exchange for lower interest payments. For similar reasons, conventional lending norms state that prepayment penalty provisions go hand in hand with reductions in interest rates.[31]

These norms enable borrowers to choose how they handle the time–price differential of money. Legitimate lenders provide that choice. Predatory lenders, in contrast, subvert this conventional trade-off by layering points or prepayment penalties on top of high interest rates on a take-it-or-leave-it basis.[32]

Loans Requiring Borrowers to Waive Meaningful Legal Redress

Subprime mortgages frequently contain nonnegotiable, mandatory arbitration clauses that bar borrowers from seeking judicial redress.[33] Other clauses forbid borrowers from joining class actions against lenders. Loans that do allow borrowers to pursue claims in court frequently shift lenders' attorneys' fees onto borrowers.[34]

The harm from predatory lending is so severe that it is necessary to ask, What would make homeowners ever agree to such one-sided, oppressive bargains? Much of the answer lies in lenders' conscious exploitation of cognitive anomalies in financial decision-making by home owners, as the remainder of this chapter discusses.

BEHAVIORAL INSIGHTS INTO CONSUMER DECISION-MAKING ANOMALIES AND MARKETING

In debates over predatory lending, those who oppose government intervention argue that aggrieved subprime borrowers should live by the bargains they strike. Such critics maintain that those borrowers are rational actors who knowingly and freely consent to the terms in their contracts.

Evidence from the new and evolving field of behavioral economics, however, suggests that this portrait of subprime borrowers misses the mark. In fact, borrowers often bring cognitive biases to the table that lenders exploit through clever marketing to manipulate them into signing abusive loan agreements, in violation of strong personal preferences to remain in their homes. The remainder of this chapter examines evidence for that proposition and considers the public policy implications.

Background: Expected Utility Theory and Its Critique

The rational actor assumption is grounded in expected utility theory, which has been the classic paradigm for decision-making under uncertainty for a half-decade or more. Neoclassical economics assumes that reasonable people seek to follow expected utility theory and that most of them actually do so.[35]

Despite its prominence, expected utility theory does not derive from empirical fact. Rather, expected utility theory reduces the complexities of human decision-making to the following mathematical formula for determining the overall utility U of a prospect:

$$U\ (x_1, p_1; \ldots; x_n, p_n) = \Sigma\ p_i u(x_i) = p_1 u(x_1) + \ldots + p_n u(x_n),$$

where $(x_1, p_1; \ldots; x_n, p_n)$ is a risky prospect having possible outcomes x_i, $\{i = 1, 2, 3, \ldots, n\}$, each with probability p_i, $p_1 + \ldots + p_n = 1$, and $u(\cdot)$ is the utility the consumer would derive from outcome x_i. Expected utility theory posits that consumers will prefer the prospect with the highest expected utility. Under that theory, consumers are said to be concerned with their final state of wealth, not with gains or losses.[36]

The Critique of Expected Utility Theory and Loss Aversion

Skeptics had long complained that expected utility theory is normative in nature, not necessarily descriptive, and eventually set out to prove it. Starting in the 1970s, psychologists and economists began to document anomalies in consumer behavior that violated expected utility theory. Experiments by Daniel Kahneman and Amos Tversky, for instance, demonstrated that when certain loss is a possible outcome, people are concerned with avoiding the certain loss instead of with their final state of wealth. For example, when people were asked to choose between

A: an 80 percent chance of losing 4,000   *or*   B: a certain loss of 3,000,

the majority of the subjects preferred the 80 percent gamble of losing 4,000 to losing 3,000 for sure. The desire to avoid a loss led the subjects to overweight the certain outcome—losing 3,000—and to opt for the risky choice, despite a bigger expected loss ($0.8 \times -4,000 = -3,200$). Conversely, when subjects were asked to choose between an 80 percent chance of winning 4,000 or a certain win of 3,000, the majority of subjects preferred the sure gain of 3,000 to an expected but risky gain of 3,200.[37]

Based on these and similar experiments, Kahneman and Tversky hypothesized that people overweight the probability of some events and underweight others, depending on whether they are confronting possible gains or losses. In addition, these results suggest that people are so loss-averse that they will take substantial risks to avoid losses, even if their total expected wealth is less as a result. The theory known as prospect theory is an attempt to explain these phenomena.[38]

Prospect theory has several important principles with implications for predatory lending. The first is *loss aversion*. Loss aversion drives consumer behavior in a number of ways. As the experiments just discussed suggest, loss aversion is the reason why people take substantial risks to avoid certain losses.[39] Similarly, loss aversion causes people to focus on minimizing out-of-pocket expenses rather than opportunity costs. The reason for this is that "[f]oregone gains are less painful than perceived losses."[40] Finally, when people face potential outcomes that entail both gains and losses, loss aversion causes them to prefer combining smaller losses with larger gains. This outcome is attractive because the outcome is perceived as a net gain.[41]

In the home mortgage context, loss aversion is apparent in the strong aversion that homeowners normally have to losing their homes. Thus, Kahneman and Tversky noted: "[A]n individual's aversion to losses may increase sharply near the loss that would compel him to sell his house."[42] This intense aversion to losing one's home is suggested by data showing that home owners are seven times less likely to file for bankruptcy than people who do not own homes. Similarly, among people who do file for bankruptcy, home ownership makes them more likely to file for protection under the workout provisions of Chapter 13, instead of under the liquidation provisions of Chapter 7, specifically in order to save their homes.[43]

The bankruptcy data provide valuable insights into the preference ordering of the average home owner. Home owners prefer to make other financial sacrifices rather than take the risk of bankruptcy and losing their homes. If debts do force home owners into bankruptcy, they prefer to remain home owners and reschedule their debts under Chapter 13, to losing their homes but obtaining total debt forgiveness under Chapter 7.

Given the strong loss aversion associated with home ownership, one would expect home owners to make financial sacrifices or delay paying other bills in order to save their homes, instead of sacrificing their homes to pay off other debts. Loss-averse home owners should be highly reluctant to enter into loan transactions that threaten their future home ownership. Yet numerous subprime borrowers do precisely that. The answer to this paradox lies in how predatory lenders frame their sales pitches in order to manipulate the preference ordering of homeowners, as I now discuss.

Reference Dependence and Framing Effects

Consumers do not evaluate gains and losses in the abstract. Instead, they evaluate their options in relation to some reference point, a phenomenon known as *reference dependence*.[44] Imagine that someone has a choice between *A*, where she has less of good *X* and more of good *Y*, and *D*, where she has more of good *X* and less of good *Y*. If her reference point is *C*, she will regard the choice as a choice between two gains, while if her reference point is *B*, she will regard it as a choice between two losses. From either reference point *A'* or *D'*, she will view it as a choice between mixtures of different proportions of two desirable goods.[45]

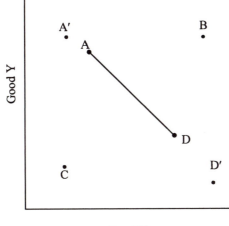

In many cases, the reference point is not fixed, but can be manipulated depending on how the choice is framed. Marketers shift reference points by relabeling and thus framing possible outcomes, which can then shape consumers' responses. Predatory lenders exploit this ability to frame borrowers' reference points. This is why reference dependence and framing effects are important concepts in thinking about predatory lending.

As the following experiment illustrates, people make different choices about identical outcomes, depending on whether the outcomes are framed as gains or losses. In the experiment, people were divided into two groups and were given different scenarios that involved choosing between two options. All of the choices would make the subjects $400 richer, but for one group the choices were framed as gains and for the other as losses.

Scenario A. Assume yourself richer by $300 than you are today. You have to choose between the following:

a sure gain of $100   *or*   a 50 percent chance to gain $200 and a 50 percent
chance to gain nothing.

Scenario B. Assume yourself richer by $500 than you are today. You have
to choose between the following:

a sure loss of $100   *or*   a 50 percent chance to lose nothing and a 50 per-
cent chance to lose $200.

In Scenario A, of 126 people surveyed, 72 percent chose a sure gain of
$100 and 28 percent chose the 50/50 wager. In Scenario B, of 128 people
surveyed, only 36 percent chose the sure loss of $100, while 64 percent
chose the 50/50 wager.[46]

As this experiment shows, whether people were risk-loving or risk-averse
depended on whether the outcome was framed as a gain or a loss. When
the choice was framed as a gain, a majority became averse to uncertainty
and chose the sure gain. But when the choice was framed as a loss, a majority sought to avoid the certain loss and chose uncertainty. A majority
behaved inconsistently, even though they would become $400 richer no
matter what choice they made. Framing dictated whether the majority was
risk-loving or risk-averse, again contradicting expected utility theory.

Framing creates an illusion that can induce inconsistent and sometimes
irrational consumer decisions. This illusion arises when two different statements of a choice are logically equivalent, but not transparently equivalent.[47] Normally, consumers are not conscious of alternative ways of
framing decisions or of the psychological effects of different frames.[48] Thus,
how a decision is framed can manipulate and momentarily shift the order
of a home owner's preferences.[49]

Framing is the alchemy that permits predatory lenders to manipulate the
order of home owners' preferences and overcome their otherwise strong
aversion to losing their homes. In reality, predatory loans are highly likely
to result in losses, in the form of staggering debt, lost home equity, and
possible foreclosure. Yet lenders never frame predatory mortgages in terms
of major expected losses. One never sees ads saying: "Take $20,000 today
in exchange for a 50 percent chance that, in two years' time, you will lose
your $50,000 home." Such a marketing strategy would unleash loss aver-
sion of profound proportions.

Instead, predatory lenders go to extreme lengths to frame their loans as
gains and to obscure potential losses. Gains are portrayed not just as fast
cash, but as fast cash in the tens of thousands of dollars. Losses, on the
other hand, are obscured by depicting them as initial monthly payments
that are manageable in size. Lenders manipulate loan terms through legal
means to give the appearance of reasonable monthly payments. They do
this through initial teaser rates, extended loan maturities, balloon clauses,

and adjustable-rate mortgages.[50] Left unsaid, or buried in fine print, is the fact that predatory loans are high-stakes ventures, with potential catastrophe looming down the road. The effect is to create the impression of huge, immediate gains offsetting small, eventual losses.

This key principle of framing—offset small perceived losses with the illusion of large gains[51]—is particularly seductive to home owners who are in financial straits but have significant home equity. For home owners desperate for lifesaving medical care, a car that works, roof repairs, or relief from bill collectors, lenders can easily shift their reference point from continued enjoyment of their homes to the creditors at the door. Despite pressing financial problems, numerous such home owners—if asked—would prefer a solution that would allow them to stay in their homes. At a minimum, if the choice were put to them openly, most home owners would delay paying other debts to avoid losing their homes.

Nevertheless, subprime marketing can manipulate a temporary preference shift among debt-ridden home owners by focusing a spotlight on their immediate financial problems while obscuring the eventual threat to their ownership of their homes. That is why predatory lenders pinpoint home owners in crisis and promise to erase their debts with offers of instant cash. There are numerous ways to identify distressed home owners. Predatory lenders monitor people's credit reports for debt problems, buy lists of delinquent debtors from debt collectors, and drive through neighborhoods looking for decrepit roofs and porches. At city halls, registries, and courthouses, they check filings daily for building code violations, tax liens, collection cases, divorce summonses, and mortgage payoffs. Lenders flush out likely victims with door-to-door sales and aggressive telemarketing campaigns. They use Home Mortgage Disclosure Act data to target low-income minority neighborhoods where Hispanics and African Americans historically have been redlined and have lost hope of qualifying for home loans.[52] Then they target home owners who appear in the crosshairs with a sales pitch. With a knock on the door or a phone call, the lenders miraculously appear and offer to wipe away the home owners' financial difficulties with the illusion of large gains from a new loan.

Lack of Transparency

Framing effects can occur when choices that are logically equivalent are not transparent.[53] In an experiment, Daniel Kahneman and Amos Tversky examined decision-making anomalies that can result from lack of transparency. They gave 150 people the following choices:

Imagine that you face the following pair of concurrent decisions. First examine both decisions, then indicate the options you prefer.

Decision (1) Choose between

A. A sure gain of $240
B. A 25 percent chance to win $1,000 and a 75 percent chance to gain nothing.
Decision (2) Choose between
C. A sure loss of $750
D. A 75 percent chance to lose $1,000 and a 25 percent chance to lose nothing.

In Decision (1), 84 percent chose A and 16 percent chose B, while in Decision (2), 13 percent chose C and 87 percent chose D. In effect, an overwhelming majority preferred A and D to B and C. However, the combined expected value of B and C exceeds that of A and D, making B and C the rational choice:

B and C: The expected value equals $(0.25 \times \$1,000) - 750 = -\$500$

A and D: The expected value equals $\$240 + (-0.75 \times \$1,000) = -\$510$.

When the options were presented transparently, people invariably chose B and C. But when the options were presented in the obscure format of the problem posed above, 73 percent of the people chose combination A and D and only 3 percent of them chose the rational combination B and C.[54]

This suggests that when the information people receive is confusing or difficult to evaluate, they cannot recognize the choice with the highest expected utility. Thus, consumer choice depends not only on loss aversion but also on transparency.[55]

Predatory lenders have multiple tools to defeat transparency. One technique involves search. A key objective of predatory lenders is to prevent home owners, once solicited for loans, from engaging in comparison-shopping. This is one reason why predatory lenders generally focus on the refinance market, not the purchase money market.[56] In the purchase money market, individuals are actively shopping for credit. In the refinance market, numerous home owners who could refinance are not seeking to do so,[57] and those are the people whom predatory lenders target. Once vulnerable prospects are identified, lenders aim to lock them in psychologically and immediately. Rapid loan approval is key. So are high-pressure closings. By accelerating the loan process, lenders reduce the chance that borrowers will comparison-shop, making it easier for lenders to insert exploitative terms into loans. Finally, lenders carefully study home owners' debt profiles to devise how to manufacture a sudden urge for a loan in home owners who previously had none.

In the rare cases when home owners shop for subprime loans, their search is unlikely to be informative. Unlike the prime mortgage market, subprime quotes by different lenders are almost never posted side by side, and when they are, the quotes do not permit meaningful comparison. It is well known that subprime interest rates go up as FICO scores go down.[58] Subprime loans are not advertised that way, however, and it is impossible for loan applicants to compare subprime loans based on FICO scores.[59] Similarly, subprime mortgage loans do not have standardized cost terms that permit easy comparison. One may have a prepayment penalty for three years; another, for five. One may offer single-premium credit life insurance; another may limit credit life policies to monthly premiums.[60] Under TILA, numerous cost elements can be excluded from the APR, hampering comparison-shopping. Even when APRs are comparable, some lenders intentionally tell borrowers that only the nominal interest rate matters, not the APR.[61] Finally, lenders generally have no obligation to inform borrowers of alternative sources of credit or to advise them to get credit counseling or legal advice before proceeding to closing.

Lack of Experience

Predatory lenders purposely target inexperienced borrowers who have not had prior opportunities for meaningful feedback regarding subprime refinance loans. Approximately 51 percent of home owners have never refinanced their mortgages.[62] Subprime borrowers, many of whom historically have been credit-constrained, are even less likely than prime borrowers to have refinanced. In addition, because subprime borrowers are less well educated on average than prime borrowers, they are more apt to be confused by subprime loan terms and the intricacies of the subprime mortgage process.[63]

Predatory lenders capitalize on this lack of education and experience to lock borrowers into products that they do not understand and cannot afford. Once locked in, borrowers who cannot keep up with the monthly payments find few, if any, avenues of relief. Struggling borrowers would like to refinance on better terms, but their worsening financial condition makes them unpalatable to other lenders. With each late payment, their credit score sinks. Many become victims of repeated loan flipping, and with each "flip," their loans mature later and have other new and abusive terms. Eventually, large prepayment penalties, interest arrears, and late fees strip their equity and, when combined with the outstanding principal, their indebtedness may exceed the value of their homes. The borrowers are locked into desperate situations and cannot get out.[64]

Choice Heuristics and Errors in Estimating Probabilities

All consumers, including subprime customers, use heuristic principles of one sort or another to simplify their financial decisions. When these principles are sound, they can provide a useful shortcut to financial decision-making. Other choice heuristics, however, can lead to grave and systematic errors in weighing risks and benefits.[65]

At least three choice heuristics lead home owners to make bad choices about subprime mortgages. The first is the relative insensitivity of subprime customers to interest-rate levels in general and annual percentage rates (APRs). These individuals tend to focus on whether the monthly payments offered are affordable rather than on lower interest rates.[66] Pessimistic about whether other lenders would be willing to lend to them and fearful that the loan at hand will vanish, these borrowers jump at the first option offered as long as the payments seem feasible. Predatory lenders exploit that tendency by using long maturities, teaser rates, balloon clauses, and sometimes fraud to advertise low monthly payments on high-cost loans.

Two additional choice heuristics cause home owners to make mistaken probability assessments. First, repeated studies have shown that people tend to overestimate the probability of compound events.[67] In order for a mortgage to be paid off successfully, a borrower must make on-time payments every month for up to thirty years. One missed payment can be enough to throw the loan into default. Under basic principles of probability, the longer the loan term and the greater the number of scheduled monthly payments, the more likely it is that the loan will go into default. Nevertheless, people tend to equate the likelihood of making the first mortgage payment—which is higher—with the likelihood of successfully paying off the entire loan. The less likely default seems, the more likely home owners are to disregard the potential loss of their homes.[68]

The last choice heuristic sheds light on the heightened propensity of subprime customers to buy credit life insurance and related insurance products at inflated prices. Experimental evidence reveals that people are willing to pay more to insure against vivid, catastrophic risks having low probability than against more general risks. In one survey, for example, subjects were willing to pay more for life insurance for death on an airplane flight due to terrorism than for death on a flight for *any* reason.[69] Thus, while predatory lending victims underestimate the risk of default in general, they may overestimate the risk of default due to isolated risks such as death or disability, and overpay for insurance for those risks.

POLICY IMPLICATIONS

Predatory lending has a certain perverse genius. That genius lies in targeting cognitive anomalies in financial decision making by individuals and masterminding marketing techniques to exploit those anomalies, all to disastrous effect for borrowers. Predatory lenders make attractive terms salient and obscure the terms that might pose concern. They hunt down home owners in financial straits and capitalize on the desperation that fuels risk-taking to snare their assent. They give a hard sell on credit life insurance, knowing that people will overpay for it. They do everything in their power to impede comparison-shopping by homeowners. And, all too often, they perpetrate fraud on victims.

These marketing techniques of predatory lenders have distinct public policy implications. Improved disclosure, for example, is often touted as the optimal remedy. However, it is hard to imagine Congress mandating a disclosure scheme so starkly plain that victims would turn down abusive, irrational loans. To do that, Congress would essentially have to mandate upfront marketing pitches of the form "If you sign this loan, you will have w percent chance of damage to your credit record, x percent chance of going into default, y percent chance of bankruptcy, and z percent chance of losing your home to foreclosure." All subprime advertising would have to be heavily regulated for content, to prevent undermining that core message. All other marketing, including oral pitches, would have to be strictly limited.

Under the Securities Act of 1933, advertising is heavily regulated in just that manner for the sale of public securities offerings. Given the current political climate and the lobbying prowess of the mortgage industry, however, it is impossible to imagine Congress enacting similar advertising restrictions for the subprime mortgage industry today.

There is a further problem with disclosure, which is that disclosure fails to address the separate and thorny issue of intentionally targeting susceptible victims. To people already in dire straits, if lenders frame the only choice as a predatory loan or no loan at all—to the exclusion of other, more appropriate options, such as government-subsidized home repair loans, home equity lines of credit, or unsecured loans from reputable lenders—disclosures of the form outlined above are unlikely to deter potential victims from bad decisions. In recognition of this problem in the boiler-room securities sales context, securities regulators have mandated not only disclosures but also more stringent measures, including a duty of suitability.[70]

Another remedy often touted is home owner education and/or counseling. In the long run, it is doubtful that sufficient financial resources will ever be devoted to effective nationwide counseling. More to the point, at a minimum, as Kahneman and Tversky pointed out, "[e]ffective learning . . . requires accurate and immediate feedback about the relation between the situational conditions and the appropriate response."[71] For the reasons discussed earlier, mortgage lending, particularly predatory mortgage lending, does not lend itself to accurate and immediate feedback or to opportunities for corrective action. Home owner education in advance of marketing pitches by lenders is too early. Neutral home owner counseling before an application is signed has the virtue of immediacy, but there are no good faith estimates or concrete loan documents available for review. Without that information, it is difficult to counteract impulsive decisions by people in financial exigency, especially when the lenders are touting the virtues of the loans. While it is true that lenders are supposed to give applicants a good faith estimate within three days after signing their loan applications, GFEs lack interest rates and finance charges, and many lenders never deliver GFEs. Home owner counseling right at closing (or during the three-day TILA rescission period afterward) would have the potential benefit of access to HUD-1s and loan documents, but would face an uphill struggle to educate home owners who are thirsting for their loan proceeds and who have already paid nonrefundable application fees.

Home owner education and counseling further assumes that cognitive anomalies can be eradicated. However, there is increasing evidence that experience and learning do not succeed in eliminating cognitive biases or improve people's ability to apply the principles they learn to specific situations.[72]

Finally, disclosure, education, and counseling ignore the crucial fact that predatory lending is the product of relentless and fiendishly clever marketing that manipulates cognitive imperfections. Predatory lenders will always be better at reaching potential victims than will legitimate lenders, community groups, churches, and the government. In large part that is because vulnerable customers often are not actively in the market for loans to begin with. As a result, the best way to pinpoint them is labor-intensive and costly: by mimicking predatory lenders and going door-to-door. Due to the high costs involved, reaching the potential victims of predatory lending thus presents an enormous hurdle for any educational campaign.[73]

In the analogous context of insurance, Eric Johnson and his colleagues concluded that the "recognition that consumer perceptions and decision processes are imperfect and manipulable . . . support[s] insurance regulation and prohibition of certain types of insurance."[74] Likewise, Kahneman and Tversky argued that framing places ethical duties on the marketer: "When framing influences the experience of consequences, the adoption of a decision frame is an ethically significant act."[75] Particularly here, since predatory lenders and brokers can obviate the harm more cheaply than the victims, the onus should fall on the purveyors of predatory loans.

In the securities context, identical considerations caused the Securities and Exchange Commission long ago to impose a duty of suitability on securities brokers. Under that duty, securities brokers must refrain from recommending securities that are unsuitable, given an individual customer's financial status, needs, and goals.[76]

The time has come for a comparable duty of suitability in subprime lending, one that is tailored to the realities of the subprime market. Such a duty would put the burden of preventing predatory lending on those who can afford it most cheaply (predatory lenders and brokers) by empowering the federal government and individual victims to sue for loan reformation, disgorgement, and damages.[77]

NOTES

The first section describing predatory lending practices is a condensed version drawn from an earlier article coauthored with Kathleen Engel. My thanks to Peter Diamond, Kathleen Engel, Botond Köszegi, Jim Rebitzer, and Elizabeth Renuart for their insights.

1. Board of Governors of the Federal Reserve System et al., "Expanded Interagency Guidance for Subprime Lending Programs" (2001), http://www.federalre serve.gov/boarddocs/press/boardacts/2001/20010131/attachment.pdf, p. 2; Board of Governors of the Federal Reserve System et al., "Interagency Guidance on Subprime Lending" (1999), http://www.federalreserve.gov/boarddocs/SRLETTERS/ 1999/sr9906a1.pdf, p. 1; U.S. Department of Housing and Urban Development and U.S. Department of the Treasury, "Curbing Predatory Home Mortgage Lending" (2000), p. 28, available at http://www.huduser.org/publications/hsgfin/curbing.html; *Predatory Mortgage Lending: Hearing Before the House Committee on Banking and Financial Services*, 106th Congress (Washington, D.C.: Government Printing Office, 2000), pp. 308–19.

2. John C. Weicher, *The Home Equity Lending Industry: Refinancing Mortgages for Borrowers with Impaired Credit* (Indianapolis, Ind.: Hudson Institute, 1997), pp. 30, 34, 60–61.

3. Mortgage Bankers Association of America, "Subprime Lending and High Cost Mortgages: Recommended 'Best Practices' and 'Legislative Guidelines' " (2000), para. 6, http://www.mbaa.org/resident/lib2000/0525b.html.

4. U.S. Department of Housing and Urban Development and U.S. Department of the Treasury, "Curbing Predatory Home Mortgage Lending," pp. 21, 22, 24–25, 27 n.12; Fannie Mae, "Lender Letter 03-00, Eligibility of Mortgages to Borrowers with Blemished Credit Records" (April 11, 2000), www.efanniemae.com/single family/forms_guidelines/lender_letters/db_lender_letters.jhtml?role=ou#03-00; National Training and Information Center, "Preying on Neighborhoods: Subprime Mortgage Lending and Chicagoland Foreclosures" (September 21, 1999), pp. 23–27, http://www.ntic-us.org/preying/preying.pdf; Patricia Sturdevant and William J. Brennan Jr., "A Catalogue of Predatory Lending Practices," *The Consumer Advocate* 5 (1999): 37.

5. Negative amortization is another practice that inflicts seriously disproportionate net harm on borrowers. In negative amortization, scheduled payments do not cover the interest due, causing the outstanding principal to grow over time. Affected borrowers who make regular payments still lose equity in their homes. U.S. Department of Housing and Urban Development and U.S. Department of the Treasury, "Curbing Predatory Home Mortgage Lending," pp. 91–92.

Reverse mortgages administered by the Department of Housing and Urban Development are an exception to the rule that negative amortization is abusive. These reverse mortgages permit elderly homeowners to cash out their home equity in exchange for an income stream. Reverse mortgages are heavily regulated and entail mandatory counseling. Ibid., p. 92.

6. Jeff Bailey, "A Man and His Loan: Why Bennie Roberts Refinanced 20 Times," *Wall Street Journal*, April 23, 1997, p. A1; U.S. Department of Housing and Urban Development and U.S. Department of the Treasury, "Curbing Predatory Home Mortgage Lending," pp. 21, 73–74; Sturdevant and Brennan, "A Catalogue of Predatory Lending Practices," p. 39.

7. Teresa Dixon Murray, "Borrower Beware: Predatory Mortgage Brokers Don't Give Terms Promised, Causing Some to Lose Their Homes," *Cleveland Plain Dealer*, August 28, 2000, p. 1C; Sturdevant and Brennan, "A Catalogue of Predatory Lending Practices," pp. 39–40.

8. Freddie Mac, "Automated Underwriting: Making Mortgage Lending Simpler and Fairer for America's Families," www.freddiemac.com/corporate/reports (September 1996), chapter 5 and nn.5–6; Sturdevant and Brennan, "A Catalogue of Predatory Lending Practices," p. 37.

9. U.S. Department of Housing and Urban Development and U.S. Department of the Treasury, "Curbing Predatory Home Mortgage Lending," p. 40.

10. U.S. Department of Housing and Urban Development and U.S. Department of the Treasury, "Curbing Predatory Home Mortgage Lending," p. 27; Weicher, *The Home Equity Lending Industry*, pp. 69, 74–88.

11. Dwight M. Jaffee and Thomas Russell, "Imperfect Information, Uncertainty, and Credit Rationing," *Quarterly Journal of Economics* 90 (1976): 651.

12. In this chapter, all references to the secondary market are to the market for the sale of mortgage-backed securities to investors, through either private placements or public offerings. Institutional investors such as banks and thrifts, and government-sponsored entities such as Fannie Mae and Freddie Mac, purchase mortgage-backed securities in private placements. The public can invest in mortgage-backed securities through public offerings.

13. U.S. Department of Housing and Urban Development and U.S. Department of the Treasury, "Curbing Predatory Home Mortgage Lending," p. 28; Weicher, *The Home Equity Lending Industry*, p. 69. Newer evidence casts doubt on this assertion. Kathleen C. Engel and Patricia A. McCoy, "Predatory Lending: What's Wall Street Got to Do with It" (2004), pp. 28–34.

14. U.S. Department of Housing and Urban Development and U.S. Department of the Treasury, "Curbing Predatory Home Mortgage Lending," p. 28; Weicher, *The Home Equity Lending Industry*, p. 67.

15. U.S. Department of Housing and Urban Development and U.S. Department of the Treasury, "Curbing Predatory Home Mortgage Lending," p. 28; Weicher, *The Home Equity Lending Industry*, pp. 61–62, 67.

16. U.S. Department of Housing and Urban Development and U.S. Department of the Treasury, "Curbing Predatory Home Mortgage Lending," p. 28; Weicher, *The Home Equity Lending Industry*, pp. 56–57 and table 4.1, 69–70, 74–88.

17. Howard Lax et al., "Subprime Lending: An Investigation of Economic Efficiency" (unpublished working paper, December 21, 2000), pp. 17–19; Mark Shroder, "The Value of the Sunshine Cure: Efficacy of the RESPA Disclosure Strategy" (unpublished working paper, April 2000), pp. 14–15, fig. 2, table 4; Sturdevant and Brennan, "A Catalogue of Predatory Lending Practices," pp. 38–39; Alan M. White, "Are Subprime Mortgages Priced According to Risk?" (unpublished working paper, 2004).

18. Sturdevant and Brennan, "A Catalogue of Predatory Lending Practices," pp. 38–39.

19. U.S. Department of Housing and Urban Development and U.S. Department of the Treasury, "Curbing Predatory Home Mortgage Lending," pp. 81, 88 and n. 85, 89, 91; Sturdevant and Brennan, "A Catalogue of Predatory Lending Practices," p. 39.

20. 15 U.S.C. 1601–1693(c) (2000).

21. 12 U.S.C. 2601–2617 (2000).

22. Board of Governors of the Federal Reserve System, "Expanded Interagency Guidance for Subprime Lending Programs," p. 10; U.S. Department of Housing and Urban Development and U.S. Department of the Treasury, "Curbing Predatory Home Mortgage Lending," pp. 79–90.

23. Patrick Barta, "Is Appraisal Process Skewing Home Values?" *Wall Street Journal*, August 13, 2001, p. A1; U.S. Department of Housing and Urban Development and U.S. Department of the Treasury, "Curbing Predatory Home Mortgage Lending," pp. 21–22, 80; Sturdevant and Brennan, "A Catalogue of Predatory Lending Practices," p. 37.

24. U.S. Department of Housing and Urban Development and Federal Reserve Board, *Joint Report to Congress Concerning Reform to the Truth in Lending Act and the Real Estate Settlement Procedures Act* (1998), http://www.federalreserve.gov/boarddocs/rptcongress/tila.pdf, Executive Summary, p. I; Ralph J. Rohner and Fred H. Miller, *Truth in Lending* (Chicago: American Bar Association, 2000), p. 179.

25. Department of Housing and Urban Development and Federal Reserve Board, *Joint Report to Congress*, Executive Summary, p. II.

26. Ibid., Executive Summary, p. X.

27. In a survey of GFEs, economist Mark Shroder found that many of the GFEs were off by "a fair amount" and that a minority of borrowers received "large underestimates." Shroder, "The Value of the Sunshine Cure," p. 12.

28. The relatively small group of HOEPA loans—now approximately 5 percent of subprime mortgages—form the exception. Under HOEPA, the lender must make specific written disclosures three days before closing.

29. Department of Housing and Urban Development and Federal Reserve Board, *Joint Report to Congress*, Executive Summary, p. XIX.

30. Kathleen E. Keest and Elizabeth Renuart, *The Cost of Credit: Regulation and Legal Challenges*, 2nd ed. (Boston: National Consumer Law Center, 2000), p. 163; Sturdevant and Brennan, "A Catalogue of Predatory Lending Practices," p. 38; Weicher, *The Home Equity Lending Industry*, p. 67.

31. Richard Boisky, "In Reality, 'Predatory Lending' Isn't Easy to Define," *News & Observer* (Raleigh, N.C.), October 24, 2000, p. A10; Weicher, *The Home Equity Lending Industry*, pp. 71–74.

32. John Farris et al., "Quantifying the Economic Costs of Prepayment Penalties to Subprime Mortgage Borrowers," December 15, 2003, p. 18.

33. Shelly Smith, "Mandatory Arbitration Clauses in Consumer Contracts: Consumer Protection and the Circumvention of the Judicial System," *DePaul Law Review* 50 (2001): 1191–92.

34. U.S. Department of Housing and Urban Development and U.S. Department of the Treasury, "Curbing Predatory Home Mortgage Lending," p. 99.

35. Daniel Kahneman and Amos Tversky, "Prospect Theory: An Analysis of Decision Under Risk," *Econometrica* 47 (1979): 263–92.

36. Ibid.; Amos Tversky and Daniel Kahneman, "The Framing of Decisions and the Psychology of Choice," *Science* 211 (1981): 453–58.

37. Kahneman and Tversky, "Prospect Theory," pp. 264, 268–69, 274.

38. Kahneman and Tversky expressed prospect theory in mathematical terms by altering the formula for expected utility to add a value function $v(\bullet)$ on gains and losses, plus decision weights $\pi(\bullet)$ on stated probabilities. The value function $v(\bullet)$

expresses the idea that people put greater value on avoiding losses than on making gains. The decision weights $\pi(\bullet)$ capture the idea that people overweight outcomes with low probabilities and underweight outcomes with moderate and high probabilities. This results in the following equation expressing the decision-making process that loss-averse people are said to employ:

$$V = \pi(p)v(x) + \pi(q)v(y),$$

where p and q are probabilities and x and y are competing choices. Kahneman and Tversky, "Prospect Theory," pp. 275–76; Amos Tversky and Daniel Kahneman, "Rational Choice and the Framing of Decisions," *Journal of Business* 59 (1986): S257; Tversky and Kahneman, "The Framing of Decisions and the Psychology of Choice," p. 454.

39. Kahneman and Tversky, "Prospect Theory," pp. 264, 268–69, 274.

40. Daniel Kahneman et al., "The Endowment Effect, Loss Aversion, and Status Quo Bias," *Journal of Economics* 5 (1991): 203–4.

41. Richard H. Thaler, "Mental Accounting and Consumer Choice," *Marketing Science* 4 (1985): 202; Richard H. Thaler, "Mental Accounting Matters," *Journal of Behavioral Decision Making* 12 (1999): 187–88.

42. Kahneman and Tversky, "Prospect Theory," pp. 278–79.

43. Ian Domowitz and Robert L. Sartain, "Determinants of the Consumer Bankruptcy Decision," *Journal of Finance* 54 (1999): 410–14.

44. Thaler, "Mental Accounting Matters," p. 185; Tversky and Kahneman, "Rational Choice and the Framing of Decisions," p. S258.

45. Kahneman et al., "The Endowment Effect, Loss Aversion, and Status Quo Bias," p. 200.

46. Tversky and Kahneman, "Rational Choice and the Framing of Decisions," p. S258.

47. Matthew Rabin, "Psychology and Economics," *Journal of Economic Literature* 36 (1998): 36.

48. Stephen E.G. Lea et al., *The Individual in the Economy: A Textbook of Economic Psychology* (Cambridge: Cambridge University Press, 1987), p. 347; Tversky and Kahneman, "The Framing of Decisions and the Psychology of Choice," pp. 453, 457–58; Tversky and Kahneman, "Rational Choice and the Framing of Decisions," p. S260.

49. Rabin, "Psychology and Economics," p. 37. The related literature on preference reversals explores situations where different methods of elicitation lead to systematically different orderings of preferences. Ibid.; Paul Slovic and Sarah Lichtenstein, "Preference Reversals: A Broader Perspective," *American Economic Review* 73 (1983): 596–605; Amos Tversky et al., "The Causes of Preference Reversal," *American Economic Review* 80 (1990): 204–17; Amos Tversky and Richard H. Thaler, "Anomalies: Preference Reversals," *Journal of Economic Perspectives* 4 (1990): 202.

50. Customers are less resistant to price increases when those increases are couched as cancellation of temporary discounts such as teaser rates. Tversky and Kahneman, "Rational Choice and the Framing of Decisions," p. S261.

51. Kahneman and Tversky, "Prospect Theory," p. 287; Tversky and Kahneman, "The Framing of Decisions and the Psychology of Choice," p. 456.

52. U.S. Department of Housing and Urban Development and U.S. Department

of the Treasury, "Curbing Predatory Home Mortgage Lending," p. 39; Kathleen C. Engel and Patricia A. McCoy, "A Tale of Three Markets: The Law and Economics of Predatory Lending," *Texas Law Review* 80 (2002): 1281–84.

53. Rabin, "Psychology and Economics," p. 36.

54. Tversky and Kahneman, "Rational Choice and the Framing of Decisions," pp. S265–66.

55. Ibid., p. S265.

56. U.S. Department of Housing and Urban Development and U.S. Department of the Treasury, "Curbing Predatory Home Mortgage Lending," pp. 30–31.

57. Glenn Canner et al., "Mortgage Refinancing in 2001 and Early 2002," *Federal Reserve Bulletin* 88 (2002): 470.

58. U.S. Department of Housing and Urban Development and U.S. Department of the Treasury, "Curbing Predatory Home Mortgage Lending," pp. 28, 33–34; White, "Are Subprime Mortgages Priced According to Risk?"

59. Thaler, "Mental Accounting and Consumer Choice," pp. 209–11; White, "Are Subprime Mortgages Priced According to Risk?"

60. White, "Are Subprime Mortgages Priced According to Risk?"

61. For instance, in *In re First Alliance Mortgage Company*, 298 B.R. 652 (Bankr. C.D. Cal. 2003), loan officers, following a company script, told unsuspecting home owners that the "interest rate is what consumers care about, APR is what the federal government cares about and yield is what the banks care about in evaluating a loan" (p. 657).

62. Canner et al., "Mortgage Refinancing in 2001 and Early 2002," p. 470.

63. U.S Department of Housing and Urban Development and U.S. Department of the Treasury, "Curbing Predatory Home Mortgage Lending," p. 37; Alan M. White and Cathy Lesser Mansfield, "Literacy and Contract," *Stanford Law and Policy Review* 13, no. 2 (2002): 233.

64. Thaler, "Mental Accounting and Consumer Choice," p. 210.

65. Amos Tversky and Daniel Kahneman, "Judgment Under Uncertainty: Heuristics and Biases," *Science* 185 (1974): 1124.

66. George S. Day and William K. Brandt, "Consumer Research and the Evaluation of Information Disclosure Requirements: The Case of Truth in Lending," *Journal of Consumer Responsibility* 1 (1974): 22–23; Thaler, "Mental Accounting Matters."

67. Tversky and Kahneman, "Judgment Under Uncertainty: Heuristics and Biases," p. 1129.

68. Kahneman and Tversky, "Prospect Theory," p. 275.

69. Eric J. Johnson et al., "Framing, Probability Distortions, and Insurance Decisions," *Journal of Risk and Uncertainty* 7 (1993): 35–51.

70. Engel and McCoy, "A Tale of Three Markets," pp. 1325–26.

71. Tversky and Kahneman, "Rational Choice and the Framing of Decisions," p. S274.

72. Rabin, "Psychology and Economics," p. 31.

73. Engel and McCoy, "A Tale of Three Markets," p. 1309.

74. Johnson et al., "Framing, Probability Distortions, and Insurance Decisions."

75. Tversky and Kahneman, "The Framing of Decisions and the Psychology of Choice," p. 458.

76. Engel and McCoy, "A Tale of Three Markets," p. 1318.

77. Ibid., pp. 1339–56.

5

Legal and Economic Inducements to Predatory Practices

Keith Ernst, Deborah N. Goldstein, and
Christopher A. Richardson

Subprime lending is not a new business. Lending to people with blemished credit histories has been around seemingly for as long as there have been creditors and debtors. Examples of the long-standing tradition of subprime lending in the United States run the gamut from pawnshops to the more positively regarded community development home loans. Subprime lending has, however, changed since the 1980s as the technological, macroeconomic, and legal frameworks in which these transactions take place have evolved, giving rise to increasingly sophisticated operations and substantial growth. Accompanying this growth has been the notable emergence of predatory home mortgage lending within the subprime credit sector. This chapter argues that deregulation and increased access to investment capital have interacted with preexisting credit market dynamics in ways that have made increases in high-fee predatory home mortgage lending among nondepository lenders predictable if not inevitable. It concludes with a discussion of whether the nation's storied depository institutions have been or may yet be similarly corrupted—and the resulting implications for American consumers.

The dramatic change in the U.S. financial sector is perhaps nowhere more evident than in the growth of the subprime home mortgage lending sector, from $35 billion volume in 1994,[1] to $134 billion in 2000,[2] and to $241 billion in 2002.[3] To the extent that this trend has given rise to a new kind of subprime lending that truly reflects the "democratization of credit,"[4] it enables tens of thousands of families each year to take either their first steps into the middle class by purchasing a home or their second and third steps in the form of home equity loans that finance small businesses and college educations. Indeed, as policy makers strive to push American home ownership rates to new heights,[5] lenders have looked with ever-increasing earnestness beyond white families, whose home ownership rates already averaged 75 percent in 2002, to families with more potential for home ownership growth, including African American families (home ownership rate of 49 percent in 2002), Hispanic families (47 percent in 2002), families headed by single parents (55 percent for men and 50 percent for women in 2000), and low-income families (48 percent in 2002).[6]

Many of these same families, however, have seemingly been targeted by lenders with less benign motives.[7] To the extent that subprime lending has created new opportunities for unscrupulous lenders to make abusive loans that strip home equity through exorbitant fees,[8] shroud transactions through deceptive disclosure techniques,[9] and may ultimately lead to declines in neighborhood wealth and stability,[10] lenders, policy makers, and consumer advocates have been all the more driven to find solutions to predatory lending. Indications are that predatory lending is more than a marginal issue, with a reported $784 million in settlements related to such practices secured by federal agencies and attorneys general in 2002 alone.[11]

For many years, subprime lending was the province of pawnshops and finance companies that were typically restricted in the amount of fees and even the rates of interest which they could charge (e.g., N.C. General Statutes 24–14). These enterprises were readily recognizable and identifiable as lenders of if not last, at least second, resort. But increasingly, household names of creditors like *Citi* and *Wells Fargo* have become attached to subprime suffixes like *Financial*. If these changes represent a transition of subprime lending into the mainstream and a commensurate increase in access to fairly priced credit, they will no doubt be widely welcomed. However, if these changes serve to leverage the formidable economic and political power of large, legally favored institutions to promote abusive lending, a contentious debate is likely to ensue.

Congress' initial response to the emergence of abuses within the subprime lending market, the Home Ownership and Equity Protection Act of 1994 (HOEPA), has been viewed by many as inadequate to stop predatory lending.[12] In fact, the law's failure to include the full range of home loans (completely omitting home purchase loans and open-end loans such as home equity lines of credit) and its numerous loopholes for points and fees (prepayment penalties in particular) provide ample opportunities for predatory lenders to evade the legislation. Despite HOEPA's enactment, the total cost of predatory lending to U.S. consumers in 1999 alone was estimated at more than $9 billion.[13]

Within subprime home lending, technological advances have given rise to fantastic increases in the cost-effectiveness of customer identification and mass marketing[14] as well as the ease with which creditors can navigate state laws.[15] These advances are important underlying factors in the story of how subprime lending and its less desirable progeny, predatory lending, have grown. This chapter focuses, however, on the more fundamental question of how the intersection of deregulation and preexisting credit market dynamics gave rise to the emergence of predatory home lending as it is understood today.

Toward this end, this chapter first describes how changes in federal laws have made predatory loans possible, particularly for nondepository lenders that are traditionally regulated by states. It then considers economic factors apart from profit maximization that influence lenders to employ predatory practices. Finally, the chapter concludes by examining the mechanisms that may draw depository institutions into predatory lending, and discusses the implications of any such development.

EVOLVING LEGAL CONSTRUCTS PROVIDE OPPORTUNITIES FOR PREDATORY LENDING

Deregulation of financial institutions, an offspring of the troubled economic times of the 1970s and the early 1980s, can be seen as a trend that continues to the present day. For the purposes at hand, deregulation through federal law can be divided into three components: (1) changes influencing the terms and structure of credit transactions, (2) changes influencing the range of charges that may be levied by certain lenders, and (3) changes that encourage borrowers to assume home-secured debt over other credit options. While many aspects of these changes have been exceedingly positive for both lenders and borrowers, each also provides opportunities for irresponsible lenders to take advantage of borrowers.

Traditionally, credit has been among the most regulated of products. Major religions and nations have set maximum permissible rates of interest, with such regulation falling under the rubric of usury.[16] It is not without reason that credit has been viewed with some skepticism and trepidation. Few other decisions have the continuing cost or the singular ability to alter an individual or family's welfare that the act of signing a loan agreement has. Borrowing to buy a home can build equity and economic security but on the other hand, lending abuses decimate families and harm whole communities.

Such abuses in recent years have taken the form of high-cost, high-fee home loans. As our colleague describes:

The problem of excessive [financed] fees for the subprime . . . borrower is two-fold: the fees seem painless at closing and they are forever. They are *deceptively costless* to many borrowers because when the borrower "pays" them at closing, he or she does not feel the pain of counting out thousands of dollars in cash. The borrower parts with the money only later, when the loan is paid off and the equity value remaining in his or her home is reduced by the amount of fees owed. In addition, the *fees are forever* because, even if another lender refinances a family . . . just one week later, the borrower's wealth is still permanently stripped away.[17]

In fact, to the extent that these high fees deter borrowers from refinancing when higher rates would not, they can properly be seen as anti-competitive terms that offer borrowers little to no offsetting advantages. If a borrower receives a loan with an interest rate that is too high for her risk profile, another lender can simply offer to refinance at a lower rate, thereby denying a would-be predatory lender the future excess interest. To be sure, the borrower loses the excessive interest paid before she refinances; however, such an outcome stands in contrast to a high-fee loan where the lender locks in profits through fees at the time of origination, effectively prohibiting any lender from competing to offer a better deal.

Unfortunately, to date, regulators and the courts have been slow to comprehend and address this distinction between interest rates and fees. For example, the Supreme Court has actually articulated a premise clearly at odds with the foregoing logic: "there is no apparent reason why home-state-approved percentage charges should be permissible but home-state-approved flat charges unlawful."[18]

In a historical context, federal policy makers' failure to act on this distinction may not have been significant, since in the United States, the structure and terms of credit have customarily been regulated at the state level.[19] While these state laws have varied in the level of protection afforded consumers, several developments at the federal level have made it easier for unscrupulous lenders to lure borrowers into abusive loans, particularly high-cost, high-fee loans. First, Congress has explicitly deregulated certain types of home loans, explicitly allowing charges that would otherwise contravene state law to be levied by a broad class of lenders. Second, federal law has blurred state boundaries by allowing certain lenders to charge rates and fees based on their home state's law in all other states. Third, and finally, federal law has provided consumers with incentives to prefer home-secured debt over nonsecured debt.

Deregulation of Certain Types of Home Loans

Perceiving a credit crisis in the home loan market resulting in part from the application of state usury caps in a rapidly escalating interest rate environment, Congress moved to deregulate and preempt conflicting state law on a broad set of first-lien home loans and laws restricting "alternative" mortgages.[20]

First, the Depository Institutions Deregulation and Monetary Control Act of 1980 (DIDA) preempted the "constitution or the laws of any State expressly limiting the rate or amount of interest, discount points, finance charges, or other charges" on extensions of credit secured by a first lien on a home (12 U.S.C. 1735f–7a(a)(1)). The legislative history of DIDA specifically provides that this provision preempts only state laws related to interest and certain other charges.[21] As a result, the corresponding regulations expressly disavow preemption of any "limitation on prepayment charges, attorneys' fees, late charges or other [charges not included in calculations of APR]."[22] Second, in a further limitation, DIDA provides that states may restore their laws on points and fees at any time through legislative action (though the deadline for states to opt out of interest rate preemption expired in 1983).[23]

Despite these limitations, by preempting prior state laws that limited fees on first lien home loans, Congress has nonetheless provided substantial leeway for lenders bent on stripping home equity through fees. In a report exceedingly critical of a state-chartered finance company, the Washington Department of Banking found that Household International was deceiving borrowers and repeatedly charging more than seven bogus discount points.[24] In another instance involving a state nondepository lender, First Alliance Mortgage Company charged borrowers 25 percent in fees, financing the fees directly into the loan amount, and enticed borrowers by representing that the loan had "no out-of-pocket costs."[25]

Following up on DIDA in 1982, Congress passed the Alternative Mortgage Transaction Parity Act (AMTPA) to give nonfederally chartered "state housing creditors" parity with federally chartered institutions with regard to "alternative" mortgage transactions (12 U.S.C. 3801). More specifically, Congress identified that state housing creditors, including nondepository finance companies in particular, were having difficulty originating fixed-rate, fixed-term loans in a high-interest-rate environment, and could not compete with federally chartered institutions that were already authorized by their regulators to offer alternative products, such as adjustable-rate mortgages, to help minimize monthly payments.[26]

The first enabling AMTPA regulations permitted state housing creditors to follow federal regulations applicable to federal thrifts regarding negative amortization and balloon payments rather than state law on these points.[27] While prepayment penalties were not initially preempted by federal regulators for state housing creditors, the federal Office of Thrift Supervision (OTS) in 1996 identified late fees and prepayment penalties as terms that state housing creditors could also consider to be governed by federal law.[28]

The 1996 policy change presented a particularly vexing problem for vulnerable home loan borrowers. Prepayment penalties have been decried as among the least transparent and most widely abused charges associated with subprime home loans.[29] The damage done by prepayment penalties in subprime home loans is threefold: they strip home equity, trap borrowers in bad loans with an increased risk of foreclosure, and facilitate kickbacks that encourage brokers to place borrowers in loans with higher interest rates than loans for which the borrowers qualify (by ensuring lenders can recoup the kickback should the loan prepay). Prepayment penalties with a lockout period of three to five years, which stipulate that a borrower must pay "six months' interest" on up to 80 percent of the original loan amount if he prepays his subprime home loan, are common.[30] On a 12 percent interest, $125,000 principal balance, 30-year home loan, such a penalty can approach $6,000, a substantial amount for families trying to build wealth. In fact, this figure represents more than one third of the 2001 median net worth of $17,100 reported for families of color.[31] Given this statistic, one might assume that few subprime home loans would include prepayment penalties.

In fact, many borrowers find themselves trapped in unattractive subprime home loans by prepayment penalties. While only 2 percent of borrowers in the competitive prime home loan sector choose mortgages with prepayment penalties, over 80 percent of borrowers in the subprime market receive loans with a penalty.[32] Borrower choice is unable to explain such a disparity, since rational borrowers in the subprime market, who may improve their credit scores and refinance into more attractive rates, should presumably prefer prepayment penalties less often than borrowers in the prime market.

Moreover, lenders who claim to be providing a reasonable benefit to borrowers in the form of decreased monthly costs in exchange for the acceptance of a prepayment penalty have been shown to provide considerably less than equitable exchanges. For example, one finance company affiliate of a national bank reported that it provided a reduction of 0.50 percent in interest for borrowers who chose a prepayment penalty.[33] Yet, a borrower who has to pay a six months' interest prepayment penalty to refinance at year three of a 12 percent interest, 30-year home loan—roughly the average life of subprime home loans for many originators[34]—will have received a benefit worth less than 2 percent of the loan amount, but may be liable for a penalty of almost 5 percent of the loan amount. In other words, for the majority of borrowers facing this prospect, such a prepayment penalty–interest rate exchange will be a losing proposition.

Subsequently, in 2002, the OTS reversed its 1996 policy change as it applied to finance companies, recognizing abuses associated with prepayment penalties and concluding that prepayment penalties were not relevant to Congress' intent to authorize alternative mortgage products. Reverting to earlier AMTPA regulations, the OTS fully restored the right of states to regulate prepayment penalties and late fees for nondepository entities.[35] The OTS's 2002 action represented a boon to consumers. While some 35 states regulated prepayment penalties on home loans as of early 2003,[36] the OTS rules from 1996 to 2002 rendered those rules moot for state housing creditors.

Still, even after this significant change, federal law provides that state housing creditors can ignore state consumer protections with regard to negative amortization and balloon payments. While this authority provides substantial flexibility that is used positively in the competitive prime market to reduce monthly payments required under a loan, it can easily be abused by lenders trying to hide a loan's true costs.

Table 5.1
How a Balloon Payment Can Obscure Loan Fees

	Borrower A	Borrower B
1. Borrower situation		
House sale price	$100,000	$100,000
Loan amount needed	$90,000	$90,000
Equity for down payment	$10,000	$10,000
2. Rate quote		
Interest rate (fixed)	8.25%	8.25%
Monthly payment	$686	$686
Term	30 years	30 years
3. Loan fees and features		
Points and fees	$1,350	$9,000
Loan amount	$91,350	$99,000
Prepayment penalty	None	4.125%/5 years
Structural Features	None	Balloon of $90,570
4. Borrower equity after year 3 refinance		
Starting equity	$10,000	$10,000
Points and fees	$(1,350)	$(9,000)
Principal repaid	$2,350	$219
Prepayment penalty	None	$(3,267)
Final borrower equity	$11,000	$(2,048)

Table 5.1 illustrates how a lender can use a balloon payment to obscure equity-stripping fees. Both borrower A and borrower B receive seemingly identical loan quotes—the same interest rate, term, and monthly payments in response to the same proposed transaction. Yet, borrower B is, in fact, borrowing substantially more money just to pay the fees the lender is financing into the loan amount. Unfortunately, borrower B is less likely to perceive this pricing differential because the monthly payments have been depressed by deferring payment until the end of the loan period, at which time a sizable balloon payment will come due. At the time both borrowers refinance—an occasion that may happen for any number of reasons, including job loss or family necessity—the economics become all too clear. While borrower A's loan has built equity in the home, borrower B's loan has stripped equity from the home.

Blurring State Boundaries

National banks, federal credit unions, federal thrifts, and state-chartered depository institutions enjoy varying degrees of preemption of state usury laws under a legal framework known as the "most-favored lender" doctrine. Under this doctrine, federally chartered institutions "located" in one state (e.g., South Dakota) can "export" the maximum permissible interest rate of that state to loans the bank makes to borrowers in another state (e.g., North Carolina), thus preempting state usury law.[37] State-chartered institutions enjoy a similar right through the Federal Deposit Insurance Act, which allows state-chartered, federally insured depositories to charge the higher of the interest rate allowed by the laws of the state where the bank is located and where the loan is made (12 U.S.C. 1831d(a)). In cases where the lender seeks to use the second state's laws, it is permitted to choose the highest rate authorized by state law even if such charges are authorized only for a specific set of lenders to which it does not belong.

While it is true that states may opt out of this preemption insofar as it applies to state-chartered banks, the inertia plaguing most legislative efforts seems, at best, to make such action difficult. Federal law thus presents state policy makers with the dilemma of whether to help state-chartered institutions compete with federally chartered lenders or to act on behalf of state consumers.

The most obvious example of this quandary today lies with payday lending. In payday lending, borrowers typically take out two-week loans of about $255 with annual percentage rates in excess of 400 percent.[38] In the absence of intervening federal law, the charging of this high a rate of interest would actually be a crime in the state of Georgia (Georgia Official Code 7-4-18). However, payday lenders routinely claim that they are making the loans on behalf of an institution that preempts state law through the "most-favored lender" doctrine.[39]

With regard to home lending, the potential for damage to be done by state-chartered lenders and their agents is equally clear. It takes little imagination to predict that home-secured credit card operations would seek to take advantage of "most-favored lender" preemption of state law regulations governing home-secured loans in the same way as payday lenders. One need only consider that payday lenders in North Carolina reported "that they earn $6.00 per dollar in capital assets, compared to $0.21 for credit card companies."[40]

Changing Consumer Perceptions of the Cost of Home-Secured Debt

Finally, Congress has changed the relative value of home loan debt by privileging it over all other debt. Prominent consumer advocates have argued that Congress' 1986 repeal of the tax deduction for interest paid on consumer debt provided tremendous incentives for borrowers to fold their other debts into mortgage loans, and too often into predatory mortgage loans.[41] These observations have been supported by empirical research that has documented the sensitivity of household debt composition to the tax treatment of different types of debt.[42]

This incentive is particularly troubling because refinancing credit card and other nonsecured debt into a home loan is among the worst financial steps possible for most families in severe economic distress. The act of securing debt with a home effectively eliminates the possibility of help in bankruptcy, since mortgages survive bankruptcy proceedings, whereas unsecured debt such as credit cards routinely does not.[43] In other words, even if a borrower files for bankruptcy, he cannot avoid home loan payments without ultimately losing the home.

Unfortunately, though, at the time of refinance, borrowers apparently are typically well informed of the tax advantages of home-secured refinances but completely in the dark with regard to bankruptcy law. There can be little doubt that debt collectors' aggressive pursuit of nonsecured debt—especially debt related to emergency medical expenses and credit cards—push borrowers to look for solutions, and may lead to bad choices made under pressure. Attorneys general routinely report debt collection complaints as among the chief concerns expressed by the consumers they are charged with protecting.[44] The combination of consolidation to make debt collectors stop calling, the promise of lower monthly payments (sometimes resulting from rate differences, but almost always a function of the longer terms commonly associated with home loans), and the tax deductibility of interest on home-secured debt provides home lenders, and consequently irresponsible outfits within their ranks, with a powerful sales pitch. Associates Home Equity Services certainly took just such an approach, advertising to prospective borrowers that "the interest you pay on a home equity line of credit may be tax deductible . . . your savings could go on year after year."[45]

WHAT MOTIVATES FIRMS TO ENGAGE IN PREDATORY PRACTICES?

The changes in the legal environment for lenders have naturally had an effect on lenders' subsequent business decisions. This section explores how the structure of consumer credit markets may encourage some lenders to engage in harmful and predatory business practices.

Standard economic theory says that firms (lenders) are motivated by the goal of maximizing their profits. As lenders pursue profit maximization, they are subject to constraints, including resource constraints on the amount of physical capital, financial capital, and labor investment necessary to produce a certain dollar volume of loans; legal constraints (for example, prepayment penalty regulations) that restrict lenders' business practices; and regulatory constraints (for example, capital constraints) that aim to promote safe, sound, and competitive markets by limiting lenders' risk profiles. Within this framework, neoclassical economic theory holds that in competitive markets with no market imperfections, lenders will allocate resources toward their most efficient and valuable uses.

But neoclassical economic theory is of limited value in helping us understand the existence of predatory lending. In the real world, some lenders refrain from employing blatantly abusive tactics, while others engage in predatory practices at the expense of unwitting customers. These lenders benefit from their harmful practices by garnering higher profits than they would have received had they "played fair." If, as described in the first section of the chapter, the law permits lenders to earn extra profit from charging customers excessive interest rates and fees, locking unsuspecting borrowers into overpriced loans with prepayment penalties, or convincing borrowers to refinance bad loans multiple times, then what causes most lenders to refrain?

Constraints on prime and legitimate subprime lenders suggest two hypotheses: (1) reputational effects make it too costly for reputable lenders to market to exploitable customers, since "competitive" pressures in the predatory market may force good lenders to use the same tactics as predatory lenders (when in Rome, do as the Romans), or (2) the direct costs of doing so are prohibitive due to the higher regulatory scrutiny faced by legitimate lenders who do not want to lose the implicit benefits of regulation, such as the value of their regulatory charter, lower funding costs, or the ability to take maximum advantage of federal preemption of state law. The final section of this chapter will explore whether such constraints are sufficient to deter at least more traditional lenders from engaging in predatory lending.

First, however, this section provides insight into the factors that encourage lenders to engage in predatory lending. We look beyond the standard neoclassical economic paradigm and consider market imperfections and behavioral aspects of lender behavior. Next, we consider two by-products of deregulation and innovation in credit markets that, while having generally positive impacts, nevertheless have provided mechanisms for some lenders to engage in predatory practices: loan securitization and third-party lending.

Market Imperfections and Lender Behavior

Beyond basic neoclassical models, a better understanding of lending in general and subprime lending in particular can be achieved by examining the role of market imperfections. Two of the most important imperfections in subprime credit markets are information asymmetries and disparate bargaining power.[46] Information asymmetries arise because lenders generally have more information about potential borrowers than vice versa. The informational advantage of lenders creates bargaining power that can be exploited when dealing with borrowers.

For example, even today, in an age where consumers can buy their credit report on the Internet, many consumers do not have a good understanding of the implications of their credit history before they start shopping for mortgages.[47] In the best-case scenario—where prime borrowers shop for credit in the prime market—the customer may settle upon one lender she believes is reasonable and start the application process, during which the lender obtains the customer's credit report. This provides the lender with an informational advantage because it has had the opportunity to scrutinize the customer's credit history to determine the mortgage terms for which the customer qualifies. The lender can then attempt to capitalize on its informational advantage by offering less favorable terms or, alternatively, by giving the customer the terms she requests, rather than giving her the "best deal."

The end result of a lender's information advantage, while potentially bad in the prime market, is much more devastating in the subprime market. Indeed, many customers in the subprime market do not even initiate the loan process themselves (particularly in the case of refinance and home-equity loans). In these cases, the lenders themselves initiate the process through the use of push-marketing tactics. Furthermore, under the Fair Credit Reporting Act, a borrower's credit history needs to be disclosed only if she is rejected (15 U.S.C. 1681(m)). This postapplication disclosure is designed to address concerns with credit discrimination, and is an insufficient deterrent for predatory lenders who are more likely to provide an abusive loan than deny an application outright. As Professor Elizabeth Warren has observed, predatory lenders routinely steer "families to higher-cost loans whenever they thought there was a chance they could get away with it."[48]

The most extreme cases of informational asymmetry occur when borrowers who could actually qualify for loans in the prime market instead apply for loans with subprime lenders. The chances of a prime customer incorrectly self-sorting into the subprime market appear greater than ever, as underwriting criteria have become increasingly complicated, including not only traditional factors such as loan-to-value and debt-to-income ratios, but additional factors such as income potential and stability, and timely payment of utility bills and rent. Since lenders have no legal obligation to inform borrowers of their prime status or refer them to prime lenders, these borrowers wind up paying substantially more for credit.

Moreover, even if borrowers accurately evaluate their creditworthiness beforehand, they still face an informational disadvantage in the subprime credit market with regard to their knowledge of relevant interest rates and fees. While the Internet has diminished this disadvantage to some extent for prime borrowers, those who respond to mail, phone, or television so-licitations for subprime loans are once again at an informational disad-vantage because the advertised interest rate will in all likelihood no longer be the "true" rate by the time the customer responds to the advertisement. In fact, customers most likely *expect* the actual interest rate to be differ-ent. Unfortunately, even if the customer knows the actual interest rate will differ from the advertised one, the customer is ill-equipped to figure out what her proper rate should be because such advertisements usually do not provide enough information to do meaningful comparison-shopping. So the customer is likely either to (a) believe her rate will not necessarily be the same, but will be "close" to what is advertised, or (b) believe the adver-tised rate is a "special" low rate that she should insist on receiving—even though, unbeknownst to her, her "proper" rate may be much lower than the advertised one. This price uncertainty leads to suboptimal outcomes for borrowers because it creates yet another opportunity for lenders to exploit their customers.

One distinction between predatory lenders and legitimate ones is that predatory lenders choose to exploit their informational advantage on "sub-prime" borrowers who, due to a host of factors including a lack of previ-ous experience with conventional lending markets, may be perceived as being less financially sophisticated than "prime" borrowers. As observed by Kathleen Engel and Patricia McCoy,[49] three types of lenders—prime, subprime, and predatory—can be defined as follows. Prime lenders are lenders who deal exclusively with "prime" customers—customers who have very good credit histories and are presumed to be financially savvy, and thus not easily exploited. Subprime lenders include lenders who cater to customers who may or may not be financially sophisticated but in most cases have blemished credit histories that preclude them from obtaining credit in the prime credit market. Predatory lenders seek to do business with customers who have blemished credit *and* who are not financially so-phisticated, two characteristics that together make such customers prone to exploitation.[50] These three categories of lenders are not mutually exclu-sive, because predatory lenders are mainly a subset of subprime lenders. (Of course, specific lenders may at various times assume all three identi-ties.) What sets predatory lenders apart is that legitimate subprime lenders seek to do business with this group of borrowers on a more or less fair basis, while predatory lenders knowingly seek to do business with subprime borrowers on an exploitative basis.

Theories of industrial organization—the branch of economics that deals with how firms interact with their economic environment and with each other—explore the dimensions upon which firms compete. Most com-monly, firms engage in either price competition, quantity competition, or product differentiation—making their product unique (either through ac-tual substantive differences or through marketing).[51] Prime lenders may engage in all of the above types of competition. Casual observations suggest that subprime lenders, on the other hand, are less likely to compete in terms of price than prime lenders but more likely to compete in terms of quantity (offering guaranteed loan approval to boost loan volume, for example) or product differentiation—touting their ability to make a loan to fit the specialized, nonstandard situation of the borrower with blemished credit.

By extending these theories, we hypothesize that predatory lenders "compete" with each other as well as with legitimate subprime lenders through marketing aimed at borrowers likely to respond to their product. Specifically, predatory lenders choose to market to people they think they can exploit. While predatory lenders make the claim that they are further differentiating their product from other subprime lenders, we argue that it is a product that no borrower would willingly and knowingly accept if provided with complete and accurate information.[52]

Loan Securitization: The Invisible Hand of Liability?

During the 1980s and 1990s, the selling and securitization of mortgages grew at a steep rate, with the amount of outstanding mortgage backed securities (MBS) increasing from $111 billion in 1980 to more than $2.2 trillion in 1999.[53] Securitization has been fueled by increased standardization of underwriting criteria brought on by automated underwriting, innovations in the use of derivatives and other financial risk management tools, and increased demand among institutional investors for new investment vehicles.[54] The widespread acceptance of securitization in financial markets has provided lenders with unparalleled access to capital with which to fund loans to a growing number of American consumers.

Historically, financial institutions have used short-term deposits and other low-cost credit (such as extensions from the Federal Home Loan Bank system) to provide a base of capital from which to conduct the business of lending. However, these sources have been supplemented by capital from investors. With some variation in forms, lenders have been selling off the revenue streams resulting from home loans in pursuit of additional capital for quite some time.

One early example of such an arrangement was the sale of participation certificates, which allow lenders to sell off interests in whole loans to investors. Structured to minimize tax liability, pass-through certificates were hampered by the inability to tailor payout schedules to meet the differing needs of investors.[55] In addition to tax restrictions, a host of other New Deal regulations imposed their own limitations, including prohibitions on forward commitments by issuers that would allow deals to be struck in advance, and a lack of special accommodations for MBS in securities regulations.[56] Each of these restrictions created uncertainty regarding interest-rate and higher regulatory costs for pass-through transactions.

By the mid-1980s, Congress apparently was persuaded that additional capital could be redirected to the market, and that by doing so, it would reduce the cost of housing and increase the percentage of Americans who owned their own homes.[57] At the time, the three large government-sponsored entities (Fannie Mae, Freddie Mac, and Ginnie Mae), which had 96 percent of the MBS market at the end of 1983, used regulatory exemptions and financial power to create superior forms of pass-through transactions. In light of these and other perceived inequities, Congress enacted the Secondary Mortgage Market Enhancement Act of 1984 (SMMEA). Though removing many of the direct legal costs to nonagency organizations interested in securitizing their home loans, SMMEA did little to make such investments more attractive to investors.[58] Congress, however, quickly revisited the issue in the Tax Reform Act of 1986, creating the now familiar Real Estate Mortgage Investment Conduit that allows for multiple classes of securities to be issued from the same pool of mortgages without triggering unfavorable tax treatment.[59]

Along the way, other changes were made to promote the flow of investment capital to home loans. For example, the Department of Labor revised regulations in 1981, permitting private pension funds greater latitude to invest in private mortgage-backed securities.[60] At the same time, market participants discovered that a credit enhancement called subordination could be applied to any type of mortgage, including those rejected by pool insurers, and that subordination could be used by any issuer to create highly rated securities, regardless of the issuer's own credit rating or even the quality of the mortgages themselves.[61] Finally, the Resolution Trust Corporation (RTC), set up to manage and liquidate the assets of failed savings and loan institutions, played a timely role in providing a critical mass to this fledgling secondary market. In fact, "the RTC was the largest issuer of nonagency MBSs in 1991 and 1992 . . . [and] in its heyday the RTC's frequent issuance and large transaction size helped consolidate the nonagency MBS investor base and transform the nonagency MBS market into a major mortgage market sector."[62]

Following these developments, Cathy Lesser Mansfield observes, "[s]ubprime lenders began to securitize pools of loans in earnest by the mid 1990's. In 1994 subprime lenders securitized approximately $10 billion worth of home equity loans. By the end of 1997, 'the amount of home equity credit in securitized pools was about $90 billion . . . [with] much of it believed to be subprime in quality.' "[63] In 2002, industry sources report that $133 billion worth of subprime home loans were securitized in a year that saw $213 billion worth of subprime home loans originated.[64]

Such growth was not fueled solely by well-capitalized subprime lenders looking to augment their returns. As one article has noted, " 'independents, starting out, were doing $50 million in underwriting the first year, $100 million the next, $1 billion the third,' said Cary Thomson, CEO of Aames

Financial Corporation, a major subprime lender."[65] As others have observed, even "thinly-capitalized mortgage bankers and finance companies can [now] originate loans for sale on the secondary market."[66]

The proliferation of securitization creates an interesting business situation for lenders: within days of origination, lenders can collect their profits from originating home loans and, in some cases, predatory loans that they sell to the secondary market. Moreover, these profits can be guaranteed and locked in ahead of time through forward commitments. Selling to the secondary market quickly frees up the capital of subprime lenders to make more potentially predatory loans.

The only thing tempering this flow of credit is the due diligence exercised by secondary market conduits to ensure that the loans being securitized meet certain standards. These standards, however, are designed to protect investors and do not provide substantial shelter for borrowers.[67] In fact, securitization frequently serves primarily to remove borrowers' claims by operation of a legal doctrine called "holder in due course," which prevents borrowers from asserting most claims against purchasers of home loans.[68] Under this doctrine of commercial law, once a loan is sold, purchasers ordinarily cannot be held liable for claims against the original party to the transaction, as long as the purchaser took the loan without knowledge of the existence of such claims (U.C.C. Article 3). As the following example shows, this doctrine creates a vacuum in which the borrower has no remedy against certain parties that benefit from the predatory loan.

The mortgage process usually proceeds as follows. The lender, either directly or through a mortgage broker, originates the loan to the borrower. The lender packages the loan with other mortgage loans and sells the loans to a securitizer in the secondary market, and receives payment. The lender may also choose to sell the rights to servicing the loans to the securitizer as well (or to another entity), or the lender may keep the servicing rights and service the loan itself. At this point, if the lender has sold off both the loan and the servicing rights, the lender is seemingly out of the picture, because it has already received its profit. All future cash flows from loan repayment are collected by the servicer, who passes them on, minus its fee, to the MBS investors.

Under normal circumstances, there is no problem for the borrower with this process. On the other hand, if the loan is predatory, the process can give rise to significant borrower concerns. For example, suppose the loan (1) charged an interest rate that was overpriced relative to the borrower's risk of default, given that the borrower qualified for a prime loan, (2) charged an excessive origination fee and additional discount points, (3) was a brokered loan that was originated at a higher interest rate than the lender required—thus netting a (yield spread) premium for the broker (yield-spread premiums are discussed below, in the section "Mortgage Brokers and Third-Party Lending," (4) contained an abusive subprime prepayment penalty, and (5) charged an interest rate that was increased further still by mortgage servicing rights that were overpriced relative to the expected costs of servicing the loan, given that the borrower qualified for a loan in the prime market, where servicing fees are lower. (Typical prime servicing fees are 25 basis points (0.25 percent), while subprime fees (including fees on FHA/VA loans) are typically much higher.)[69]

Who profits excessively from this loan? The answer is, of course, *everyone*. Let us divide the spoils:

- The *lender* gets a higher selling price for the loan in the secondary market as a result of the higher interest rate and extra profit from the excessive front- and back-end fees.
- The *broker* gets the yield-spread premium and possibly some of the excessive fees paid.
- The *secondary market purchaser* of the loan/MBS security issuer gets additional income from investors for being able to securitize a higher-yielding MBS or pass-through security.

It is also possible, but perhaps less likely, that:

- The *loan servicer* gets a higher servicing fee than otherwise and frequently will retain late fees.
- The *MBS investors* get a higher risk-adjusted return on their investment than if the loan had been properly originated in the prime market and was not over-priced.

Here, typical deductive reasoning might suggest that if one were asked "*Who is liable for the harm caused to this borrower of the predatory loan?*," the answer would logically be, at least to some extent, *everyone*, because all parties had a hand in the excessive charges from the loan. In fact, however, under the "holder in due course" doctrine, a borrower typically could only pursue a claim of abusive lending practices against the original broker.[70] For the reasons discussed below, borrowers should be especially concerned when the sole liable party is the broker.

Mortgage Brokers and Third-Party Lending

Mortgage brokers reportedly account for one-half of all subprime home loan originations.[71] Mortgage brokers usually choose the mortgage lender and the terms of the mortgage for the customer.[72] For this reason, customers typically perceive mortgage brokers as their "agent" and expect their broker to act in their best interests.

Brokers introduce the opportunity for yet another market imperfection, what is referred to as the "principal–agent problem" in economics.[73] The agency problem in this case is that the customer (principal) pays the broker (agent) either directly or indirectly, or both, to act in her best interest by securing a suitable mortgage loan, yet the customer cannot completely monitor the actions of the broker. This lack of monitoring provides the broker with an opportunity to operate in conjunction with a third party (the lender) to take advantage of the customer. An additional complication is that the amount of payment the broker receives is determined not by the borrower but by the lender, through the payment of a yield-spread premium.[74] While it is preferable (in theory) from an efficiency standpoint to allow customers to "contract out" the job of obtaining the mortgage to professionals with greater expertise than theirs, this arrangement allows abusive brokers to steer unsuspecting borrowers into bad loans, aided and abetted by lenders willing and able to pay extravagant yield-spread premiums. Furthermore, in reality, brokers probably see themselves as agents of the lender rather than the broker, thus leaving the consumer even more vulnerable to abuse, as the consumer has no one to act reliably in her best interest.

This example illustrates how the specialization of tasks involved in the mortgage process can lead to larger and more efficient credit markets, on one hand, but at the same time create greater pitfalls and problems for vulnerable borrowers. Consequently, not only do mortgage brokers represent a double-edged sword in the home ownership battle, but they make it more difficult to hold accountable the perpetrators of predatory lending. Borrowers seeking a remedy find that brokers typically have substantially fewer assets than lenders (one recent study put the average size of brokerages at ten employees)[75] and are more likely to go out of business and be judgment-proof.[76] When this is combined with the holder-in-due-course doctrine, borrowers may find themselves without the ability to hold anyone responsible for the damages they have suffered.

The unintended consequences of deregulation and increased market efficiency create a legal conundrum. Deregulation and specialization in modern capital markets push economies toward even more specialization, which economic theory suggests will lead to greater market efficiency because deregulation presumably gives each participant in the market the latitude to do what it does best. Yet specialization also makes it harder to track down the sources of abuse in capital markets because everyone can point the finger at someone else. Laws help, of course, but to be most effective, they have to be tailored to the ways in which lending markets operate in particular submarkets. Suppose, for instance, that mortgage brokers are used more frequently in, say, Maryland than in Minnesota, or that Montana lenders keep their loans in portfolio more often than Massachusetts lenders. Given such diversity, it would come as no surprise to find substantial disparities not only in the prevalence of predatory lending among states but also in the varying degrees of culpability among market participants in each state. As the next section discusses, such questions become complicated—particularly for state policy makers—when federal law trumps state law and creates opportunities for regulatory arbitrage.

FUTURE OF DEPOSITORY INSTITUTIONS AND SUBPRIME LENDING

In addition to the market failures addressed earlier, the fact that not all lenders are subject to the same degree of regulatory scrutiny creates yet another market imperfection with consequences for consumers. Surprisingly, in fact, lenders who cater primarily to low- and moderate-income or minority neighborhoods tend to be subject to less regulation than lenders operating in more affluent areas or areas with low minority populations.[77] In recent years, however, depository lenders have increasingly moved into the subprime market. This section discusses whether additional legal and reputational constraints faced by such depositories are sufficient deterrents to predatory lending or, instead, whether the entry of depositories into the subprime market will create additional pressure to reduce consumer protections for vulnerable borrowers.

In the early years of subprime mortgage lending, the industry consisted largely of finance companies that either borrowed in order to fund loans or securitized pools of mortgage loans to create a revolving source of capital with which to make new loans.[78] Much, if not all, of the funding for subprime lenders during this period came from Wall Street, with banks and other financial institutions reluctant to take the risk of funding subprime companies.[79]

By the mid-1990s, however, factors such as economic incentives, reduction in legal and reputational risks, and decreased costs associated with subprime lending, attracted larger depository institutions with experience in prime lending to the subprime market. Between 1993 and 1998, the number of subprime mortgages originated by banks and thrifts increased 551 percent, and by 1998 banks, thrifts, and affiliates accounted for 25 percent of all subprime mortgage originations.[80]

Decreasing risks of participating in the subprime market came at a time when subprime lenders needed a new source of funds and lenders traditionally involved in prime lending were interested in expanding into new markets. Frightened by failures in the industry, institutional investors and brokerage houses had become more averse to purchasing securitized subprime loans or extending additional credit to subprime companies.[81] Depositories saw that they could offer more competitive pricing (particularly for borrowers in the least risky tier of the subprime market) and give subprime companies more stable access to capital markets.[82]

The resulting entrance of banks into the subprime market might have a positive impact by providing more expertise in risk management, better systems for monitoring and standardizing loan products, and increased control over delivery channels. Furthermore, increased scrutiny of subprime lending activities by federal regulators has the potential to set standards and establish supervision over loan products.

Unfortunately, it is not at all clear that such improvements have occurred. Regulators have increased supervision of subprime lending, but to date have largely focused such supervision on risks to the lender and investors, rather than sufficient consumer protections. The desire of regulators to make federal charters more attractive to financial institutions has had an impact on their willingness to address consumer protections. In some cases, this balancing has had positive effects for consumers—for example, in the context of regulating prepayment penalties by nondepository lenders (see discussion in "Deregulation of Certain Types of Home Loans"). In other instances, regulatory action on behalf of subprime lending by depositories has been directly against consumer interests—the most recent example being the preemption of state anti-predatory lending laws as they apply to national banks.[83]

The consequences of regulatory decisions at the federal level have the potential to harm consumers in two ways. First, rather than improve subprime lending, depository lenders and their affiliates may find the combination of deregulation and market dynamics attractive and, consequently, engage in many of the practices already under scrutiny in the subprime sector. Second, because depositories enjoy a greater degree of preemption of state consumer protection law, finance companies that wish to compete in the subprime industry have accelerated their push for relief from state laws, creating the potential for a "race to the bottom" in terms of consumer protections. Without substantive consumer protections to counterbalance economic incentives and reduced legal risk through securitization, abusive practices likely will only increase and permeate the subprime market.

The degree to which these potential harms are realized turns largely on the willingness of policy makers to create an effective system that protects consumers at multiple levels, both through state and federal regulation and at different points during the loan transaction process. Ultimately, federal legislators and regulators will decide whether to permit experimentation with a multifaceted approach or to preempt state efforts by adopting a monolithic approach at the federal level.[84] A consideration of whether federal regulators have effectively discouraged predatory lending under the authority of depository lenders and their affiliates suggests that, unfortunately, regulators currently are falling short. As illustrated below, their approach to safeguarding investors and deposit insurance funds has been narrow, accounting only for short-term risks arising from unsafe and unsound practices at the expense of longer-term risks arising from predatory lending's damage to reputations of lenders and damage to the markets where loans are made. As a result, the meager protections put in place are nonspecific and may be inadequate.

Due to concerns with risks inherent in subprime lending, regulators wary of depositories' entry into the market tightened capital standards to make it harder to own a risky affiliate. In 1997 the Federal Deposit Insurance Corporation (FDIC) first issued an advisory letter, warning lenders to "ensure prudent controls are implemented to mitigate . . . risks [associated with subprime lending]." Focusing on lenders' failures to properly assess default risk, the FDIC cautioned that lenders should monitor credit-scoring models, establish operational controls, ensure specialized management expertise, and prepare staff to manage higher delinquencies. The FDIC also encouraged lenders to set policies regarding third-party transactions, such as acquisitions from brokers or extending lines of credit to subprime finance companies.[85]

Two years later, the FDIC joined with the Office of Thrift Supervision (OTS), OCC, and Federal Reserve Board to jointly issue additional guidance on subprime lending, and the OCC issued supplemental guidance later in the same year. This more refined guidance addressed factors such as capitalization, credit-risk management, and policies and practices designed to monitor risks of subprime lending that each agency would examine to determine whether supervised institutions were appropriately managing risks of subprime lending through capital adequacy requirements.[86] The agencies' approach was subsequently adjusted in 2001, by providing far greater specificity with regard to capital requirements and their application. The guidance applies to specific institutions whose subprime loans comprised more than 1 to 2 percent of assets, sets specific requirements for loss allowances, and details requirements for maintaining adequate regulatory capital.[87]

Perhaps concerned by growing claims of predatory lending, regulators also shook a fist at predatory lending through several iterations of guidelines, but have ultimately failed to provide specifics that would give teeth to consumer protections. The 1997 FDIC guidance makes no mention at all of consumer protections laws, while the 1999 interagency guidance warns banks to bear in mind existing federal laws such as HOEPA, RESPA, and fair lending laws, but does not suggest that regulators intend to take any affirmative steps on behalf of consumers, either by promulgating new regulations or through enforcement powers.[88]

Further, the interagency guidance tends to be very permissive with respect to the terms of credit, without regard to whether the costs of such terms outweigh benefits to consumers. Instead, the guidance makes broader, more ambiguous statements discouraging abusive conduct by lenders. The 1999 guidance does acknowledge that high rates and fees can create incentives for discriminatory steering of borrowers to higher-priced products, but does not take on the issue of whether such fees or rates themselves are unfair or otherwise abusive. Similarly, the 2001 guidance defines predatory lending purely in terms of lender conduct, such as equity-based lending, loan flipping, and fraud, rather than addressing unfair terms like abusive fees or credit insurance.[89] One notable exception was the Federal Reserve's 2002 decision to specifically mandate the inclusion of financed credit insurance in HOEPA's definition of points and fees, a ruling which greatly curtailed this abusive product.

Banking regulators are certainly permitted by Congress, if not expected, to go much further than they have in providing guidance to banks on consumer protections against predatory lending. In fact, they are responsible for enforcing the Federal Trade Commission Act (the FTC Act) as it applies to federally insured lenders. The FTC Act, which prohibits unfair or deceptive practices, applies to federally insured financial institutions, and grants rulemaking authority to the Federal Reserve Board (for banks), OTS (thrifts) and National Credit Union Administration (federal credit unions), and enforcement power for both the act itself and banking agency regulations to respective supervisors.[90]

In recognition of this responsibility, in March 2002 the OCC issued an advisory letter to national banks, informing them that certain lending and marketing practices could constitute unfair or deceptive acts or practices.[91] Again, however, the letter was silent with regard to specific predatory lending terms of credit. The letter summarized the standards for finding a practice deceptive or unfair under the FTC Act and listed examples of practices that may violate the act. Some of the examples included were failure to provide sufficient information to allow consumers to understand the terms of the product or service being offered, failure to adequately disclose significant fees, and failure to adequately disclose material limitations affecting the service offered.[92]

The following year, in conjunction with a proposal to preempt a state anti-predatory law enacted in Georgia, the OCC added to its guidance by providing a second advisory letter that included discussion of FTC Act concerns. The OCC provided further clarification of its understanding of the FTC Act, but continued to refrain from addressing specific abusive credit terms.[93]

The combination of state anti-predatory lending laws and federal regulatory efforts have created pressure to make the latest stage of debate over predatory lending about preemption and the boundaries of preemption. State reforms aimed at equity stripping and loan flipping provide significant and effective protections for consumers.[94] However, if such protections are preempted with respect to federally chartered depositories, what remedies will consumers have when such depositories are involved in abusive practices? Furthermore, it is possible that such preemption would add to pressure from finance companies that compete with depositories to weaken existing consumer protections. These issues will have to be addressed with regard to specific actors (e.g., extension of preemption to brokers), credit terms (e.g., permitting prepayment penalties for finance companies), and different types of financial entities (e.g., parity between state-chartered and federally chartered depositories or the extension of preemption to affiliates of depositories).

CONCLUSION

This chapter has shown that deregulation has made possible, and to a certain extent has encouraged, predatory high-fee home mortgage lending through nondepository lenders, despite contrary state law. Furthermore, existing market dynamics, particularly the trend toward greater credit market specialization, have made such abusive practices predictable, if not inevitable. While this chapter has put forward the general underlying economic incentives behind predatory lending, much more empirical research is needed to evaluate which factors are most central to the development of predatory lending. Currently, this question is being played out in a new way, as depository lenders are increasingly investing in subprime lending and are facing choices regarding their involvement in potentially abusive practices. There is a real risk that existing regulation of these entities will be insufficient to combat predatory lending, and may, by preempting state laws intended to improve protections for borrowers, make borrowers even more vulnerable to abuse.

NOTES

1. Elizabeth Laderman, "Subprime Mortgage Lending and the Capital Markets," *Federal Reserve Bank of San Francisco Economic Letter,* no. 2001-38 (December 28, 2001): 1.

2. Paul Maulo, "Top 100 Subprime Lenders: Subprime Comes on Like a House on Fire," *2004 Mortgage Industry Directory*, http://www.nationalmortgagenews.com/mid_demo/chap9.htm (accessed June 20, 2004).

3. Ibid.

4. Eugene Ludwig, "Statement of Eugene Ludwig, Comptroller of the Currency, Before U.S. Congresswoman Maxine Waters' 'Forum on Community Reinvestment and Access to Credit: California's Challenge,' on the Community Reinvestment and Development Activities of Commercial Banks in California, Los Angeles, California, January 12, 1998," Office of the Comptroller of the Currency, *Quarterly Journal* 17, no. 2 (June 1998): 31.

5. George W. Bush, "A Home of Your Own: Expanding Opportunities for All Americans," http://www.whitehouse.gov/infocus/homeownership/homeownership-policy-book-whole.pdf (June 2002).

6. Rachel Bratt, *Housing for Very Low-Income Households: The Record of President Clinton, 1993–2000* (Cambridge, Mass.: Joint Center for Housing Studies of Harvard University, 2002), p. 6; U.S. Bureau of the Census, "More Householders Than Ever Own Their Own Homes According to Census 2000," press release (November 27, 2001); Joint Center for Housing Studies of Harvard Uni-

versity, *The State of the Nation's Housing: 2003* (Cambridge, Mass.: Joint Center for Housing Studies of Harvard University, 2003).

7. Calvin Bradford, *Risk or Race? Racial Disparities and the Subprime Refinance Market* (Washington, D.C.: Center for Community Change, 2002), http://www.communitychange.org/housing.

8. Eric Stein, "Quantifying the Economic Costs of Predatory Lending" (Center for Responsible Lending, revised October 2001), http://www.predatorylending.org/pdfs/Quant10-01.PDF, pp. 4–9.

9. U.S. Department of Housing and Urban Development and U.S. Department of the Treasury, "Curbing Predatory Lending," http://www.hud.gov/library/bookshelf18/pressrel/treasrpt.pdf (June 2002), p. 60.

10. Harold L. Bunce et al., "Subprime Foreclosures: The Smoking Gun of Predatory Lending?" in *Housing Policy in the New Millennium* (Washington, D.C.: U.S. Department of Housing and Urban Development, 2000), http://www.huduser.org/publications/pdf/brd/12Bunce.pdf.

11. Steven W. Kuehl, "High Profile Predatory Lending Cases," *Profitwise News and Views* (Federal Reserve Bank of Chicago, Spring 2003).

12. Michael Schroeder, "Summers Calls for Legislation to Curb Predatory Lending in Mortgage Markets," *Wall Street Journal*, April 13, 2000, p. A2.

13. Stein, "Quantifying the Economic Costs of Predatory Lending," p. 3.

14. Deborah Bach, "Online Banking: E-Loan CEO: Diversification Is Key to Staying Profitable," *American Banker* 167, no. 19 (January 29, 2002).

15. Eric Bergquist, "Some Lenders Turning to Compliance Software," *American Banker* 168, no. 62 (April 1, 2003).

16. Shimon A. Berger, "Adding Insult to Injury: How IN RE Venture Mortgage Fund Exposes the Inequitable Results of New York's Usury Remedies," *Fordham Urban Law Journal* 29, no. 8 (August 2002): 2198.

17. Stein, "Quantifying the Economic Costs of Predatory Lending," p. 4.

18. *Smiley v. Citibank (South Dakota), N.A.*, 517 U.S. 735 (1996).

19. Berger, "Adding Insult to Injury," pp. 2205–6.

20. Cathy Lesser Mansfield, "The Road to Subprime 'HEL' Was Paved with Good Congressional Intentions: Usury Deregulation and the Subprime Home Equity Market," *South Carolina Law Review* 51, no. 3 (2000): 476.

21. Senate Report no. 96–368, reprinted in U.S.C.C.A.N. 236 (1980): 254.

22. Ibid., p. 255.

23. DIDA, sec. 501(b)(4).

24. Washington Department of Financial Institutions, "Remarks: Attorney General Christine Gregoire Relating to the Preliminary Settlement with Household International," http://www.atg.wa.gov/householdfinance/remarks.shtml (October 11, 2002).

25. Federal Trade Commission, "Federal Trade Commission's Second Amended Complaint for Permanent Injunctive and Other Equitable Relief," file no. SACV 00-964 DOC (EEx), U.S. District Court, Central District of California, Southern Division (November 26, 2001), http://www.ftc.gov/os/2002/03/famco2acmp.pdf, p. 4.

26. Public Law 97-320, 96 Stat. 1469 (October 15, 1982).

27. Federal Home Loan Bank Board, 48 *Federal Register* 23,032 (May 23, 1983).

28. Office of Thrift Supervision, 61 *Federal Register* 50,951 (September 30, 1996).

29. Debbie Goldstein and Stacy Strohauer Son, "Why Prepayment Penalties Are Abusive in Subprime Home Loans" (Center for Responsible Lending, April 2, 2003), http://www.predatorylending.org/pdfs/PPP_Policy_Paper2.pdf.

30. Frank Fabozzi, *The Handbook of Fixed Income Securities* (New York: McGraw-Hill, 2001), pp. 563–64.

31. Ana M. Aizcorbe et al., "Recent Changes in U.S. Family Finances: Evidence from the 1998 and 2001 Survey of Consumer Finances," *Federal Reserve Bulletin* 89 (January 2003), http://www.federalreserve.gov/pubs/bulletin/2003/0103lead.pdf.

32. Goldstein and Son, "Why Prepayment Penalties Are Abusive in Subprime Home Loans," p. 2.

33. CitiFinancial, "Real Estate Lending Initiatives Progress Report" (October 2001), http://www.citigroup.com/citigroup/press/2001/data/011211b.pdf, p. 15 (accessed October 16, 2003).

34. Jess Lederman et al., "A– Breaks Away from the Subprime Pack," *Secondary Marketing Executive* (May 2000), http://www.sme-online.com/sme/aralending.phtml.

35. Office of Thrift Supervision, 67 *Federal Register* 60,542 (September 26, 2002).

36. Goldstein and Son, "Why Prepayment Penalties Are Abusive in Subprime Home Loans," p. 8.

37. *Marquette Nat. Bank of Minneapolis v. First Bank of Omaha*, 439 U.S. 299 (1978), pp. 310–11.

38. Peter Skillern, *Small Loans, Big Bucks* (Durham: Community Reinvestment Association of North Carolina, 2002), p. 2.

39. Jean Ann Fox and Edmund Mierzwinski, "Rent-a-Bank Payday Lending: How Banks Help Payday Lenders Evade Consumer Protections" (Consumer Federation of America and U.S. Public Interest Research Group, November 2001), http://www.consumerfed.org/paydayreport.pdf.

40. Sharon Hermanson and George Gaberlavage, *The Alternative Financial Services Industry*, AARP Public Policy Institute Issue Brief (August 2001), http://research.aarp.org/consume/ib51_finance.pdf, p. 6.

41. Margot Saunders, "The Increase in Predatory Lending and Appropriate Remedial Actions," *North Carolina Banking Institute* 6 (2002): 116.

42. Dean M. Maki, "Household Debt and the Tax Reform Act of 1986," *American Economic Review* 91, no. 1 (March 2001): 305–19.

43. Elizabeth Warren and Amelia Warren Tyagi, *The Two-Income Trap: Why Middle-Class Mothers and Fathers Are Going Broke* (New York: Basic Books, 2003).

44. For example, Dan Morales, "Find Out Who Placed in the 1996 Rip-off Top 10," http://www.stp.uh.edu/vol62/61/OpEd/op1/op1.html (last modified November 12, 1996).

45. Federal Trade Commission, "Complaint for Permanent Injunction and Other Equitable Relief," *Federal Trade Commission v. Citigroup, Inc., Citifinancial Credit Company, Associates First Capital Corporation, and Associates Capital Corporation of North America*, U.S. District Court for the Northern District of Georgia, Atlanta Division (2001), http://www.ftc.gov/opa/2001/03/associates.htm, Exhibit A.

46. For applications of information asymmetries to credit markets, see Xavier

Freixas and Jean-Charles Rochet, *Microeconomics of Banking* (Cambridge, Mass.: MIT Press, 1997).

47. Howard Lax, Michael Manti, Paul Raca, and Peter Zorn, "Subprime Lending: An Investigation of Economic Efficiency," working paper (December 21, 2000), p. 10.

48. Warren and Tyagi, *The Two-Income Trap*, p. 136.

49. Kathleen C. Engel and Patricia A. McCoy, "A Tale of Three Markets: The Law and Economics of Predatory Lending," *Texas Law Review* 80, no. 6 (May 2002): 1255–1381.

50. Ibid., pp. 1258–59.

51. Massimo Motto, "Endogenous Quality Choice: Price vs Quantity Competition," *Journal of Industrial Economics* 41, no. 2 (June 1993): 113–31; Marcel Canoy and Martin Peitz, "The Differentiation Triangle," *Journal of Industrial Economics* 45, no. 3 (September 1997): 305–28.

52. Christopher A. Richardson, "Predatory Lending, Consumer Behavior, and Housing Disinvestment," *Housing Policy Debate* (forthcoming).

53. Fabozzi, *The Handbook of Fixed Income Securities*, p. 619.

54. Kurt Eggert, "Held Up in Due Course: Predatory Lending, Securitization, and the Holder in Due Course Doctrine," *Creighton Law Review* 35, no. 3 (April 2002): 534–45.

55. Patricia Prim Biller, "The Significance of Income Taxation for Securitized Mortgages and the Secondary Market," *American Journal of Tax Policy* 9, no. 2 (Fall 1991): 293.

56. Eric Bruskin, Anthony B. Sanders, and David Sykes, "The Nonagency Mortgage Market: Background and Overview," in *The Handbook of Nonagency Mortgage-Backed Securities*, ed. Frank Fabozzi et al., 2nd ed. (New York: McGraw-Hill, 2000), p. 9.

57. David Abelman, "The Secondary Mortgage Market Enhancement Act," *Real Estate Law Journal* 14 (1985): 141.

58. John W. Alexander and David Culp, "Taxable Mortgage Rules Now in Effect," *The Tax Adviser* 23 (June 1992): 360.

59. Ibid.

60. Louis Colosimo, "Statement of Louis Colosimo, The Bond Market Association, for the Subcommittee on Employer-Employee Relations, Committee on Education and the Workforce, U.S. House of Representatives, March 10, 2000," *Legislative Issues*, The Bond Market Association, http://www.bondmarkets.com/legislative/t106-014.shtml.

61. Bruskin, Sanders, and Sykes, "The Nonagency Mortgage Market," pp. 9–10.

62. Ibid., p. 10.

63. Lesser Mansfield, "The Road to Subprime 'HEL' Was Paved with Good Congressional Intentions," p. 531.

64. Inside Mortgage Finance, *2002 Mortgage Market Statistical Annual* (Bethesda, Md.: Inside Mortgage Finance Publications, 2002).

65. Lesser Mansfield, "The Road to Subprime 'HEL' Was Paved with Good Congressional Intentions," p. 579.

66. Engel and McCoy, "A Tale of Three Markets," p. 1274.

67. Ibid., p. 1286.

68. Eggert, "Held Up in Due Course."

69. Paul Muolo, "Economies of Scale Are Questioned," *U.S. Banker* (December 2000), http://www.us-banker.com.

70. Eggert, "Held Up in Due Course."

71. OCC Advisory Letter 2003-3, "Avoiding Predatory and Abusive Lending Practices in Brokered and Purchased Loans" (2003), http://www.occ.treas.gov/ftp/advisory/2003-3.pdf, p. 3.

72. Howell E. Jackson and Jeremy Berry, "Kickbacks or Compensation? The Case of Yield-Spread Premiums," working paper, Harvard Law School, January 8, 2002, http://www.law.harvard.edu/faculty/hjackson/pdfs/january_draft.pdf, p. 2.

73. Sanford J. Grossman and Oliver D. Hart, "An Analysis of the Principal–Agent Problem," *Econometrica* 51, no. 1 (January 1983): 7–41.

74. Jackson and Berry present a detailed example to illustrate how yield-spread premiums are calculated as a function of the amount over "par value" a lender is willing to pay to obtain a mortgage. See their "Kickbacks or Compensation?" p. 4.

75. Wholesale Access, "New Research About Mortgage Brokers Published," (August 6, 2003), http://www.wholesaleaccess.com/8.6.03.mb.shtml.

76. Eggert, "Held Up in Due Course," pp. 523, 556.

77. Kathleen C. Engel and Patricia A. McCoy, "The CRA Implications of Predatory Lending," *Fordham Urban Law Journal* 29, no. 4 (April 2002): 1582.

78. Evan M. Gilreath, "The Entrance of Banks into Subprime Lending: First Union and the Money Store," *North Carolina Banking Institute* 3 (April 1999): 152–53.

79. Ibid., p. 155.

80. U.S. Department of Housing and Urban Development and U.S. Department of the Treasury, Curbing Predatory Lending, p. 45.

81. Gilreath, "Entrance of Banks into Subprime Lending," pp. 155–56.

82. U.S. Department of Housing and Urban Development and U.S. Department of the Treasury, "Curbing Predatory Lending," p. 45.

83. OCC Notice of Proposed Rulemaking, 68 *Federal Register* 46,119, 46,120 (August 5, 2003).

84. Gary Nelon, Chairman, Conference of State Banking Supervisors, Bankers Advisory Board, letter to the editor, "Federalization Would Maul State Banking System," *American Banker*, October 3, 2003.

85. Federal Deposit Insurance Corporation, "Subprime Lending," *Financial Institution Letters*, May 2, 1997, http://www.fdic.gov/news/news/financial/1997/fil9744.html.

86. Board of Governors of the Federal Reserve System et al., "Interagency Guidance on Subprime Lending," *Financial Institution Letters* (March 1999), http://www.fdic.gov/news/news/financial/1999/FIL9920a.html.

87. Joseph A. Smith, "The Federal Banking Agencies' Guidance on Subprime Lending: Regulation with a Divided Mind," *North Carolina Banking Institute* 6 (April 2002): 83–87.

88. Federal Deposit Insurance Corporation, "Subprime Lending"; Board of Governors of the Federal Reserve System et al., "Interagency Guidance on Subprime Lending."

89. Smith, "The Federal Banking Agencies' Guidance on Subprime Lending," p. 105.

90. 15 U.S.C. 45(a), 57a(f)(1); 12 U.S.C. 1818.

91. OCC Advisory Letter AL 2002-3, "Guidance on Unfair or Deceptive Acts or Practices," http://www.occ.treas.gov/ftp/advisory/2002-3.doc (2002).

92. Ibid.

93. OCC Advisory Letter 2003-3, "Avoiding Predatory and Abusive Lending Practices in Brokered and Purchased Loans," http://www.occ.treas.gov/ftp/advisory/2003-3.pdf.

94. Roberto Quercia, Michael Stegman, and Walter Davis, *The Impact of North Carolina's Anti–Predatory Lending Law: A Descriptive Assessment* (Center for Community Capitalism, University of North Carolina at Chapel Hill, June 25, 2003), http://www.kenan-flagler.unc.edu/assets/documents/CC_NC_Anti_Predatory_Law_Impact.pdf.

REFERENCES

Abelman, David. "The Secondary Mortgage Market Enhancement Act." *Real Estate Law Journal* 14 (1985): 136.

Aizcorbe, Ana M. et al. "Recent Changes in U.S. Family Finances: Evidence from the 1998 and 2001 Survey of Consumer Finances." *Federal Reserve Bulletin* 89 (January 2003), http://www.federalreserve.gov/pubs/bulletin/2003/0103lead.pdf.

Alexander, John W., and David Culp. "Taxable Mortgage Rules Now in Effect." *The Tax Adviser* 23 (June 1992): 359.

Bach, Deborah. "Online Banking: E-Loan CEO: Diversification Is Key to Staying Profitable." *American Banker* 167, no. 19 (January 29, 2002).

Berger, Shimon A. "Adding Insult to Injury: How IN RE Venture Mortgage Fund Exposes the Inequitable Results of New York's Usury Remedies." *Fordham Urban Law Journal* 29, no. 8 (August 2002): 2193–232.

Bergquist, Eric. "Some Lenders Turning to Compliance Software." *American Banker* 168, no. 62 (April 1, 2003).

Biller, Patricia Prim. "The Significance of Income Taxation for Securitized Mortgages and the Secondary Market." *American Journal of Tax Policy* 9, no. 2 (Fall 1991).

Board of Governors of the Federal Reserve System et al. "Interagency Guidance on Subprime Lending." *Financial Institution Letter* (March 1999), http://www.fdic.gov/news/news/financial/1999/FIL9920a.html.

Bradford, Calvin. *Risk or Race? Racial Disparities and the Subprime Refinance Market*. Washington, D.C.: Center for Community Change, 2002. http://www.communitychange.org/housing.

Bratt, Rachel. *Housing for Very Low-Income Households: The Record of President Clinton, 1993–2000*. Cambridge, Mass.: Joint Center for Housing Studies, Harvard University, 2002.

Bruskin, Eric, Anthony B. Sanders, and David Sykes. "The Nonagency Mortgage Market: Background and Overview." In *The Handbook of Nonagency Mortgage-Backed Securities*. Edited by Frank Fabozzi et al. 2nd ed. New York: McGraw-Hill, 2000.

Bunce, Harold L., et al. "Subprime Foreclosures: The Smoking Gun of Predatory Lending?" In *Housing Policy in the New Millennium*. Washington, D.C.:

U.S. Department of Housing and Urban Development, 2000. http://www.huduser.org/publications/pdf/brd/12Bunce.pdf.

Bush, George W. "A Home of Your Own: Expanding Opportunities for All Americans." http://www.whitehouse.gov/infocus/homeownership/homeownership-policy-book-whole.pdf. June 2002.

Canoy, Marcel, and Martin Peitz. "The Differentiation Triangle." *Journal of Industrial Economics* 45, no. 3 (September 1997): 305–28.

CitiFinancial. "Real Estate Lending Initiatives Progress Report" (October 2001), http://www.citigroup.com/citigroup/press/2001/data/011211b.pdf (accessed October 16, 2003).

Colosimo, Louis. "Statement of Louis Colosimo, The Bond Market Association, for the Subcommittee on Employer-Employee Relations, Committee on Education and the Workforce, U.S. House of Representatives, March 10, 2000." *Legislative Issues*, The Bond Market Association. http://www.bondmarkets.com/legislative/t106-014.shtml.

Dixon, Robert W. "The Gramm–Leach–Bliley Financial Modernization Act: Why Reform in the Financial Services Industry Was Necessary and the Act's Projected Effects on Community Banking." *Drake Law Review* 49 (2001): 671–88.

Eggert, Kurt. "Held Up in Due Course: Predatory Lending, Securitization, and the Holder in Due Course Doctrine." *Creighton Law Review* 35, no. 3 (April 2002): 507–640.

Engel, Kathleen C., and Patricia A. McCoy. "The CRA Implications of Predatory Lending." *Fordham Urban Law Journal* 29, no. 4 (April 2002): 1571–1605.

Engel, Kathleen C., and Patricia A. McCoy. "A Tale of Three Markets: The Law and Economics of Predatory Lending." *Texas Law Review* 80, no. 6 (May 2002): 1255–1381.

Fabozzi, Frank. *The Handbook of Fixed Income Securities*. New York: McGraw-Hill, 2001.

Federal Deposit Insurance Corporation. "Subprime Lending." *Financial Institution Letters* (May 2, 1997). http://www.fdic.gov/news/news/financial/1997/fil9744.html.

Federal Home Loan Bank Board. 48 *Federal Register* 23,032 (May 23, 1983).

Federal Trade Commission. "Federal Trade Commission's Second Amended Complaint for Permanent Injunctive and Other Equitable Relief." File no. SACV 00-964 DOC (EEx). U.S. District Court, Central District of California, Southern Division (November 26, 2001). http://www.ftc.gov/os/2002/03/famco2acmp.pdf.

Federal Trade Commission, "Complaint for Permanent Injunction and Other Equitable Relief." *Federal Trade Commission v. Citigroup, Inc., Citifinancial Credit Company, Associates First Capital Corporation, and Associates Capital Corporation of North America*. U.S. District Court for the Northern District of Georgia, Atlanta Division (2001). http://www.ftc.gov/opa/2001/03/associates.htm.

Fox, Jean Ann, and Edmund Mierzwinski. "Rent-a-Bank Payday Lending: How Banks Help Payday Lenders Evade Consumer Protections." Consumer Federation of America and U.S. Public Interest Research Group, November 2001. http://www.consumerfed.org/paydayreport.pdf.

Freixas, Xavier, and Jean-Charles Rochet. *Microeconomics of Banking*. Cambridge, Mass.: MIT Press, 1997.

Gilreath, Evan M. "The Entrance of Banks into Subprime Lending: First Union and the Money Store." *North Carolina Banking Institute* 3 (April 1999): 149–68.

Goldstein, Debbie, and Stacy Strohauer Son. "Why Prepayment Penalties Are Abusive in Subprime Home Loans." Center for Responsible Lending, April 2, 2003. http://www.predatorylending.org/pdfs/PPP_Policy_Paper2.pdf.

Grossman, Sanford J., and Oliver D. Hart. "An Analysis of the Principal–Agent Problem." *Econometrica* 51, no. 1 (January 1983): 7–41.

Hermanson, Sharon, and George Gaberlavage. *The Alternative Financial Services Industry*. AARP Public Policy Institute Issue Brief (August 2001). http://research.aarp.org/consume/ib51_finance.pdf.

Jackson, Howell E., and Jeremy Berry. "Kickbacks or Compensation? The Case of Yield-Spread Premiums." Working paper, (Harvard Law School. http://www.law.harvard.edu/faculty/hjackson/pdfs/january_draft.pdf (January 8, 2002).

Joint Center for Housing Studies of Harvard University. *The State of the Nation's Housing: 2003*. Cambridge, Mass.: Joint Center for Housing Studies of Harvard University, 2003.

Kuehl, Steven W. *Profitwise News and Views* (Federal Reserve Bank of Chicago, Spring 2003).

Laderman, Elizabeth. "Subprime Mortgage Lending and the Capital Markets." *Federal Reserve Bank of San Francisco Economic Letter*, no. 2001-38 (December 28, 2001).

Lax, Howard, Michael Manti, Paul Raca, and Peter Zorn. "Subprime Lending: An Investigation of Economic Efficiency." Working paper (December 21, 2000).

Lederman, Jess et al. "A– Breaks Away from the Subprime Pack." *Secondary Marketing Executive* (May 2000). http://www.sme-online.com/sme/ar/alending.phtml.

Lesser Mansfield, Cathy. "The Road to Subprime 'HEL' Was Paved with Good Congressional Intentions: Usury Deregulation and the Subprime Home Equity Market." *South Carolina Law Review* 51, no. 3 (2000): 473–587.

Ludwig, Eugene. "Statement of Eugene Ludwig, Comptroller of the Currency, Before U.S. Congresswoman Maxine Waters' 'Forum on Community Reinvestment and Access to Credit: California's Challenge,' on the Community Reinvestment and Development Activities of Commercial Banks in California, Los Angeles, California, January 12, 1998." Office of the Comptroller of the Currency, *Quarterly Journal*, 17, no. 2 (June 1998): 25–44.

Maki, Dean M. "Household Debt and the Tax Reform Act of 1986." *American Economic Review* 91, no. 1 (March 2001): 305–19.

Marquette Nat. Bank of Minneapolis v. First Bank of Omaha, 439 U.S. 299 (1978).

Morales, Dan. "Find Out Who Placed in the 1996 Rip-off Top 10." http://www.stp.uh.edu/vol62/61/OpEd/op1/op1.html (last modified November 12, 1996).

Motto, Massimo. "Endogenous Quality Choice: Price vs Quantity Competition." *Journal of Industrial Economics* 41, no. 2 (June 1993): 113–31.

Muolo, Paul. "Economies of Scale Are Questioned." *U.S. Banker* (December 2000). http://www.us-banker.com.

Muolo, Paul. "Top 100 Subprime Lenders: Subprime Comes on like a House on Fire." In *2004 Mortgage Industry Directory*. http://www.nationalmortgagenews.com/mid_demo/chap9.htm (accessed October 22, 2003).

Nelon, Gary, Chairman, Conference of State Banking Supervisors, Bankers Advisory Board. "Federalization Would Maul State Banking System." *American Banker*, October 3, 2003.

OCC Advisory Letter AL 2002-3. "Guidance on Unfair or Deceptive Acts or Practices." http://www.occ.treas.gov/ftp/advisory/2002-3.doc (2002).

OCC Advisory Letter 2003-3. "Avoiding Predatory and Abusive Lending Practices in Brokered and Purchased Loans." http://www.occ.treas.gov/ftp/advisory/2003-3.pdf (2003).

OCC Notice of Proposed Rulemaking. 68 *Federal Reg. Register* 46119, 46120 (August 5, 2003).

Office of Thrift Supervision. 61 *Federal Register* 50,951 (September. 30, 1996).

Office of Thrift Supervision. 67 *Federal Register* 60,542 (September. 26, 2002).

Public Law 97-320, 96 Stat. 1469 (October 15, 1982).

Quercia, Roberto, Michael Stegman, and Walter Davis. *The Impact of North Carolina's Anti–Predatory Lending Law: A Descriptive Assessment*. Center for Community Capitalism, University of North Carolina at Chapel Hill, June 25, 2003. http://www.kenan-flagler.unc.edu/assets/documents/CC_NC_Anti_Predatory_Law_Impact.pdf.

Richardson, Christopher A. "Predatory Lending, Consumer Behavior, and Housing Disinvestment." *Housing Policy Debate*, forthcoming.

Saunders, Margot. "The Increase in Predatory Lending and Appropriate Remedial Actions." *North Carolina Banking Institute* 6 (2002): 111–44.

Senate Report no. 96–368. Reprinted in U.S.C.C.A.N. 236 (1980).

Schroeder, Michael. "Summers Calls for Legislation to Curb Predatory Lending in Mortgage Markets." *Wall Street Journal*, April 13, 2000, p. A2.

Skillern, Peter. *Small Loans, Big Bucks*. Durham: Community Reinvestment Association of North Carolina, 2002.

Smiley v. Citibank (South Dakota), N.A., 517 U.S. 735 (1996).

Smith, Joseph A. "The Federal Banking Agencies' Guidance on Subprime Lending: Regulation with a Divided Mind." *North Carolina Banking Institute* 6 (April 2002): 73–109.

Stein, Eric. "Quantifying the Economic Costs of Predatory Lending." Center for Responsible Lending, rev. October 2001). http://www.predatorylending.org/pdfs/Quant10-01.PDF.

U.S. Bureau of the Census. "More Householders Than Ever Own Their Own Homes According to Census 2000." Press release. November 27, 2001.

U.S. Department of Housing and Urban Development and U.S Department of the Treasury. "Curbing Predatory Lending." http://www.hud.gov/library/bookshelf18/pressrel/treasrpt.pdf (June 2000).

Warren, Elizabeth, and Amelia Warren Tyagi. *The Two-Income Trap: Why Middle-Class Mothers and Fathers Are Going Broke*. New York: Basic Books, 2003.

Washington Department of Financial Institutions. "Remarks: Attorney General Christine Gregoire Relating to the Preliminary Settlement with Household International." http://www.atg.wa.gov/householdfinance/remarks.shtml (October 11, 2002).

Wholesale Access. "New Research About Mortgage Brokers Published." http://www.wholesaleaccess.com/8.6.03.mb.shtml (August 6, 2003).

6

Community Organizing and Advocacy: Fighting Predatory Lending and Making a Difference

Maude Hurd and Lisa Donner,
with Camellia Phillips

Since subprime mortgage lending took off in the 1990s, organized, grassroots community resistance has provided an important challenge to the industry's massive expansion and its all-too-frequent predatory lending practices. In response to the exponential growth of subprime lending, particularly in low- and moderate-income and minority neighborhoods, in 1999 ACORN (Association of Community Organizations for Reform Now)[1] launched a grassroots campaign to fight predatory lending in our communities. Motivated by the experiences of our members, ACORN's campaign against predatory lending demonstrates the critical role that community organizing can play in revealing abuses in the financial services sector, and in forcing change within the industry.

In our predatory lending campaign, as in ACORN's other campaigns, our core philosophy is that lasting, progressive change will not occur in this country until low- and moderate-income people are organized on a large scale. Based on this belief, our primary strategy to curb predatory lending has been to identify and mobilize predatory lending victims and their neighbors to demand change and accountability from the institutions, both government and financial, that impact their lives and take advantage of their communities. From knocking on doors and holding neighborhood meetings, to campaigning for passage of city and state legislation and filing class action lawsuits, what has driven this campaign has been engaging predatory lending victims themselves and designing legislative, regulatory, and legal reforms directly informed by their needs and experiences.

One good example of how grassroots organizing is working to force changes in the subprime lending market is ACORN's campaign against

Household Finance, one of the nation's largest subprime lenders. Employing a diverse array of strategies, from direct action to shareholder action, ACORN's multiyear campaign against Household led to record-breaking legal settlements and practice changes that are helping reduce losses to borrowers from abusive loans. This chapter details the origins, strategies, and impact of this campaign.

IDENTIFYING THE PROBLEM OF PREDATORY LENDING

ACORN's campaign to fight predatory lending arose from our longtime commitment to increasing home ownership opportunities for low- and moderate income and minority families. Home ownership is a crucial part of building neighborhood stability and of helping low- and moderate-income families and communities to acquire and control assets. Building on a broader commitment to increasing the health and wealth of the neighborhoods in which we work, the goal of our predatory lending campaign has been to win comprehensive changes in the lending market. This includes changing lender behavior, changing policy, improving the range of choices available to low- and moderate-income families, and engaging affected borrowers and their neighbors actively in this fight. At the same time, following the model of ACORN's other issue-based community organizing work, the campaign has endeavored to help residents work together to build the power to protect and improve their communities. This diverse approach has built both an effective campaign and the organizational and community capacity to take on other predatory financial scams and continue to fight for a more level financial playing field overall.

The explosion of predatory lending in low- and moderate-income communities came to our attention in a variety of ways. Through ACORN's ongoing organizing work in low- and moderate-income and minority neighborhoods, our members began to report their own, their families', and their neighbors' growing problems paying their mortgage loans. Also, as neighborhood leaders got together to talk about what to do about vacant homes, and how they had gotten that way, more and more stories of abusive loans began to emerge. Another set of warning signs about the expanding scope of predatory lending came from the experiences of ACORN Housing Corporation clients.

ACORN Housing Corporation (AHC) was established in 1986 as an outgrowth of ACORN's work pressuring banks to expand their lending in low- and moderate-income and minority communities. Rather than simply pushing lenders to make broad commitments to increase lending, ACORN worked to create a mechanism to actually make banks deliver loans on fair terms to residents of ACORN neighborhoods. Through this program, including specially modified underwriting and rate or fee discounts negotiated with lenders, since 1986 AHC has provided loan counseling to more than 130,000 borrowers, and helped more than 50,000 families become first-time home owners.

With increasing frequency in the mid- to late 1990s, however, AHC clients who had begun as home owners with good, affordable loans were returning to AHC offices in serious trouble because of high-cost refinance loans. These borrowers had been pushed to refinance out of low-cost loans, into high-cost loans—more often than not having been seriously misled about the costs and consequences of the refinance loans they were sold.

Recognizing the growing and harmful impact of predatory lending in already struggling neighborhoods, ACORN developed a comprehensive campaign to curb predatory lending which included a number of key elements.

First, we began a broad campaign to educate home owners and prospective home owners about the dangers and warning signs of abusive loans. To reach these families, we utilized ACORN's established presence in the most affected communities, promoted the message through media generated by other aspects of our campaigns, and worked with AHC to provide information about predatory loans and how to avoid them as a key and repeated piece of the mortgage counseling it provides. AHC also went on to add postpurchase counseling to its programs in order to help borrowers find good refinance loans.

Second, ACORN, working closely both locally and nationally with the AARP and the Coalition for Responsible Lending, as well as many other organizations in each state, has fought for significant new legislation against predatory lending practices at the state and local levels. Along with these other groups, our members lobbied their legislators, testified at hearings, spoke to the press, and mobilized in state capitals and in their home districts as major participants in successful legislative efforts in the states of New Mexico, New York, California, and New Jersey, and cities of New York, Oakland, and Los Angeles, among others.

Third, ACORN has worked to communicate our members' and their communities' experiences with predatory lending to national policy makers in Washington, D.C., and elsewhere. Our members have tried to push legislators and regulators to take action by repeatedly confronting them with the problem and its victims, and by showing them that their constituents care about—and will hold them accountable for—the specific policy changes needed to address the problem. Such meetings with officials at HUD and the Treasury, for example, ultimately helped push these agencies to hold field hearings about predatory lending in 2000, and to publish a report on their findings[2] (which in turn was useful both as a tool in state legislative fights and in moving other federal regulatory change). Once the hearings were scheduled, hundreds of ACORN members turned out to attend them and to testify. Their voices have added an important element both of actual experience and of connection to community residents on the ground back home, as we have joined with other national groups in demanding regulatory changes such as pressuring the Federal Reserve Board to crack down on financed credit insurance products.

Combining research with grassroots organizing and direct action, in 2001 we released the first national and city-by-city study of the proportion of purchase and refinance loans made by subprime lenders in lower-income and minority neighborhoods,[3] and we have produced annual updates since. We have released these studies at local press conferences where ACORN members, often accompanied by local and state elected officials, speak about their own loans and about the problems being caused in their communities. Each year, these events and the studies' findings have been covered by 70 or more major publications and television and radio stations around the country.

Finally, ACORN spearheaded a series of national campaigns targeting individual lenders that are major players in the subprime market. By focusing on specific companies, we have been able to force these lenders to make major changes in their business practices while also illustrating the problems that demand legislative and regulatory solutions.

HOUSEHOLD FINANCE

Since the late 1990s, Household Finance, along with Beneficial (an independent lender purchased by Household in 1998), has been either the largest or the second largest subprime lender by loan volume every year. By 2000, the company was making $15.3 billion in mortgage loans a year.

As ACORN heard a growing volume of stories from our members about problems with Household loans, and we realized how large a player the company was, a campaign to force changes at Household emerged as a key part of our overall effort against predatory lending. When the campaign began, there had been virtually no public scrutiny of Household's lending practices, and the company was growing fast and doing well. The level of outrage provoked in our members by the practices they experienced, or that they heard about from neighbors and friends, and the significance of the company in the market as a whole made it an attractive campaign target. It was also clear, however, that it was a formidable one—we would be demanding nothing short of major revisions in a corporate giant's basic business practices.

ACORN's grassroots campaign against Household used a wide variety of tactics and strategies:

- Through outreach and organizing, the campaign identified community residents who had problems with Household loans, and involved them in the campaign.
- In order to build and communicate a picture of the company's business practices, we carefully documented hundreds of borrowers' loans, and their experiences in getting those loans.

- In more than 40 cities across the country, local ACORN chapters coordinated direct actions and other protests targeting Household lending offices, processing centers, and even the homes of senior executives.

- To draw attention to Household's practices locally and nationally, we organized an extensive media campaign which worked to get articles exposing the problems with Household loans into newspapers and on the radio and television around the country.

- We promoted a shareholder resolution on predatory practices, and pressed government and private shareholders to push the company to change.

- Working with the law firm of Miner, Barnhill & Galland, P.C., we filed two class action lawsuits charging Household with unfair and deceptive trade practices.

- Taking the fight to Wall Street, we successfully worked to get the problems with the company's loans—and the possible legal and public relations consequences of these problems—onto the radar screens of Wall Street analysts covering the firm.

- Working on a regulatory strategy, ACORN pushed state attorneys general and banking regulators around the country to investigate Household and take action against them.

- Using a legislative strategy, we continued fighting for passage of both local and state legislation. These fights provided additional forums to expose the company's practices, allowing us to use the company as an example to help drive legislative change to make their own and other lenders' tactics illegal.

Building and Engaging a Base

Engaging individuals and families who have dealt personally with the problem has been crucial to our activities against predatory lending. As an organization, our work on this issue is part of a broader effort to build power and capacity in low- and moderate-income communities—and moving people to come together to make change is at the heart of that.

Because there is relatively little numerical or other "hard" data publicly available on many predatory lending problems, documenting the individual experiences of borrowers themselves—and then connecting these experiences to demands for and campaigns to win change—has been especially important. Active leaders in the campaign included ACORN members who had joined the organization in connection with other issues but later began to talk about their problems with predatory lenders, people who joined ACORN specifically because of the predatory lending campaign, and other ACORN and community members who were concerned about the overall impact of predatory lending on their neighbors and communities. As the campaign grew, in order to engage even more Household borrowers, we reached out to residents through daily door-knocking, holding neighborhood meetings and events, and sending out letters asking people who had had problems with their loans to contact the ACORN office.

Talking to people about their loans in the context of a community-based campaign was a critical part of what made it possible for many people to share their experiences with predatory lending. Absent this context and message, many homeowners feel that the problems with their loans are their own fault. They often believe that if they *were* taken advantage of, it is a reflection on their own foolishness or ignorance, and are often deeply embarrassed about being in any kind of financial difficulty, and about how they got there. Participating in a larger campaign allows people to hear from others who have had similar experiences, and together to redefine what happened and identify patterns of abusive lending as the problem. Giving a detailed story about your refinance loan to another member, an organizer, or the public in general requires sharing extremely personal information. Often it means talking about personal business like health crises, family crises, job problems, and more. People are more willing to take such risks if they are actively involved in a larger plan to use their accounts to make change and win some justice from the lender which wronged them.

Members involved in the Household campaign were active in all aspects of campaign activities: they organized events in their cities and states, planned and attended demonstrations, met with regulators and legislators, talked to the press, spoke at public meetings, and more.

For example, in Minnesota, Paul Satriano, who is a former auditor and currently an accounts payable clerk at a national hotel chain, sought assistance from ACORN and AHC after receiving a predatory loan from Household Finance. As Satriano realized how abusive his loan really was, and met other people struggling with the same abusive loans, he became an outspoken leader in the fight against predatory lending, and in the Household campaign in particular. At the same time, he also became such an active leader in his local Minnesota ACORN chapter that he was elected to the ACORN board. As part of the Household campaign in particular, Satriano testified at hearings in Minnesota and elsewhere, and in July 2001 he testified before the Senate Committee on Banking, Housing and Urban Affairs. He told senators:

What's surprised me most in all this is that I'm not alone in getting a predatory loan. Since my story has been covered by the press in the Twin Cities, I've heard from a lot of people who've also been hurt by bad home loans—from Household and from other lenders. . . . A lot's been said about how the most vulnerable are especially targeted, and I think that's true. But I think I've got a decent understanding of finances—like I said, I deal with it every day at my job—yet I got taken by a predatory loan.[4]

Similarly, Nancy Cook and her daughter Abbey came to Boston ACORN in January 2002, overwhelmed with problems caused by a Household loan which, after multiple refinances, was at a 15 percent interest rate and required payments they could not afford. As Nancy and Abbey worked with

AHC to eventually get a better loan with an interest rate close to 6 percent, they became increasingly active in ACORN's campaign against Household. They led rallies, organized actions, spoke to the press, reached out to other predatory lending victims, and coordinated other campaign events and activities. Since then, their community activist work has broadened to include organizing to get the code violations in their local supermarket addressed, fighting for better services in their neighborhood, and even lobbying at the state capitol to push for state anti-predatory lending legislation.

There are, of course, challenges as well as advantages for a community organization in focusing its efforts on individual lenders. However large a particular target may be, most borrowers who are worried about their loans in any given neighborhood do not have loans from that individual company. Such borrowers will participate only to the extent that they are convinced that making a difference with this company will make a difference with the industry as a whole.

Another challenge of a campaign addressing a set of problems which can be immediately and individually devastating—in this case threatening families with the loss of their homes—is that people may be desperate for individual solutions faster than such a campaign can possibly deliver them, or need solutions that are so large that even a relatively successful campaign will not be able to achieve them. Over the course of the campaign against Household we referred some individuals with pressing claims to individual lawyers for help (although in some parts of the country there were virtually no lawyers who would handle such cases), and were able to use the ongoing pressure of the campaign to force loan modifications and payment reductions for many others. We also referred borrowers to ACORN Housing Corporation to help them refinance into much better loans, while continuing the work to recapture the equity lost through their transactions with Household. Nonetheless, the tensions created by the urgency of the problems caused by abusive loans remain.

Building the Case

Along with involving Household borrowers in the campaign, ACORN worked to document and record as precisely as we could what the terms and conditions of their loans were. Understanding what happened in each individual case involves collecting a lot of information. Of course, many borrowers were never given a clear picture of the terms and conditions of their loans—and many no longer have, or never had, all of the paperwork associated with their loans. In putting together a picture of people's loans, the company was often not forthcoming in responding to borrowers' requests for new copies of this paperwork. Other loan features require understanding what the lender said to the borrower, and when. Still others depend on constructing a detailed picture of what the borrower's financial situation was before the loan, including the amount and rates of other debts, and what reasons they may have had, or not had, for wanting to refinance or to take cash out of the equity in their homes.

Collecting this kind of information from borrowers around the country allowed us to develop an increasingly clear picture of what the company was doing, how it was doing it, and how it needed to change.

Some issues were obvious quickly. The company was charging more than 7.5 percent of the loan amount (excluding the fees themselves) in financed fees which went directly to it on virtually every first lien. Average points and fees on "A" or prime refinance mortgages at the time were below 1 percent. These high fees were charged as a matter of course, on the largest loans as well as smaller ones, and could amount to $10,000, $15,000 or even $20,000 on a single loan. Borrowers were often not aware of what they had been charged in fees, or not aware until closing, and although these fees were called "discount points," borrowers certainly had not negotiated them in exchange for a lower rate. Like other major subprime lenders, Household was also aggressively selling financed single-premium credit insurance with their loans—a particularly abusive loan product that is often unnecessary, overpriced, misleadingly sold to borrowers, and actually financed into the loan itself, meaning that borrowers pay interest on the insurance for the life of the loan.

Other issues became clear only as we talked to more borrowers. For example, we learned over time that Household was regularly extending extremely high-rate second mortgages to borrowers along with their first mortgages. Between the two loans, borrowers frequently owed Household more than their homes were worth, and were thus effectively trapped. In addition, the combination of the extremely high rates and the way they were amortized meant that borrowers were making virtually no progress in paying them down. Some borrowers were even seeing their balances increase over time, despite making their monthly payments. Similarly, only later in the campaign did we see a copy of the sales materials that documented Household's practice of selling loans based on a misleadingly low "effective interest rate." This rate promised illusory interest savings, based on a bimonthly payment plan, took advantage of borrowers' confusion about the difference between twice-monthly payments and payments every two weeks to pitch a rate almost half as low as the actual interest rates.

As the campaign progressed, our knowledge was supplemented with information from former, and occasionally current, Household employees who called to talk about what they did and how they did it.

Direct Action

ACORN members around the country planned and participated in scores of demonstrations at Household offices over the course of the campaign.

With signs and props including sharks made of cardboard or paper, and even inflatable pool floats, they marched and chanted in front of and inside local Household offices in central cities and suburban malls, often refusing to leave until evicted by the police. Members at these actions all demanded that Household change its practices and give back what it had taken from borrowers in the past, as well as immediate resolution of individual borrowers' concerns. Employees virtually never responded with changes in loans at the actions themselves, but the accompanying publicity often did result in loan adjustments.

Besides disrupting work at particular offices and warning away potential customers, these actions presented additional problems for the company by provoking anxiety among employees and CEOs, and exacerbating morale problems. Employees told us that memos and calls on how to deal with ACORN became a frequent subject of interoffice communication, and some loan officers began to ask more questions regarding work and sales practices.

In addition to these local actions, members took advantage of opportunities provided by particular Household activities to make sure that the company could not escape ACORN's criticism. When we got word, for example, that Household was holding a press conference to announce a window-dressing set of "best practices" as an effort to head off demands for real changes, a group of ACORN members arrived at the event as uninvited guests. ACORN distributed fliers, and chanted and marched outside loudly enough to be heard clearly inside. Household, the press, and other invited guests could not avoid encountering our point of view, and coverage of the event focused on the criticisms of the company as much as on Household's own claims.

Similarly, when we learned that the company was holding one of a series of regional conferences to reassure investors, ACORN members traveled to the meeting site, where they handed out flyers and demanded to be heard. At the 2002 ACORN convention in Chicago, nearly 2,000 members from around the country divided into a few groups, and by the hundreds paid visits to the luxurious suburban homes of senior Household executives. They marched to the front doors, asked to speak with the executives, and when they were unable to do so, distributed flyers explaining why they were there and what they wanted to neighbors and in nearby exclusive shopping areas.

Media

Exposing Household's practices via the media was a key element of the campaign, and in two years more than 300 articles discussing problems with Household's lending practices appeared in newspapers or on television or radio around the country. Some of these stories resulted from coverage of demonstrations, some from press conferences held at the homes of borrowers, some from hearings or similar events at city council meetings or in neighborhoods, and still others from meetings with reporters to explain the issues. Two key elements of generating powerful media coverage of the campaign were having detailed information about individual loans which we could provide to reporters, and being able to connect reporters with borrowers who were willing to talk about their experiences with Household in order to help others avoid suffering the same.

In addition to stories covering particular events, intensive work over a longer period with reporters from a number of major publications helped produce a few key feature pieces. A long investigative article in *Forbes*[5] which focused on concerns about Household's lending practices and a feature in the *New York Times*[6] on the front page of the business section, as well as articles in the *Wall Street Journal*, the *Washington Post*, the *Los Angeles Times*, and most of the other major dailies in the country, depended on material, including loan paperwork, information, and borrower and employee contacts, that we provided.

This media coverage served the multiple functions of putting pressure directly on the company, encouraging regulatory and other action against them, and helping to engage additional borrowers in the campaign. As coverage increased, growing numbers of borrowers contacted ACORN after having seen a television report, heard a radio interview, or read something in the newspaper.

Shareholder Strategy

We made a shareholder strategy a part of this campaign in order to expand the range of fronts on which Household would have to respond to concerns about its lending practices, and to generate additional interest in the campaign through the relative novelty of this approach with regard to a domestic, low-income consumer issue.

With help from United for a Fair Economy/Responsible Wealth, which drafted the text and found socially responsible shareholders willing to file it, we twice had resolutions introduced calling for executive compensation at the company to be tied to clear and measurable efforts to fight predatory lending. In 2001 the resolution received about 5 percent of the vote— a respectable share on the first attempt—and in 2002 it received more than 30 percent of the vote. The 30 percent shareholder vote represented an extremely high degree of support for such a critical resolution. It reflected the public battering the company was taking from other aspects of the campaign, as well as specific efforts to communicate with major shareholder groups.

Along with the resolutions "inside" the shareholder meetings, ACORN members traveled to out-of-the-way locations to demonstrate at the events.

Both years, but especially in 2002, Household chose to hold its meetings far from both major media markets and cities where ACORN was organized. Despite having to travel significant distances, members, and angry Household borrowers in particular, eagerly made the trip. In 2002 the shareholder meeting was held in a nearly empty business park outside of the small town of London, Kentucky, where Household's back office operations were among the largest employers in town. Despite the location, borrowers came to town from as far away as Pennsylvania, Michigan, and Illinois. The protest was covered in large city papers in many parts of Kentucky and Tennessee, places where there had not been any campaign activity against Household in the past, along with a few national papers reporting on shareholder activism.

Also as part of a shareholder strategy, ACORN leaders in New York used their political connections with Comptroller Carl McCall, who later ran for governor, to communicate with him about problems with Household loans. As a result, the comptroller—who is the sole trustee of the giant New York State retirement fund—issued a statement of concern about the company's abusive lending practices and their potential impact on reputation and earnings. California ACORN members similarly worked to communicate with the California state treasurer, and the state employees' retirement fund there. In cities including St. Louis and Boston, local chapters successfully had resolutions passed calling on the city government to divest from Household, and in many parts of the country we worked with local union allies to pass similar resolutions with regard to union pension funds.

One additional piece of business-related pressure that was brought to bear on Household was from the AFL–CIO. Household had a substantial contract with the AFL to provide credit cards and other loans to union members at discounted rates through the Union Privilege program. When we became aware of this relationship, ACORN sat down with staff and elected leaders at the AFL and Union Privilege, and explained our concerns about Household. They followed the progress of the campaign, and added their voices to the call for Household to change its practices, using the leverage provided by the profitable line of business for which they had hired Household.

Legal Action

Large-scale legal action has not often been a key part of ACORN's campaign strategies, but in our Household campaign the class action lawsuits were a very important element in increasing pressure on the company, and in ensuring that ACORN retained a role in the resolution of the issue. The lawsuits also helped make the campaign more concrete and easier to talk about for the press. Most reporters for daily papers have little time to learn about, much less write about, the ongoing series of actions that has brought a campaign to the point at which they encounter it, but a class action lawsuit is a "thing" to which they can repeatedly refer. The lawsuits lent further weight to the ongoing public campaign, and the other elements of the campaign gave the lawsuits a much higher public profile than the legal action alone would have had.

Taking on the formidable risks of a major case with complicated facts, and one in which virtually all borrowers had signed a mandatory arbitration clause, the law firm Miner, Barnhill & Galland, P.C., worked with ACORN to file two class action lawsuits[7] against Household, one in California[8] in February 2002 and the second in Illinois[9] in May 2002, charging the company with unfair and deceptive trade practices, and outlining exactly the same conduct which was the focus of the campaign. The lawsuits spelled out a detailed set of allegations based on the understanding of the company's business practices we had gathered from talking with so many borrowers. Along with individual borrowers, ACORN was named as a plaintiff in the California suit.

Negotiations toward a settlement began before any of the charges were litigated, but after the firm had successfully cleared an important legal hurdle in the first case, which was filed in California. Household, like the majority of other subprime lenders, typically includes mandatory arbitration clauses in all of its subprime loans. As a result, the first challenge facing any legal action is defeating these mandatory arbitration provisions. Miner, Barnhill & Galland successfully argued in California state court that the Household mandatory arbitration clauses were unconscionable. In a decision that has since been cited as a significant victory in this area, in July 2002 U.S. District Court Judge Claudia Wilkin agreed that the clauses were so unfair, both procedurally and substantively, that they could not be enforced.

It is interesting to note that despite the huge volume of Household's lending, and the seriousness of the problems with its lending, there had not been other broad class action complaints filed against the company. Between mandatory arbitration clauses and paperwork that at least in some respects complied with the forms of the law, Household, like other subprime lenders, had successfully protected itself from having to respond to major class claims.

Wall Street

The campaign's ability to have a significant financial impact on the company—and to present the threat of an ever greater influence—was enormously increased by the fact that we developed the ability to get our message directly to the Wall Street analysts who covered Household. It became a deliberate part of our campaign to keep these analysts updated on campaign developments.

As the volume of press and other public criticisms increased, some analysts decided to investigate the claims against Household and their impact on the company. The combination of continuing media attention, a compelling case that what the company was doing was outrageous, documented stories of hundreds of borrowers who had received predatory loans from the company, and a credible threat that through legal and other means we were going to force the company to change its practices, moved some analysts to report increasingly frequently on Household's predatory lending problem or to start asking questions on company conference calls and in meetings with management. Of course, many other analysts dismissed the charges as meaningless. However, interest in and concern about the company's practices were high enough that more than 50 investors and analysts listened in when Morgan Stanley invited ACORN to speak on a conference call for its investment advisory service clients. As it became clearer that regulatory action was under way against the company in relation to allegations of predatory lending (see the section "Regulatory Strategy" for more details on this aspect of the campaign), the combination of legal and reputational risk, and the possible costs of changing business practices to adjust to criticisms, began to play a significant role in casting doubt on the company's future financial strength.

Over the period of this campaign, the stock market as a whole fell markedly, but Household's stock fell much more than that of others in the consumer finance sector—from a high above 60 to a low close to 20. Perhaps even more important, in substantial part as a result of concerns about predatory lending, the company's cost of funds went up dramatically and Household was forced to pay a much higher rate to raise funds on the bond market. Household essentially became a subprime borrower, having to pay rates as high as 9 percent.

Together, these constituted an extremely serious financial difficulty which it is reasonable to assume was a major force influencing Household's decision to try to settle the investigation against it by state attorneys general, to begin talking with ACORN, and to sell out to HSBC. Despite the forcefulness of the arguments against the company's practices, had these not been accompanied by a serious threat to its ability to do business, it is very possible to imagine that Household would have chosen a more protracted legal battle.

Legislation

While ACORN's efforts, in collaboration with other groups, to win legislative change to fight predatory lending continued independently of our campaign against Household Finance, these two pieces of work also supported each other.

Legislative change provided another angle from which to alter a number of Household's practices by making them illegal. Indeed, the laws against predatory lending which ACORN and our allies worked to pass in a growing number of states made financed points and fees and prepayment penalties, at the level Household was charging them, against the law. This in turn helped support the argument that they were illegitimate business practices everywhere. In the process, these legislative campaigns, including hearings, meetings, and media attention, provided additional opportunities to expose abusive practices to people with power and influence.

Members who had joined ACORN because of their problems with Household loans participated actively in these efforts, including testifying at legislative hearings, doing countless lobbying visits, and talking to the press about why legislation was needed to keep people from getting loans like theirs. Along with longtime ACORN leaders, leaders in the predatory lending campaign participated in putting together community meetings and actions to put pressure on particular elected officials. They also helped other ACORN leaders, who had not experienced this particular problem, understand why it mattered, and moved them to work on this issue as well.

The broader campaign against Household also helped get out the message about why there was such a pressing need for legislative change. Being able to document a pattern of abusive practices by such a large lender was particularly useful as we worked to make the case in state legislatures that predatory lending is a significant problem demanding serious solutions. ACORN's growing body of evidence about the pattern of problems with Household's loans allowed us to make the important point that the individual examples of predatory loans which we were presenting to legislators, the press, and regulators were not simply occasional anecdotes. This has been a frequent charge of industry defenders, who suggest that occasional sob stories do not warrant a major response. ACORN and other groups opposing predatory lending have used a variety of responses to this claim—but it was exceptionally powerful and effective to be able to draw on the documented experiences of borrowers across to country to demonstrate the abusive loan terms that Household included as a matter of course in its loans, and then point out that the company which made a practice of this made roughly 10 percent of all subprime loans in the country.

Regulatory Strategy

In addition to the pressure our campaign put directly on Household, another important part of our strategy to win changes in its business practices was pressing state regulators to take action against the company. ACORN systematically brought Household cases to state regulators, laid out the problems and patterns we were seeing with Household loans, and asked them to take action. We also took advantage of our relationships with political allies to encourage them to pressure state regulators to investigate our complaints.

Action by state regulators was ultimately an extremely powerful element in winning changes from Household, and a number of states, most notably Washington, began major investigations of Household early in the process. In April 2002, the Washington State Department of Financial Institutions produced a report from this investigation which was based on extensive documentation of problems with Household loans on which they had received borrower complaints and which had a tremendous impact on the state and national investigations into Household.

In too many states, however, at the beginning of this process we found that regulators' standard practice was to review subprime loans and lenders based on their paperwork alone, and to assume that if a lender's paperwork and official procedures were in order, there were no major problems. In many states there was not even a record kept of how many complaints were received about which company, much less a plan to follow up on these complaints with the borrower interviews necessary to really understand what was going on.

To move regulators to act, ACORN worked with our members, and with any Household victims who contacted us, to submit complaints to state attorneys general and bank regulators. We most often delivered groups of these complaints in fairly gentle "actions," where Household borrowers and other ACORN members went in a group to the regulator's office, held a press conference outside, and asked to speak to senior officials to present the complaints. Sometimes, when we had already received a relatively interested response, regulators knew in advance that we were coming. In other cases, regulators did not know of our plans in advance, and the event held to submit the actual complaints served as part of a plan to pressure regulators to take action, as well as to continue to expose the lender's practices. We then pressed for meetings with staff to review legal issues in the loans, and pressed for staff to meet individually with borrowers.

In many states we also worked to bring state regulators to community hearings and other public events, where they listened to borrowers talk about their experiences with predatory lending and Household. In Minnesota, for example, we invited the banking commissioner who had been recently appointed by Governor Ventura, Jim Bernstein, to come to a community meeting to listen to the concerns of Household borrowers. The commissioner was reluctant, but eventually agreed to attend, with the caveat that he would not appear onstage. Once there, he listened along with more than 100 ACORN members who had gathered to hear their neighbors talk about the problems with their loans. Then, rather than staying in the audience, he did in fact come up on stage, and pledged to investigate the company. Over the next several months, Commissioner Bernstein became extremely committed to working on this case, and his office was among those which took the lead in the national investigation. The commissioner's concern about predatory lending extended well beyond the Household investigation. He worked hard with ACORN, AARP, and legal services in our ultimately unsuccessful effort to get comprehensive anti-predatory lending legislation passed in Minnesota, although he was able to secure passage of a provision which limited fees to 5 percent of the loan amount.

It was particularly important that such activities took place in a number of states, rather than just one or two, because many states would have been unwilling to take on a lender the size of Household on their own. It was the cooperation across states (although this of course presented some difficulties for the regulators involved) which made action possible at all in some areas.

Starting in early 2002, a number of state attorneys general began working together to conduct a larger national investigation into the company. These steps put enormous additional pressure on Household. Meanwhile, the broader public campaign not only continued to highlight the issues surrounding predatory lending to regulators, but also helped magnify the threat of the attorneys general's investigation and the pressure on the company to settle. The connections cultivated with the press and on Wall Street helped make sure that word that an investigation might be under way was broadly circulated. Widespread rumors of the attorneys general's and state regulators' investigation of Household gave enormous additional credibility to the arguments we were making and helped to increase the financial pressure on Household, as speculation mounted that it would be forced to make a substantial settlement. In fact, in October 2002 Household did agree to a settlement with all 50 state attorneys general.[10] This relatively quick settlement was surely due to both the convincing power of multiple state regulatory agencies and the heightened vulnerability created by all other aspects of the campaign.

Household's settlement with the attorneys general and state regulators distributed $484 million to borrowers. While no settlement of a case of this kind, which involved such extensive damage to so many borrowers, will ever come close to making borrowers whole, it was the largest settlement ever of a lending case, and represented a serious and damaging rebuke to the lender. The settlement provided an average of $2,000 to borrowers, most of whom would never otherwise have seen any recovery.[11] In addition to the monetary payments to borrowers, the settlement formalized in an enforceable agreement significant changes in the company's practices. These changes included both making permanent and enforceable the improvements Household had made over the course of the campaign in its attempts to stem criticism, and other new changes to deal with particularly problematic practices the campaign and investigations had identified. The settlement also marked the first time all 50 state attorneys general had worked together on the issue of predatory lending, and we hope that the success of the settlement will inspire attorneys general and state regulators to take a more activist stance on reining in the predatory practices of additional lenders. Certainly, since the investigation and settlement many states which had not kept track of what complaints they received about what lenders, have begun to do so.

Legal Settlement

Shortly before the attorneys general settlement was announced, Household also began negotiations directly with ACORN and our lawyers both to settle the pending lawsuits and to end our public campaign against them. We began these discussions before we knew exactly what shape the attorneys general settlement would take, and finished them once it was already announced. As a result, part of our work was shaping a proposal that would add to what was already accomplished between Household and regulators. Meanwhile, the company was under such tremendous financial pressure that in November 2002 it was sold to a larger bank—the England-based HSBC—making it part of a more highly regulated financial institution.

Announced in November 2003, ACORN's settlement with Household was designed to build on the attorneys general settlement, both by adding to the best practices and by providing additional relief for injured borrowers.

The attorneys general settlement allowed each state to determine its own formula to distribute its share of the $484 million. The private legal settlement added about $120 million to the pot, with these dollars mostly allocated to a foreclosure prevention fund (FAP) for Household borrowers. Funds from the pool can be used to buy down the rate or the principal of loans which are unaffordable to borrowers, either temporarily because of a change of circumstance or permanently, if they were not affordable when the loan was made or as a result of other specific problems. Permanent changes in loans can dramatically alter the terms and payments on borrowers' loans, while the temporary changes can provide thousands of dollars of relief and allow borrowers to catch up—giving them the opportunity to refinance into a better loan from a more stable and creditworthy position. This FAP program allows the additional funds to be directed in a concentrated way to those borrowers who are most in need, and who would otherwise be most likely to lose their homes, to be forced into additional damaging loans to temporarily save their homes, or otherwise to have unmanageable debt prolonged by payment plans which they cannot afford.

The legal settlement also required Household to spend millions of dollars to fund outreach and education to protect borrowers from predatory lending. These dollars join the millions the company gave out during the campaign in various attempts to clean up their image or seek cover from broader criticisms by funding groups in return for praise of its practices.

The FAP program has already provided substantial relief to hundreds of borrowers in its first few months of existence. Following are just a few examples:

- Susan and Brian H. had two loans with Household. Through the FAP program, their second mortgage of $26,000 was forgiven, and they were approved for a permanent 2 percent interest rate on their first mortgage.

- Denise S. is a single mother with two children. Through the FAP program, Denise's second mortgage of $10,000 was forgiven, and the rate on her first mortgage was permanently reduced to 6 percent. Her payment decreased from $1,825.39 to $881, saving her nearly $1,000 per month and $169,920 over the life of the loan.

- When Kim J. became permanently disabled and lost her job, her husband, Melvin, took on three jobs to try to bring their mortgage current. Through the FAP, they qualified for a permanent interest rate reduction from 10.5 percent to 3.9 percent. Their payments have been reduced from $1,270 to $647.42, a savings of $112,140 over the life of the loan.

- Benita H. called ACORN Housing in February 2004, when her home was scheduled for sheriff's sale the coming month as a result of payment problems due in part to a family crisis. Through the FAP program, the sale of Benita's home was stopped immediately, her account was brought current, the interest rate on the loan was reduced to 4.9 percent for six months, and her monthly payment lowered from $585 to $324.57.

Cumulatively, among the most important practice changes accomplished over the course of the campaign and by the attorneys general and ACORN settlements were the following:

- A reduction in points and fees from more than 7.5 percent of the loan amount on every loan, to a maximum of 5 percent.

- A reduction of prepayment penalties from five years to three years on all loans, both new and existing.

- A prohibition on making loans for substantially more than borrowers' homes are worth, and thus effectively trapping them in a high-cost loan, and on making multiple loans at the same time.

- Ending the sale of financed credit insurance and similar products.

- Ending deceptive sales practices, including designating loans as revolving lines of credit in order to evade restrictions on the highest-cost fixed-rate loans, promising lower "effective rates" through bimonthly payment plans, and hiding the points, fees, or prepayment penalties charged on a loan; Household is now required to provide much clearer information about the costs of the loans at every step of the process, including providing key loan paperwork in a language the borrower understands.

- An end to billing practices which essentially encouraged borrowers to fall behind on their high-rate second loans, meaning that they often made little if any progress in paying them off.
- Sharply curtailing the use of "live check" solicitations to sell refinance loans.
- A legally binding requirement that loans carry not just a benefit, but a *net* benefit, to borrowers, considering both the costs and the advantages of the loan.

In addition, HSBC, Household's new owner, has pledged to move quickly to implement policies which assure that borrowers with "A," or very good, credit receive loans at "A" rates.

These changes do not produce a perfect set of lending practices by any means. For example, five points remains extremely high as a standard charge, as does a standard prepayment penalty of six months' interest. But on a volume of lending as high as Household's, these changes nonetheless add up to hundreds of millions of dollars in reduced costs to borrowers every year. The changes also contribute substantially to making certain practices—though still perfectly legal in many states—less legitimate for the industry as a whole.

CONCLUSION

Much remains to be done to even the playing field in the mortgage lending world, and to arrive at a point where predatory lending abuses are not allowed to perpetuate and amplify differences in wealth, assets, and power. But campaigns like the one described here targeting Household have made a real difference. As a result of this effort, hundreds of millions of dollars were returned to borrowers, thousands of borrowers will be able to keep homes they were otherwise in danger of losing, and a giant corporation was required to make changes in business practices which will save consumers hundreds of millions of dollars a year. At the same time, the campaign contributed to the drive for legislation in states around the country, helped move state regulators to take unprecedented concerted action in this area, and increased capacity in our neighborhoods to take on these and similar problems in the future. It did this last by engaging thousands of people in efforts to protect their rights and by increasing their experience, and ACORN's experience as an institution, with a broad range of tactics that can be used to demand changes in corporate policy and win accountability to our communities from legislators and regulators. It thus also left us in a stronger position to continue this and other battles.

NOTES

1. ACORN is the nation's largest community organization of low- and moderate-income families, with over 150,000 member families organized into 750 neighbor-

hood chapters in more than 65 cities across the country. Since 1970 ACORN has taken action and won victories on issues of concern to our members. Our priorities include better housing for first-time home buyers and tenants, living wages for low-wage workers, more investment in our communities from banks and governments, and better public schools. We achieve these goals by building community organizations that have the power to win changes—through direct action, negotiation, legislation, and voter participation.

2. U.S. Department of Housing and Urban Development and U.S. Department of the Treasury, "Curbing Predatory Home Mortgage Lending" (June 2000), http://www.huduser.org/publications/hsgfin/curbing.html. Based on information gathered at five field forums by the joint task force.

3. ACORN, ACORN Fair Housing Organization, and ACORN Housing Corporation, "Separate and Unequal: Predatory Lending in America" (October 2001). For annual updates, see www.acorn.org.

4. Paul Satriano, testimony before the U.S. Senate Committee on Banking, Housing, and Urban Affairs, hearing on "Predatory Mortgage Lending: The Problem, Impact and Responses" (July 26, 2001), http://banking.senate.gov/01_07hrg/072601/satriano.htm.

5. Bernard Condon, "Home Wrecker," *Forbes* (September 2, 2002).

6. Peter Eavis, "Lawsuits and Regulators Shadow Big Lender's Future," *New York Times*, August 17, 2002.

7. A Massachusetts class action suit was filed in August 2002, based on violations of a specific set of state regulations.

8. *ACORN et al. v. Household International, et al.* (later consolidated with subsequent actions and renamed *In re Household Lending Litigation*), case no. C 02-1240, Northern District of California, filed February 6, 2002.

9. *Murelin and James Bell et al. v. Household International et al.*, case no. 02CH8640, Circuit Court of Cook County, Illinois, filed May 15, 2002.

10. For additional details on the settlement, see http://www.household-beneficial-settlement.com/.

11. It is important to note that both the attorneys general settlement and the private legal settlement preserved all borrowers' rights to sue in the event that they are threatened with foreclosure. In addition, the campaign, the press coverage, and the accompanying legal notices surely also helped increase the number and degree of successful individual lawsuits to recover damages.

7

Designing Federal Legislation That Works: Legal Remedies for Predatory Lending

John P. Relman, Fred Rivera, Meera Trehan, and Shilpa S. Satoskar

The 1990s witnessed an unprecedented rise in residential mortgage lending. Low interest rates, available housing, and an improved economy throughout the 1990s resulted in more loans for more Americans than at any time in our history. The lending boom, however, has not been good for everyone. The rise in mortgage lending has coincided with a sharp increase in predatory lending practices. These practices disproportionately harm minorities and the elderly, stripping equity from communities that can least afford it.

Since the 1980s, federal and state legislators have struggled to pass laws that would make it more difficult for unscrupulous brokers and lenders to engage in predatory lending. Out of these efforts a patchwork regulatory scheme has emerged that has managed to curb some abuses, but has left others wholly unaddressed. The Truth in Lending Act (TILA), Real Estate Settlement Procedures Act (RESPA), and Home Ownership and Equity Protection Act (HOEPA), for example, all require disclosures to help educate consumers entering into loans, but impose no real penalties for those found in violation and offer no truly "make whole" remedies for those who are robbed of their assets or home. Anti-discrimination laws such as the Fair Housing Act and the Equal Credit Opportunity Act do provide such penalties and remedies, but require proof that the predatory lending practices are directed against a protected minority group. State consumer fraud or unfair and deceptive trade laws offer some useful protection from predatory practices, but the coverage of these laws is uneven because they vary widely from state to state. And while the Federal Trade Commission has brought a handful of important cases under the Federal Trade Commission

Act that have had an important deterrent effect for some rogue lenders, government enforcement actions have been few.

It would not be fair to suggest that this patchwork of laws has not been utilized to good effect in many instances. Enforcement of all of these laws—by both public agencies and private litigants—has resulted in notable settlements and provided some measure of relief to victims of predatory lending. Moreover, some responsible lenders have instituted strong fair lending policies or practices that have curbed predatory lending. But as the mortgage boom continues, the rise in abusive lending practices for the most part has continued unabated. Better enforcement tools are clearly needed.

In recent years, congressional proponents have introduced new federal legislation that would fill many of the gaps in the regulatory and enforcement framework. All of these efforts, however, have ended in legislative failure. A handful of progressive state legislatures have managed to enact laws that strengthen borrower protections, but these laws are necessarily limited in geographic scope, and opponents claim that they are in large part preempted by federal law and thus inapplicable to a large segment of the lending industry.

The current regulatory framework serves no one's interests. For consumer and civil rights advocates, the enforcement scheme is simply not up to the task of systematically and effectively curbing abusive practices. And for lenders, the scheme is unworkable because it subjects a lender with offices around the country to a byzantine and inconsistent set of requirements in different states and localities. New, comprehensive federal legislation to combat predatory lending is desperately needed.

This chapter focuses on the issues that model federal legislation will need to address if it is to bring order and efficiency to the enforcement process and provide borrowers with meaningful protection from predatory practices. The next section reviews the current federal laws and regulatory scheme, pointing out their practical and legal limitations and deficiencies. The third section attempts the same analysis at the state level, focusing in particular on states where advocates have managed to pass remarkably progressive anti-predatory lending legislation. The final section sets out some of the basic elements that model federal legislation will need to contain if true progress is to be made in the battle to curb abusive lending practices.

THE EXISTING FEDERAL REGULATORY SCHEME

Defining "Predatory Lending"

"Predatory lending," as the term is used by the lay public, is difficult to define because it encompasses an unusually wide range of fraudulent and unscrupulous conduct. HUD and the Department of the Treasury have described predatory lending as "engaging in deception or fraud, manipulating the borrower through aggressive sales tactics, or taking unfair advantage of a borrower's lack of understanding."[1] These practices are often combined with loan terms that typically make the borrower more vulnerable to financial exploitation.

While there is no definitive list of predatory practices, three basic types of abusive lending practices are commonly associated with predatory lending. The first is fraud or deception in the presentation of the terms of the loan. Predatory lenders or brokers frequently alter loan application information or loan terms after obtaining borrower signatures, or simply forge the signatures. A second common predatory practice involves lending without consideration of the borrower's ability to repay the loan. In these situations, a predatory lender is more concerned with taking the collateral—the borrower's home—through foreclosure than in securing steady and timely repayment of principal and interest. Foreclosure is accomplished by encouraging the borrower to commit to a loan at a price he or she cannot afford. The third—and perhaps hallmark—practice associated with predatory lending is equity stripping. This is achieved through exorbitant (and often hidden) fees and costs. This practice can be devastating, for even those borrowers who recognize their error and ultimately refinance the loan (which may be costly if the loan contains a prepayment penalty) have lost the large up-front fees that the broker or lender skimmed from the transaction at closing. Fee abuse gives the lender or broker added incentive to "flip" or repeatedly refinance the loan. Each refinancing results in more up-front fees for the lender while the borrower continues to lose her equity in the property.

These basic and common predatory practices are reflected in the following hypothetical mortgage transaction. Imagine the following facts:

Acme Mortgage (a fictitious name) operates in the African American neighborhood of a major American city. Through one of its cooperating brokers, it identifies a young African American woman (Mary) who is in urgent need of a modest loan ($30,000) to repair and renovate her home. Mary has limited formal education. She inherited her house from her mother without any mortgage or lien on the property. The house is a modest, older row house, fairly appraised at $175,000. Mary has no credit history, no credit cards, pays cash for all purchases, and has never applied for or obtained a loan. She earns $2,000 per month. From the broker, Mary learns that she can have the loan in one week. All she has to do is come to the closing and sign the papers. The broker tells her that the interest rate will be high at first (15 percent), but that he will make sure that after a few months she gets a lower rate. Mary arrives at the closing to find no one but a notary. She signs where told to, but does not understand the fine print of the loan documents.

Little does Mary know that she has signed her name to a loan in the amount of $60,000 at an annualized interest rate of 18 percent. The loan terms contain broker fees in the amount of $8,000, an escalator clause taking the APR to 18 percent if she is late in paying one time, a "no-insurance" penalty of 1 percent for each month she fails to have homeowners' insurance, and mandatory attorneys' fees should the lender move to foreclose. Mary's monthly payments are more than half her monthly income. Mary is also unaware that this is a "balloon" note, meaning that her monthly payment covers only the interest on the loan, and does not go to pay back principal. She will have to pay back the entire principal of the loan in seven years.

Within six months Mary is temporarily laid off from work. She has no reserves and quickly falls behind in her loan payments. Three months later Acme moves to foreclose on the property, asserting late fees, interest on interest (at 24 percent), no-insurance penalties, attorneys' fees, and unpaid principal totaling $100,000. The property goes to foreclosure sale at a market price of $175,000, and Acme obtains the deed to Mary's house for a payment of $65,000 (after deducting for foreclosure costs and expenses). Two months later, Acme resells the property for $185,000 to an unsuspecting neighbor of Mary's. The sale is financed by an Acme loan with terms similar to Mary's.

Step back for a moment and consider the elements of this transaction: a fraudulent inducement to sign a loan document with false promises of affordability; no effort by the underwriter of the loan to determine Mary's ability to pay; hidden fees and terms designed to get Mary behind on her payments quickly and irreparably; and foreclosure of the property designed to strip the equity quickly from Mary's home and flip the property, recycling the abuse on another unsuspecting member of a minority community starved for hard money credit. This is traditional predatory lending at its (not uncommon) worst.

Virtually all predatory lending occurs in the subprime market. The converse, however, is not true. Subprime lending, of course, need not be predatory and does in some instances provide a necessary and valuable service by increasing the amount of credit available to borrowers who would not qualify for products at the prime rate. When done responsibly and transparently, subprime lending can offer consumers with higher or nontraditional credit risk profiles loan products that are priced according to their relative risk. The subprime market, however, lacks comprehensive and efficient regulation. This fact, coupled with the limited choices available to borrowers who are forced to rely on subprime lending, has fostered an environment where predatory practices are free to flourish.[2]

Federal Statutes

Seven major federal statutes provide borrowers with varying degrees of protection against predatory lending. Each, however, falls short in critical respects. Each of these laws—the Truth in Lending Act (TILA), the Home Ownership Equity Protection Act (HOEPA), the Real Estate Settlement Procedures Act (RESPA), the Equal Credit Opportunity Act (ECOA), the Fair Housing Act (FHA), the Racketeer Influenced and Corrupt Organizations

Act (RICO), and the Federal Trade Commission Act (FTC Act)—is discussed below.

Truth in Lending Act (TILA)

Enacted in 1968, the Truth in Lending Act represents Congress' first major effort of the modern era at regulating consumer credit transactions.[3] Its purpose is to protect borrowers from inaccurate and unfair credit billing and credit card practices by requiring a meaningful disclosure of credit terms in the credit transaction. Congress' own findings, which appear in the preamble to the Act, leave no doubt that Congress understood the importance of disclosure to the efficient and fair operation of the consumer credit market:

The Congress finds that economic stabilization would be enhanced and the competition among the various financial institutions and other firms engaged in the extension of consumer credit would be strengthened by the informed use of credit. The informed use of credit results from an awareness of the cost thereof by consumers. It is the purpose of this subchapter to assure a meaningful disclosure of credit terms so that the consumer will be able to compare more readily the various credit terms available to him and avoid the uninformed use of credit, and to protect the consumer against inaccurate and unfair credit billing and credit card practices.[4]

TILA applies broadly, regulating most forms of consumer credit, including home mortgages, personal loans, and credit cards.[5] Four conditions must be met for TILA to apply. *First*, credit must be offered or extended to consumers. *Second*, the lender must offer or extend credit regularly. *Third*, credit must be subject to a finance charge and/or be payable by a written agreement in at least four installments. *Fourth*, the credit sought must be primarily for personal, family, or household purposes, not business or commercial purposes.[6]

TILA's key provisions require that certain information be disclosed in a uniform manner in order to allow consumers to compare the cost of credit. The two core pieces of data are (1) the finance charge, which is the total dollar cost of credit, and (2) the APR, or annualized simple interest rate of the finance charge, which informs borrowers of the cost of credit over time.[7]

For purposes of TILA, "finance charge" is defined broadly to include "any charge payable directly or indirectly by the consumer and imposed directly or indirectly by the creditor as an incident to or a condition of the extension of credit."[8] There are, however, significant exceptions to this definition. For example, in real estate and mortgage lending transactions, the finance charge need not include fees for credit reports, notary costs, property appraisal and inspection, title examination, title insurance, property survey, and the preparation of deeds of trust or settlement documents.[9] In addition, the creditor need not include charges for consumer credit or property insurance in the finance charge if the creditor does not require insurance coverage and informs the borrower of that fact.[10]

TILA grants an automatic right of rescission in transactions where "a security interest . . . is or will be retained or acquired in any property which is used as the principal dwelling of the person to whom credit is extended."[11] During a three-day "cooling-off period" following the loan closing, the borrower may elect to rescind or cancel the loan by sending notice of the decision to the lender. The lender must then cancel all notes, mortgages, and other instruments and return to the borrower all funds or other property received.

Notwithstanding these disclosure requirements and the right of rescission, TILA does not always ensure "the informed use of credit." In residential mortgage lending transactions, consumers are inundated with scores of forms and dozens of pages of paperwork, of which TILA disclosures are just one small part. TILA forms are often lost in this avalanche of paperwork, adding little to the borrower's true understanding of the costs of the transaction or the loan over its life. This is particularly true for borrowers who are targeted by predatory lenders for their lack of financial sophistication. Ironically, the lender is often the only party assisted by the small print of TILA disclosures buried in the paperwork of the loan transaction. As HUD and the Department of the Treasury recognized, "written disclosure requirements, without other protections, can have the unintended effect of insulating predatory lenders where fraud or deception may have occurred."[12]

Our hypothetical with Mary and Acme illustrates the point. TILA's disclosure requirements would be unlikely to make any difference in the outcome of that loan transaction. Assuming that Acme included the disclosure forms among the many documents Mary was required to sign, without proper advice and guidance there is little chance that Mary would either read or understand those disclosures. Worse, her signature on the forms would, if anything, potentially help Acme argue that Mary's subsequent dilemma was one of her own making, and that the terms of her loan agreement were known to her from the beginning.

Even if TILA's substantive protections were effective in providing meaningful protection to the borrower, violations result in no real cost to the lender. The monetary remedies available for a TILA violation are relatively modest and do not have a deterrent effect. A prevailing plaintiff may recover actual damages, statutory damages, and attorneys' fees and costs.[13] Actual damages for disclosure violations may be calculated in one of two ways: the borrower may show that, but for the inaccurate disclosures, he or she could have received equivalent credit at a lower rate elsewhere.[14] Or, if disclosure documents understate, for example, a finance charge, the borrower may recover the sum of the undisclosed charges.[15] But these damages may be small, and are difficult for the borrower to prove in most situations. History shows that this type of claim is unlikely to be pursued.[16]

TILA's limited remedies and emphasis on paperwork make the statute, from the lender's perspective, more of a nuisance than a deterrent to deceptive and fraudulent practices. TILA represented a step in the right direction when it became law in 1968, but in the current climate of abusive practices, it remains of marginal use in stopping predatory lending or remedying its harms.

Home Ownership Equity Protection Act (HOEPA)

In 1994, Congress amended TILA to provide for additional disclosures and increased protection for loans defined as "high cost." The result was the Home Ownership and Equity Protection Act of 1994.[17] The statute defines high-cost loans as those with (1) an APR greater than 10 percent above the yield on Treasury securities with a maturity date comparable to the term of the loan or (2) points and fees exceeding the greater of 8 percent of the total loan amount or $400 (which is adjusted up for inflation).[18] After the Act was passed, the Federal Reserve Board lowered the interest rate threshold to eight points above the Treasury yield.[19]

For loans that fall within the definition of "high cost," HOEPA precludes certain types of balloon payments; forbids negative amortization; restricts payments prepaid from proceeds; outlaws increased interest payments after default; and limits prepayment penalties.[20] Fixed-rate HOEPA loans must disclose the APR and monthly payment amount. Adjustable-rate HOEPA loans must disclose the APR, the regular monthly payment, the amount of the highest monthly payment based on the allowable interest rate, and make clear that the interest rate and payment may increase.[21] HOEPA also prohibits lenders from engaging in a "pattern or practice" of issuing high-cost loans without regard to a borrower's ability to repay.[22] While TILA defines a "creditor" as one who regularly (by six or more transactions) extends consumer credit secured by a dwelling, HOEPA defines "creditor" as any entity that has made two high-cost mortgages. If the transaction involved a broker, one high-cost mortgage may be sufficient to trigger the Act.[23] Creditors that violate HOEPA are liable for actual and statutory damages, attorneys' fees and costs, and "enhanced" damages in an amount equal to the total finance charge and fee paid by the borrower.[24]

Like TILA, HOEPA has proven to be a relatively ineffective tool for controlling predatory lending. The vast majority of subprime loans do not meet the definition of "high-cost," and therefore are not subject to any of HOEPA's protections or prohibitions.[25] HOEPA excludes some questionable costs—such as high prepayment penalties—from its points and fees threshold, and does not cover purchase money mortgages, reverse mortgages, or home equity lines of credit.

In addition, although HOEPA bans some predatory practices for covered loans, its prohibitions are either too limited or too onerous to provide adequate protection for borrowers. HOEPA, for example, appears to recognize that asset-based lending is abusive, but applies only when there is a "pattern or practice" of asset-based lending, and not when a lender fails to consider the plaintiff's ability to pay in any one instance. HOEPA thus insulates from prosecution all but the worst asset-based lenders. In short, although HOEPA targets the worst loans, it has not been able to stem the rise in abusive lending practices.

Returning again to our hypothetical, Mary's loan would likely qualify as a HOEPA loan, but insofar as most of HOEPA's protections center on disclosures, this statute would offer her little more than TILA. And to the extent that the required disclosures were in fact made by Acme (albeit in legal fine print not understandable to Mary), as with TILA, Acme would be in a position to argue that when Mary signed the documents, she was on notice of her obligations. Equally problematic, in order to seek relief from Acme for abusive asset-based predatory lending practices, Mary would need to show that Acme was engaged in a pattern or practice of abusive conduct. Gathering this type of evidence is complicated and difficult. Mary certainly would not have the resources to hire an attorney with the expertise to undertake this kind of investigation. In short, were Mary to rely solely on HOEPA to seek relief, she would face some very difficult proof issues.

Real Estate Settlement Procedures Act (RESPA)

The Real Estate Settlement Procedures Act (RESPA) ensures that borrowers obtain basic information about their loan during the transaction, prohibits certain practices that may increase settlement costs, and imposes certain requirements on loan servicing practices.[26] RESPA applies to "federally related mortgage loans" secured with a mortgage on a one-to-four-family residential property, which includes most home purchase loans, assumptions, refinances, home improvement loans, and equity lines of credit.[27]

RESPA requires that lenders detail the costs associated with settlement, outline lender servicing and escrow account practices, and disclose any business relationships between settlement service providers.[28] RESPA also prohibits certain potentially predatory practices that could increase settlement costs to the borrower. For example, RESPA makes it illegal to give or accept any item of value for referrals of settlement services or to give or accept charges for services not actually performed.[29]

Finally, RESPA requires loan servicers to follow certain practices related to the servicing of the loan and any escrow account used for paying property taxes, insurance, and the like. Servicers must respond to the borrower's written questions or complaints about servicing of the loan within 60 days, and must provide the borrower advance written notice before servicing of the loan is transferred to a new servicer.[30] Although RESPA does not require lenders or servicers to maintain escrow accounts, where such an account is maintained, RESPA places limits on the amount of money the servicer may require the borrower to pay into the account, and requires that the servicer make payments on time to avoid late charges.[31]

As important as these protections may be, RESPA's reach is limited. Although some of its provisions create an explicit federal cause of action, thus allowing borrowers to file private suits, others (including some of the disclosure provisions) do not. Furthermore, disclosures offer only partial protection, for the simple reason that many borrowers do not understand the content of the notices they are given. In addition, settlement costs and servicing practices—while they can be unfair and abusive—are not the primary methods by which predatory lenders strip equity from their victims. Thus, for a predatory loan victim like Mary, who is in need of a statute that will offer her meaningful protection and relief, RESPA presents many of the same practical shortcomings as TILA and HOEPA.

Equal Credit Opportunity Act (ECOA) and Fair Housing Act (FHA)

Predatory lenders are by no means even-handed in where they ply their trade and whom they choose to target with their fraudulent practices. Often these lenders focus their exploitative practices on traditionally underserved populations where minorities, women, and the elderly are disproportionately represented. This practice, known as "reverse redlining"—defined as marketing bad loans to an area because it is home to members of a certain racial, ethnic, or other group protected under the law—is a civil rights issue, because it causes significant harm to minority communities in particular.

Like traditional redlining—the practice of denying prime or good loans to a minority area or community—reverse redlining has, in recent years, been held to violate both the Fair Housing Act (FHA) and the Equal Credit Opportunity Act (ECOA).[32] Where these two laws can be used to combat predatory lending practices, the effect may be considerable, in large part due to the extraordinary range of remedies and procedural options these statutes offer.

In the broadest sense, the FHA and ECOA prohibit discrimination in the extension of credit and real estate-related transactions (defined to include mortgage lending). Both statutes permit recovery of compensatory damages (that is, money to make a victim whole for the injury suffered), punitive damages, and attorneys' fees, in addition to "injunctive relief" (a legal term for nonfinancial steps that the court can order to right the wrong done or to prevent future harm).[33] The FHA, in particular, provides a far more generous statute of limitations than most other federal statutes,[34] and grants an automatic right to a jury trial.[35] In addition, both the FHA and ECOA permit a finding of liability not just where discrimination is intentional, but also where a lending practice has an unnecessary disparate impact (a disproportionately negative effect) on a protected group. Given the right facts and a receptive court, these are powerful tools—far more effective than anything offered by TILA, HOEPA, or RESPA.

For all that these statutes offer, however, they also pose problems for those seeking to prosecute predatory lenders. First, the FHA and ECOA were designed to provide a remedy for discriminatory conduct—that is, conduct that treats protected groups differently from nonprotected groups. To prevail under these statutes, it is not enough to show that a lender subjected an individual to unfair or fraudulent practices; the victim must prove that she was subjected to the practices because of her race (or some other protected characteristic). That means, of course, that "equal opportunity" predatory lenders—those who prey equally, for example, on white and African American communities, young and old, men and women—may fall outside the reach of these laws.

Second, even where a lender has engaged in discrimination, it is not always easy to prove, especially for an individual without significant time and resources. For example, proof of discriminatory marketing usually requires evidence of how a lender treats a larger group of borrowers within a metropolitan community. An individual victim facing foreclosure may well lack the time or resources to marshal this kind of evidence or otherwise build a winning FHA or ECOA case.

Mary offers precisely such an example. Her individual experience with Acme would not, in and of itself, provide sufficient evidence to support a racial targeting claim under the FHA or ECOA. Mary would need to marshal evidence of how others in her minority community were treated, and examine whether Acme markets its predatory practices in similarly situated white neighborhoods. This requires access to skilled attorneys with investigative resources, something that most individuals in Mary's position do not have.

Racketeer Influenced and Corrupt Organizations Act (RICO)

Although enacted to target organized crime, the Racketeer Influenced and Corrupt Organizations Act (RICO) has been used to combat various forms of consumer abuse.[36] RICO authorizes civil suits by individuals who have been injured by certain criminal activity known as "racketeering," including mail or wire fraud. RICO prohibits persons employed by or associated with an "enterprise" (which may be a corporation or other legal entity, or an informal association of individuals) from using the enterprise to engage in a pattern of racketeering activity.[37]

Predatory lending frequently involves mail or wire fraud. This has allowed creative attorneys to assert RICO claims against lenders engaged in abusive practices.[38] The remedies offered under RICO make it a potentially powerful legal weapon: where a borrower succeeds in proving a RICO violation, he or she may collect treble damages (three times the damages actually suffered) and attorneys' fees and costs, which may be substantial.[39] Courts have interpreted RICO broadly, to cover many different types of illegal schemes, with the result that the statute offers the potential to reach a wide range of predatory lending practices. RICO's prohibition on conspiracy to violate its provisions also opens the door to claims against third parties (such as brokers) that may have assisted the lender in implementing the predatory scheme.[40]

Despite the protections and relief available under RICO, its utility in the arena of predatory lending has limitations. First, RICO requires proof of far more than abusive loan practices. In general, proving the complex elements of a RICO claim is difficult and costly, and there is considerable disagreement among the courts regarding the proof required to establish a RICO violation.[41]

Second, certain requirements of a RICO claim can be particularly difficult to meet in a predatory lending case. For example, "racketeering activity" usually requires proof of fraud, which as a legal matter can be difficult to show.[42] RICO also requires proof of a "pattern" of racketeering activity, which means that an individual like Mary, who may be victimized through a single instance of illegal conduct, cannot take advantage of RICO's protections. And even where such a pattern of illegal activity exists, it may be difficult to establish the existence of an "enterprise" through which the illegal activity was conducted.[43]

Finally, although RICO offers significant monetary remedies, the statute leaves some remedial gaps. It is unclear, for example, whether RICO authorizes injunctive relief.[44] Thus, even where a borrower wins a RICO action, the court may not be able to order the lender to cease its predatory practices or to require forgiveness of the loan.[45]

The Federal Trade Commission Act

Section 5 of the Federal Trade Commission Act prohibits unfair or deceptive trade practices.[46] An "unfair" practice is one that causes or is likely to cause consumers "substantial injury" that is not reasonably avoidable and is not outweighed by countervailing consumer benefits.[47] A "deceptive" practice is a material representation, omission, or practice that is likely to deceive consumers acting reasonably under the circumstances.[48] The FTC Act's broad prohibition against unfair or deceptive practices has been applied to a wide range of actions, including abusive lending and loan servicing practices.

The FTC Act grants the FTC authority to bring administrative and judicial enforcement actions to attack unfair or deceptive practices by individuals, partnerships, or corporations, with certain exceptions (including banks that are regulated by other federal agencies).[49] In the administrative context, the FTC issues a complaint and conducts its own investigation. Where it concludes that an individual or entity has engaged in illegal practices, the FTC may issue a cease-and-desist order to halt the illegal activity, and may then seek consumer redress in federal court for consumer injury.[50] The FTC may also pursue other individuals or entities that knowingly violate the standards in a particular cease-and-desist order by suing in federal court to recover civil penalties.[51]

Independent of its own administrative process, the FTC also has the power to challenge unfair or deceptive trade practices by filing a lawsuit directly in federal court, without first making a finding of illegal conduct. Under Section 13(b) of the FTC Act, the FTC may sue in federal court when it believes that the statute has been, or is about to be, violated.[52] The court may issue an order prohibiting the illegal practices or requiring certain action, and also may award restitution and rescission of contracts.[53]

Where the FTC has chosen to exercise its enforcement power to attack predatory lending practices, it often has been very effective.[54] The FTC Act's ultimate effect on predatory lending is limited, however. The FTC Act does not authorize lawsuits by individual consumers; only the FTC (and other agencies, in the case of some banks) can pursue potential violations of the law. Enforcement is therefore constrained significantly by practical considerations facing the FTC or any other agency, including political pressure and scarce resources. Although the FTC may be able to use its limited resources to prosecute some egregious instances of predatory lending involving a widespread pattern of predatory practices, only a small fraction of individual victims obtains relief under the FTC Act, and the vast majority of predatory lenders escape its reach. Thus, a borrower like Mary would be unlikely to be the beneficiary of relief from the FTC unless Acme's practices were sufficiently egregious that the company independently had come to the attention of the agency's investigators, or sufficient numbers of complaints had already found their way to the FTC to warrant a decision by the Commission to invest the agency's resources in an enforcement action. In practice, the FTC is simply not a reliable source of redress for the average abused borrower.

National Secondary Market "Regulations"

Although technically not part of the federal statutory or regulatory scheme, the country's two largest secondary market players, Fannie Mae and Freddie Mac (known as government sponsored enterprises or GSEs), wield enormous influence on lenders in both prime and subprime markets. Where these two large lending institutions have issued rules or guidelines about the types of loans they will and will not purchase, their pronouncements have had a profound effect on the behavior of primary lenders.

Anxious to increase their secondary-market share of the growing subprime market, Fannie Mae and Freddie Mac have in recent years responded to concerns about abusive lending practices by issuing their own guidance about the types of practices they consider predatory. In addition to requiring that lenders always determine a borrower's ability to pay, and refrain from steering borrowers toward high-cost loans, Fannie Mae and Freddie Mac have compiled lists of prohibited characteristics that make loans ineligible for purchase by these two secondary market giants.

Fannie Mae's predatory lending loan guidelines, issued in April 2000, include requirements that a subprime loan must meet with respect to five specific practices before it will be considered for purchase.[55] First, the total points and fees charged to the borrower (including origination fees, underwriting fees, broker fees, finder's fees, and charges imposed as a condition of the loan, whether paid to the lender or a third party) generally may not exceed 5 percent of the mortgage amount.[56] Second, the lender may not sell a prepaid single-premium credit life insurance policy to the borrower in connection with origination of the loan. Third, the lender must report the borrower's full payment history (both positive and negative) to credit repositories on a monthly basis. Fourth, loan servicers generally must maintain escrow accounts for the monthly deposit of funds for taxes, ground rents, mortgage insurance premiums, and the like.

Finally, the Fannie Mae guidelines place certain conditions on loans containing prepayment penalty provisions. The borrower must gain some benefit (such as a fee reduction) in return for accepting the penalty provision; the terms of the penalty provision must be adequately disclosed; the borrower must be offered the choice of another mortgage without prepayment penalties; and the prepayment penalty must not be charged when the mortgage debt is accelerated due to default.

Shortly after Fannie Mae issued its predatory lending guidelines, Freddie Mac followed suit, issuing an anti-predatory lending policy in December 2000.[57] Freddie Mac's policy contains guidelines very similar to Fannie Mae's, including prohibition of points and fees over 5 percent of the mortgage amount, prohibition of prepaid single-premium credit life insurance, a full file credit reporting requirement, and conditions on mortgages with prepayment penalty provisions.[58] Since the issuance of this policy, Freddie Mac also has ceased investing in subprime mortgages with prepayment penalty terms greater than three years.[59] And at the end of 2003, Freddie Mac announced that it will no longer invest in subprime mortgages with mandatory arbitration clauses requiring that borrowers go to arbitration, rather than court, to make a claim that the lender has violated their rights.[60] In early 2004, Fannie Mae announced a similar policy on mandatory arbitration.[61]

Fannie Mae and Freddie Mac's ability to change behavior within capital markets through such voluntary "regulatory" efforts should not be underestimated. The GSEs' stance against predatory lending has done more than just send a strong signal to the subprime market that predatory lending practices will not be tolerated; it has clearly begun to alter the playing field, bringing some real measure of order to subprime practices. The effect has been felt particularly in areas of the market where large conventional lenders who traditionally sell to Fannie Mae and Freddie Mac have acquired subprime mortgage companies. These lenders—desirous of continued good relations with the GSEs—have strong incentives to abide by Fannie Mae and Freddie Mac's predatory lending guidelines.

Still, voluntary private market regulation by the GSEs cannot solve the problem of predatory lending. It does not provide a proper substitute for an effective private right of action in the courts for victims of predatory practices, and it does not guarantee that secondary market capital will be kept from unscrupulous subprime and predatory lenders. Although Fannie Mae and Freddie Mac are the two largest secondary-market participants, they are not the only ones, and other secondary-market players have not signed on to the GSEs' predatory lending guidelines. As long as capital finds its way to those engaged in predatory practices, self-regulation by the private sector offers only a partial solution.

THE EXISTING STATE REGULATORY SCHEME

Traditional State Causes of Action

In addition to the federal laws and regulations that offer some protection against predatory lending practices, state law—consisting of both common law (judge-made law) and state statutes—may provide a basis for challenging abusive practices. The state law claims made most often in predatory lending cases are based on common law fraud and state consumer protection statutes that prohibit unfair or deceptive trade practices. Each of these causes of action can be useful, but each has drawbacks and limitations.

Borrowers victimized by predatory lending practices often are victims of fraudulent misrepresentation, which long has been prohibited by state common law. Common law prohibitions against fraud in many instances are broad enough to cover predatory lending practices. A borrower who is successful in a fraud suit may recover compensatory damages and, in most states, punitive damages. The availability of punitive damages is particularly important where the actual damages resulting from the lender's illegal conduct are relatively small; in such a situation an order limited to reimbursement will have no deterrent effect.

Fraud claims, however, are surprisingly difficult to win. Federal courts and many state courts require that allegations of fraud contain greater detail than allegations in a typical lawsuit.[62] A plaintiff in a fraud case is commonly required to prove his or her case by "clear and convincing evidence," rather than the customary "preponderance of the evidence" standard applicable in most civil cases.[63] And many of the specific elements of fraud are particularly difficult to show. For example, a fraud claim requires a plaintiff to prove that the lender intentionally deceived him or her, and that he or she reasonably relied on the intentional misrepresentation.[64] The need to prove individual reliance, in particular, may make it very difficult as a practical matter to bring a class action.[65]

Even when they are successful, plaintiffs in fraud cases generally cannot recover attorneys' fees. This fact, coupled with the general difficulty of proving fraud, creates a strong disincentive for private attorneys to bring fraud claims on behalf of individuals like Mary, who do not have the means to pay an attorney and are also most likely to be the victims of predatory lending.[66]

A second state law option for combating abusive lending practices rests with the many state statutes prohibiting unfair or deceptive trade practices. All 50 states and the District of Columbia have enacted statutes to prevent consumer deception and abuse. These statutes (known generally as "UDAP laws" because they prohibit unfair and deceptive acts and practices) tend to be both broad and flexible enough to cover a wide range of abusive practices.

State UDAP laws are generally enforced through state-initiated actions, but frequently include provisions for a private right of action by consumers.[67] In a state enforcement action, state officials may seek an order preventing a company from engaging in illegal practices, and in most states may seek civil or criminal penalties, as well as restitution for injured consumers.[68] In states that offer a private right of action, this need not prevent an individual borrower from suing a lender directly.

In general, state UDAP laws offer a variety of useful remedies to borrowers who file a private suit. Courts may order injunctive relief (i.e., an order that a company cease illegal practices),[69] actual damages, and treble or other multiple damages (actual damages multiplied by three or some other factor).[70] A minority of statutes explicitly authorize punitive damages.[71] Most state UDAP laws also permit prevailing plaintiffs to recover attorneys' fees.[72]

Claims based on state UDAP laws are generally easier to prove than common law fraud claims because the standards that define the "deceptive," "unfair," "unconscionable," "misleading" or "fraudulent" practices prohibited under these statutes are typically less stringent than the requirements of common law fraud.[73] In most states, for example, a consumer need not prove an intent to deceive, actual deception, or reliance on a misrepresentation.[74] The standard of proof is generally the typical "preponderance of the evidence" rather than "clear and convincing evidence."

Although helpful, UDAP laws are not the answer to predatory lending. These laws vary by state, providing borrowers in some jurisdictions with a lower level of protection against predatory practices, or fewer remedies, than borrowers in other states. Some state UDAP laws offer little to no protection against predatory lending, due to specific exemptions for credit transactions, real estate transactions, financial institutions, or banks,[75] or as a result of preemption by federal laws regulating credit transactions.[76] Other UDAP laws may require consumers to file a complaint with a state agency before a state enforcement action can be initiated,[77] and most lack provisions for punitive damages, significantly diminishing the impact these laws may have on a lender.

In short, state causes of action based on either common law fraud or UDAP laws are useful additions to available federal causes of action, but standing alone will not provide Mary with the protection she needs when confronted with the abuses of a lender like Acme. UDAP coverage is too uneven and unpredictable from state to state, and a fraud claim may well set too high a legal bar for an individual victim lacking experienced legal counsel. Clearly, neither is a proper substitute for comprehensive federal anti-predatory lending legislation.

Recent Efforts at State Law Reform

In recent years, a handful of state legislatures have taken the lead in passing progressive new anti-predatory lending legislation. These efforts reflect both frustration and dissatisfaction with the current federal and state enforcement schemes. North Carolina, New Jersey, New Mexico, California, and New York are among the states that have enacted important laws with wide-ranging protections that in many instances go beyond anything advocates have seen to date. These developments are welcome, for they have thrust state legislatures back into their traditional role as local laboratories for the development of new, experimental remedies and causes of action. For most of these states, the catalyst has been the steep increase in the number of foreclosures and the loss of equity among home owners.[78]

Foremost among these new laws is the legislation enacted in North Carolina. In 1999, North Carolina became the first state to pass anti-predatory lending legislation.[79] Consumer groups and all major financial trade associations in the state endorsed the law, which passed overwhelmingly.[80] The North Carolina law contains a number of key provisions: it prohibits flipping—refinancing a loan without creating a net tangible benefit to the borrower—and the financing of up-front single-premium insurance for all home loans; it prohibits prepayment penalties for home loans of $150,000 or less; and it expands the definition of and the protections for high-cost loans.

The provision dealing with high-cost loans is particularly interesting. Although the statute defines high-cost home loans to include loans where the borrower is charged more than 5 percent in points, fees, or other charges, it defines the covered fees quite broadly, including any prepayment penalty in excess of 1 percent and any fees paid directly by the borrower to the mortgage broker. In addition, any loans with a prepayment penalty longer than 30 months or greater than 2 percent of the amount prepaid are also considered high-cost. Balloon payments, negative amortization, lending without consideration of the borrower's ability to repay, and the financing of up-front fees and insurance premiums are all prohibited for high-cost loans, and counseling is required.[81]

Several years into operation of the new law, the response has been largely positive. Consumer advocates contend that it has put a stop to the worst predatory practices without retarding the growth of the subprime market within the state. Although preliminary research indicated that the law might reduce the availability and increase the price of loans, subsequent research has shown that the law has in fact worked to decrease predatory lending without any negative impact on the availability or price of subprime loans generally.[82] Even the conservative American Enterprise Institute grudgingly concedes that notwithstanding the new law, North Carolina's banking industry has continued to prosper and credit continues to be available in ample and competitive supply.[83]

New Jersey and New York were quick to build upon the North Carolina experience. In 2003, both states passed legislation similar to that enacted in North Carolina. In certain respects, however, the protection offered by the New Jersey and New York laws goes beyond the protections of the North Carolina statute. Both New Jersey and New York define points and fees to include the compensation from a lender to a broker for purposes of determining whether a loan is high-cost.[84] This is important, for it will help to stop the practice of using yield-spread premiums as an end run around more traditional protections. In addition, both laws prohibit high-cost home loan agreement provisions that require borrowers "to assert any claim or defense in a forum that is less convenient, more costly, or more dilatory for resolution than a judicial forum . . . or limits in any way any claim or defense the borrower may have."[85]

Perhaps the most notable provisions of the New Jersey and New Mexico legislation are those on assignee liability. Both statutes strike a careful compromise between the interests of the secondary market and a victim's need for recourse regardless of whether the loan has been sold to a secondary-market purchaser. If a secondary-market participant exercises reasonable due diligence to avoid purchasing high-cost loans (for example, by establishing a policy against such purchases and sampling the pools of loans it purchases to ensure compliance with that policy), then its liability is limited to the amount necessary to extinguish the borrower's liability under the home loan plus costs and attorneys' fees.[86] If, however, a secondary-market player intentionally purchases high-cost home loans, it will be subject to full assignee liability.[87]

As important as these state legislative developments are, they do not constitute a comprehensive solution to the enforcement problem. First, each of these laws is limited in geographic reach and scope. Victims in Pennsylvania, for example, cannot avail themselves of remedies created by North Carolina law. Second, gaps in coverage around the country are profound. Most states have not proved as progressive as New York, New Jersey, New Mexico, and North Carolina. Indeed, most states offer no additional protection beyond local UDAP statutes or existing common law causes of action such as fraud. Third, while experimentation at the state level may produce some excellent local laws, it also breeds inconsistency between states in the nature and type of requirements to which lenders will be subjected. This variation has led many national lenders to throw up their hands and opt for withdrawal from states they deem to be outside the enforcement mainstream. This cannot be a good result from anyone's perspective.

Finally, and most important, state legislation is increasingly subject to preemption by federal regulation or legislation. Recent actions by the Office of the Comptroller of the Currency (OCC) have limited the reach of state anti-predatory lending laws. In August of 2003, the OCC issued an order concluding that federal banking laws and regulations prohibited Georgia from enforcing its anti-predatory lending law against national banks and their subsidiaries.[88] Other states now face a similar obstacle. In early 2004, the OCC promulgated nationwide regulations that preempt the application of many provisions of state anti-predatory lending laws to national banks and their subsidiaries.[89] In addition to the OCC's actions, at least one pending federal bill—the Responsible Lending Act—contains a provision that would broadly preempt state anti-predatory lending law.[90]

DEVELOPING THE COMPONENTS OF MODEL FEDERAL LEGISLATION

For consumer and civil rights advocates, it is clear that the existing patchwork of federal and state law is simply not up to the task of providing meaningful protection for borrowers trapped by abusive lending practices. With subprime lending on the rise, the problem is getting worse, not better. These sentiments are shared by others in both the public and private sectors. In 2000, the Departments of Treasury and Housing and Urban Development convened a task force to study the problem. After meeting with consumer and industry representatives, government officials, and borrowers themselves, the task force concluded that "new legislation and new regulation are both essential components of a coordinated strategy to combat predatory lending," and proposed numerous reforms.[91]

As the government study illustrates, there is a pressing need for new, comprehensive federal legislation that will close the gaps that currently exist within the fractured enforcement scheme, and bring consistent and uniform application to lending markets across the country. The issuance of the HUD-Treasury report has at least started this process. Since the publication of the report, at least four anti-predatory lending bills have been in-troduced in Congress: the Predatory Lending Consumer Protection Act, in-troduced by Sen. Sarbanes and Rep. LaFalce;[92] the Predatory Lending Deterrence Act, introduced by Sen. Schumer;[93] the Save Our Homes Act, introduced by Rep. Schakowsky;[94] and the Responsible Lending Act, in-troduced by Rep. Ney.[95]

The bills vary in scope and strength. Some, like the Predatory Lending Consumer Protection Act, focus on expanding the costs included in the cal-culation of points and fees for high-cost loans, and protecting borrowers with such loans.[96] One bill in particular, the Responsible Lending Act, ap-pears to be at least as concerned with catering to industry demands as pro-tecting the consumer. This bill would narrow the definition of points and fees and roll back many of the disclosure requirements for HOEPA loans. It would also explicitly preempt state legislation that provides additional protection to borrowers. At present, however, none of the pending bills ap-pears likely to pass.

If there is a consensus that new legislation is needed, there is no con-sensus as to what this new legislation should contain. That has been the subject of vigorous debate by advocates and industry and government rep-resentatives over many months. Yet for those truly familiar with the cur-rent regulatory scheme, it is clear that if there is to be a consistent national enforcement framework offering meaningful protection for borrowers, model federal legislation must include provisions that address certain basic issues: preemption; expanded protections for high-cost loans; flipping; mandatory arbitration; procedural issues (such as private rights of action, statutes of limitations, standards of proof, and attorneys' fees); assignee li-ability; and servicing issues. Each of these issues is discussed in turn below.

Preemption

As a preliminary matter, any future federal legislation must address the issue of preemption (the displacement of state law by federal law govern-ing the same issue). Industry representatives often complain about the dif-ficulty of complying with a multitude of state and local lending laws. The current patchwork of predatory lending regulation, however, is the logical outgrowth of the absence of strong federal legislation. Were new federal legislation passed, it would necessarily have some preemptive effect; the real question is its nature and degree. A strong, express preemption provi-sion coupled with weak consumer protections would be especially harmful to borrowers.[97] It would strip states of the ability to develop new and in-novative ways to close the gaps in the federal scheme, but would not pro-vide meaningful federal protection to supplant state experimentation. In short, it would establish a low ceiling for anti-predatory lending compli-ance. It is crucial that a preemption provision not simply serve as a tool for lenders to escape the reach of cutting-edge state laws in the absence of meaningful federal reform.

Balancing the equities on this issue requires a true compromise. Federal legislation must contain enough of the meaningful reforms found in the most progressive of the new state laws to satisfy advocates, but it must at the same time guarantee a uniform floor of protection nationwide. The essence of this compromise will require using a carefully drafted preemption provision to create a national floor consisting of the most important protections, without imposing a federal "ceiling" on the development or implementation of enhanced protections by more progressive state legislatures.

Expanding Protections for High-Cost Loans

As discussed above, HOEPA reaches only a small subset of subprime loans and fails to provide adequate protection to borrowers. Anti-predatory lending legislation should address both of these issues by expanding the definition of covered loans and providing additional protections for such loans.

HOEPA's coverage turns upon the level of the interest rate or points and fees on a given loan. An obvious way to expand the coverage of HOEPA is to reduce the threshold interest rate or amount of points and fees. The current interest rate and fee thresholds permit lenders to charge far more than necessary to cover the additional risk posed by most borrowers without complying with HOEPA.

Some of the legislation that has been proposed sensibly addresses this problem by lowering the interest rate threshold for first mortgages to five or six points above U.S. Treasury rates and lowering the points and fees to three points of the total loan amount.[98] In most circumstances, lenders would likely adjust their interest rates and fees to fall below a lowered HOEPA threshold.

Likewise, HOEPA provisions must be revised to define more broadly the types of costs and fees that are included in the fee threshold. In fact, the latter is more important than the former; if the charging of fees is not addressed, lenders will continue to evade HOEPA by cleverly labeling equity-stripping charges as "fees" not covered by HOEPA. State laws have addressed this issue by defining covered fees to include such charges as yield-spread premiums or any other compensation paid to a broker, prepayment penalties over a percentage point, and all premiums financed by a lender for credit insurance.[99] Ultimately, the effectiveness of a new law will hinge upon the inclusiveness of its definition of fees.

New predatory lending legislation also should provide additional protections for borrowers of high-cost loans. First, lenders should be prohibited from making any asset-based high-cost loans. This can be achieved simply by eliminating HOEPA's "pattern or practice" requirement, which has the effect of protecting lenders who improperly make loans without considering the borrower's ability to repay if the victim lacks the ability to prove widespread abuse. Congress could easily provide additional guidance to lenders on this issue by following North Carolina's lead and enacting a presumption that a borrower has an ability to repay a loan if his total debts are less than 50 percent of his monthly income. This change alone would make it far more likely that someone in Mary's situation would be able to use HOEPA (or a similar provision contained in new federal legislation) to obtain relief from a lender like Acme.

Second, in order to prevent lenders from hiding costly points and fees from the borrower, new legislation should limit the amount of fees that a lender can finance. For example, the Save Our Homes Act would prohibit the financing of points and fees over 3 percent of the loan amount.[100] State laws include similar provisions with even lower thresholds.[101] This limitation protects borrowers from unknowingly agreeing to fees on which they will pay interest for the life of the loan. If the borrower lacks the resources to pay high fees up front, she will not find herself trapped in what would have been a high-cost loan with fees beyond her ability to pay. This provision, too, would have provided enormous help to Mary, who did not realize the kickback her broker was getting, or the points and fees hidden in her loan transaction.

Finally, model legislation should require all borrowers entering into high-cost loans to take part in home ownership or credit counseling, a practice that some responsible lenders already require.[102] These borrowers, like Mary, often do not fully understand the actual terms and conditions of their loans. Credit counseling by a HUD-approved counselor ensures that borrowers entering into potentially abusive loans have an educated, neutral evaluator advising them whether the loan is appropriate for them.

Anti-Flipping Provisions

Lowering the threshold definition for high-cost loans would be meaningless without a strong prohibition against loan flipping. "Flipping" refers to the practice of encouraging unnecessary refinancings in order to recoup added fees and inflate the overall loan amount, often achieved by locking borrowers into a balloon or adjustable-rate mortgage or by offering to lower monthly payments. In the end, redundant fees and costs are added to the monthly statement, and borrowers lose equity in their homes.

Although HOEPA contains some prohibitions against flipping, a truly effective anti-flipping provision must apply to all loans.[103] Otherwise, a lender can circumvent the law by repeatedly refinancing a loan with fees just below the HOEPA threshold. A lender who has twice recouped fees of, for example, 4.99 percent can strip virtually as much equity from a borrower's home as a lender who has charged 10 percent in fees. Legislation permitting such a practice would be of little use to consumers.

The most difficult problem posed by this provision is determining how to protect borrowers from equity-stripping practices without limiting legitimate refinance options. North Carolina and a handful of other states have met this challenge by enacting a "reasonable tangible net benefit" standard. Under this approach, a lender is deemed to have engaged in illegal flipping if it makes a loan that does not provide a reasonable tangible net benefit to the borrower, given the circumstances of the loan.[104]

Model legislation must provide specific examples of circumstances under which flipping would be presumed. Under New Jersey law, for example, a loan is presumed "flipped" if (1) the primary tangible benefit is a lower interest rate and it will take more than four years for the borrower to recoup the cost of the points, fees, and other closing costs through savings resulting from the lower interest rate, or (2) the new loan refinances an existing special mortgage originated or subsidized by a government agency or nonprofit organization, and the borrower will lose one or more of the benefits of the special mortgage as a result of the refinance.[105] Like the New Jersey law, federal legislation would also need to make clear that any list of presumed flipping conduct is not exclusive.

In our hypothetical, of course, Acme did not "flip" the property in this sense—it resold the property for financial gain after forcing a foreclosure. But Acme could easily have attempted to "flip" in the manner contemplated here by forcing Mary to refinance to avoid foreclosure. This provision would protect her against exactly this type of abuse.

Using the New Jersey approach is certainly not the only way to differentiate between legitimate and predatory refinancing, but it has proven workable for lenders and borrowers in practice at the state level. Model legislation and/or accompanying regulation would likely need to further elucidate this standard to ensure that lenders have proper guidance.

Mandatory Arbitration

At the core of the congressional debate over recent legislative efforts has been the issue of mandatory arbitration. Anxious to limit the financial risk that may come with a court proceeding and jury trial, some in the lending industry have pushed for a provision in the new legislation that would preclude victims from seeking relief in court and require them instead to go to binding arbitration.

From the borrower's perspective, mandatory arbitration is problematic. Binding arbitration forces a borrower into a forum that is potentially more costly, limits the relief available, and retains an institutional bias toward the lender, who is often a repeat player. At the time of closing, most borrowers are concerned with the terms of the loan itself, and do not know whether they are agreeing to a mandatory arbitration clause. Like Mary, many borrowers are unfamiliar with their basic legal rights and do not understand the possible difference between a judicial and an arbitral forum. They do not realize that arbitration may cost more, that it may limit their discovery rights, and that an arbitrator chosen by the lender may be biased in the lender's favor. For a lender to mandate that a borrower agree to a certain type of dispute resolution as a condition of the loan raises concerns about fundamental fairness to the borrower. Mandatory arbitration clauses may also run afoul of the public interest. Unlike court proceedings, which are typically open and accessible to the public, arbitrations are frequently confidential. Requiring that all allegations of wrongdoing be heard in a confidential forum may allow a lender to hide systemic abuses. Secrecy also hinders private enforcement efforts, making it even more difficult for a borrower to prove a pattern and practice under HOEPA, to bring a class action, or to establish or rely on a decision against a lender.[106]

Of course, a borrower and a lender are always free to agree voluntarily to enter arbitration or some other form of out-of-court dispute resolution in order to resolve their differences. But that is very different from a requirement that a borrower forgo his right to a judicial forum at the time he agrees to a loan. Although federal legislation need not discourage alternative dispute resolution generally, it should prohibit mandatory arbitration clauses in loan agreements.[107]

Private Rights of Action, Statute of Limitations, and Remedies

Procedural protections must not be forgotten amid the debate over the substantive protections to include in the new legislation. Four procedural issues are of paramount importance. First, federal legislation should expressly codify the "continuing violations" and "discovery" theories applied by many courts in determining the timeliness of claims. Victims like Mary often do not know they have been taken advantage of until long after the time for filing a claim has run out. Given the inequities in bargaining power that inherently exist when unscrupulous lenders negotiate with uneducated borrowers, many courts have decided to start the statute of limitations clock running when the victim learned of the abusive practice, not when it actually occurred. Other courts, particularly in the discrimination context, have held that where there is a "continuing" pattern of violations involving more than one person, and at least one illegal act occurred in the limitations period, the statute of limitations may be extended back in time to cover all of the wrongdoing, even if it covers a period of time that is longer than the statute of limitations itself. Both of these theories would protect someone like Mary, who may have been part of a larger pattern of wrongdoing by Acme and who did not know the manner in which she had been cheated at the time it occurred.

Second, federal legislation should make clear that the standard of proof for establishing a violation of the new law is the same as that used in most civil litigation—proof by preponderance of the evidence. This is the standard applied in the discrimination context. If the new law expressly authorizes suit under existing civil rights statutes to challenge the practices of predatory lenders who target minority communities, it should also make clear that the well established standards of proof and burden-shifting framework used under those laws should continue to apply.

Likewise, the new legislation must contain provisions expressly authorizing the recovery of compensatory and punitive damages, and giving victims the right to a jury trial. As we have seen, the current regulatory scheme offers a confusing patchwork of remedies. It is critical that federal legislation provide a right to damages without caps and a trial by one's peers that applies everywhere—without regard to the geographic location of the forum or the statute invoked. Mary should not have to find an attorney skilled in statute- and forum-shopping in order to win full relief from Acme.

Fourth and finally, federal legislation must codify a victim's right to file a private action, without requiring the "exhaustion" of certain preliminary steps, such as the filing of an initial complaint with an administrative or governmental agency. State and federal enforcement actions are important and, where undertaken, they have had an important deterrent effect. But they cannot meet the rising need for relief that currently exists. Equally important, the private right of action must also contain a provision allowing a prevailing plaintiff to recover reasonable attorneys' fees. Civil rights statutes have proved that awarding reasonable fees to a prevailing plaintiff sends the right message to both sides: for those with a meritorious case, an attorney will be available; for those who have committed a wrong, beware—the costs will include the plaintiff's fees.

Assignee Liability

Because mortgages often are sold on the secondary market, an assignee liability provision is necessary to ensure, on the one hand, that borrowers are not locked into predatory loans and have recourse to defend against foreclosure, and on the other hand, that secondary-market participants can assess with some measure of certainty their exposure on a given loan or pool of loans.

Model federal legislation can and should balance these competing interests by enacting an assignee liability provision similar to that found in the New Jersey and New Mexico statutes. Such a provision would contain two key components. First, it would ensure that borrowers have a right of action against a secondary-market participant that, at a minimum, would allow the borrower to extinguish his liability under a predatory loan and protect his home from foreclosure. Second, it would provide a strong incentive to secondary-market participants to engage in due diligence to avoid purchasing predatory loans, by limiting the liability for purchasers who have done so and subjecting those who have not, to the same liability as a loan originator. This type of provision would fairly punish those purchasers who recklessly continue to provide the capital necessary for predatory lenders to profit from their activities, while limiting liability for secondary-market players who purchase loans responsibly.

For Mary, this would simply mean that were Acme to sell her loan on the secondary market, she would have some additional measure of protection from foreclosure and exorbitant fees. And to the extent Acme relied on secondary-market capital to engage in its abusive practices, this provision would increase the chance that funding for Acme would be cut off at its source.

Servicing Issues

Abuses perpetrated by predatory lenders can be compounded by the actions of aggressive loan servicers. In recent months, the conduct of one loan servicer, Fairbanks Capital Corp., has made headlines. Fairbanks recently settled lawsuits brought by the FTC, HUD, and private plaintiffs alleging that the company locked borrowers into inappropriate loans or accelerating foreclosure by routinely counting on-time payments as late in order to impose penalties, "force-placing" hazard insurance on borrowers' homes at a cost well above market rates even though the homes already had insurance coverage, and threatening borrowers with rapid foreclosure unless they paid substantial fees.

The facts appeared to support the claims against Fairbanks. Of its 600,000 customers, Fairbanks listed 200,000 as at least two payments behind on their foreclosure and was in the process of foreclosing on 45,000. After initially denying the claims against it, Fairbanks entered into preliminary agreements with HUD and the FTC, as well as with private plaintiffs, that required it to change its practices, pay $40 million to a consumer redress fund, and reverse or reimburse certain charges on borrower accounts.[108]

As illustrated by the allegations against Fairbanks, loan servicers may engage in various types of abusive practices. One of the most abusive is the charging of unauthorized fees, including fees that are clearly not owed, fees that are inflated and bear no relation to the service provided, and hidden fees that seem to exist only to prevent the borrower from becoming timely on the account. Such fees may include payment for the servicer's overhead expenses, and pyramid late fees (late fees on unpaid late fees).

Another abusive practice is the "force-placing" of insurance even when the borrower already has insurance, as alleged in *Fairbanks*. Lenders commonly require that borrowers insure the homes that secure their mortgages. If a borrower does not have homeowners insurance, a lender may "force-place" such insurance (purchase the insurance and charge the borrower for it). Typically, such insurance is more expensive and offers less coverage than insurance purchased directly by the homeowner. The practice of force-placing insurance becomes abusive when the cost of insurance is unreasonably high and/or the consumer is not given a sufficient opportunity to prove that the home is insured.

Even servicing practices that are not intentionally deceptive or fraudulent may be harmful to borrowers. One example is the reporting of negative, but not positive, payment information. Servicers who engage in this practice unfairly lock a borrower into higher-priced subprime loans. The reason for this is straightforward. Most subprime borrowers end up in the subprime market because they have blemished credit. Credit ratings are not static, however. Subprime borrowers can improve their credit rating by making timely payments, and improved credit may result in the ability to refinance a subprime loan on more favorable terms. Unscrupulous servicers seek to profit from the more expensive subprime loan as long as possible by not reporting the borrower's timely payments. Under those circumstances, the borrower appears to be a greater credit risk than he actually is, and is precluded from refinancing on more favorable terms.

Many of these practices were used by Acme to take advantage of a borrower like Mary. All of these practices can and should be addressed through legislation. In order to be effective, federal legislation not only must prohibit specific abusive servicing practices, but also must require affirmative steps to prevent unjustified foreclosure or unjustifiably unfavorable loan terms. For example, servicers should be required by statute to post borrower payments in a timely manner, accept partial payments, report full payment information to credit bureaus every month, and clearly notify borrowers of the payments due and how they can dispute charges. The legislation must also contain express safeguards against unjustified foreclosure, such as protection from foreclosure for failure to make a payment for which there is a pending dispute, or for failure to pay fees and costs extraneous to the principal and interest charge.

CONCLUSION

Advocates on all sides of the issue agree on one thing: the time has come to pass new federal legislation aimed at curbing predatory lending practices. Subprime lending is growing at an exponential rate, and with it the potential for abuse of unsuspecting borrowers who have little experience with credit and financial institutions. Abusive practices hurt responsible lenders and borrowers alike. Closing the gaps in the current regulatory framework is essential if we, as a nation, are to ensure that capital will find its way to neighborhoods and communities that are desperately struggling to create better housing, businesses, schools, and jobs for their residents.

This chapter has attempted to provide an overview of existing laws and regulations in an effort to identify where the current patchwork falls short.

Protections vary widely by state and by statute. Some federal and state laws focus narrowly on particular issues but lack breadth and meaningful remedies; others, like the Fair Housing Act, contain powerful remedies but require considerable legal knowledge and resources to marshal the necessary evidence and prevail in court. All of these laws offer something to our prototypical borrower Mary, but no single statute gives her the full protection that she needs when faced with a predatory lender like Acme.

Not every component of the proposed model legislation discussed in this chapter need be enacted for borrowers like Mary to begin to see a difference in their lives. But it is vitally important that politicians, advocates, and the industry find a way to reach common ground on this important issue. Ultimately, the protection Congress affords will be only as good as the legal rights and remedies afforded to victims of abusive practices.

Our federalist system has done its job well, allowing state legislatures to experiment with a variety of new protections. Now the time has come for the hard part—meshing the progress that has been made at the local level with the best of the existing federal statutory scheme. Forging a consensus will not be easy, but it must be done. The current system leaves responsible primary lenders and secondary-market players at risk, and innocent borrowers without proper recourse. The starting point, of course, is understanding what protections we have, and where they fall short. That is what we have tried to do here. Only in that context can one begin to assess the provisions that model legislation must contain if it is to put a stop to the abuses that all agree must end.

NOTES

1. U.S. Department of Housing and Urban Development and U.S. Department of the Treasury, "Curbing Predatory Home Mortgage Lending," http://www.huduser.org/publications/hsgfin/curbing.html (2000).

2. Many borrowers in the subprime market should not be there. For example, a 1996 study by Freddie Mac showed that between 10 percent and 35 percent of all subprime borrowers actually qualified for conventional loans. Freddie Mac, "Automated Underwriting: Making Mortgage Lending Simpler and Fairer for America's Families," www.freddiemac.com/corporate/reports (1996), ch. 5. Moreover, subprime borrowers, particularly minorities and the elderly, are commonly steered to overpriced products.

3. Truth in Lending Act, 15 U.S.C. 1601ff. (2004).

4. 15 U.S.C. 1601(a).

5. 15 U.S.C. 1602; 12 C.F.R. 226.2.

6. 12 C.F.R. 226.1(c). If a credit card is the vehicle for extending credit, certain provisions of TILA apply even if the credit is not subject to a finance charge or is not payable by written agreement in four or more installments. 12 C.F.R. 226.1(c)(2).

7. 12 C.F.R. 226.22(a)(1) (closed-end credit); 12 C.F.R. 226.14(a) (open-ended credit).

8. 12 C.F.R. 226.4(a).

9. 12 C.F.R. 226.4(c)(7).

10. 12 C.F.R 226.4(d)(1).

11. See 15 U.S.C. 1635; 12 C.F.R. 226.15 (open-end credit); 12 C.F.R. 226.23 (closed-end credit).

12. U.S. Department of Housing and Urban Development and U.S. Department of the Treasury, "Curbing Predatory Home Mortgage Lending," p. 67.

13. 15 U.S.C. 1640(a).

14. See *Perrone v. Gen. Motors Acceptance Corp.*, 232 F. 3d 433, 435–36 (5th Cir. 2000); *Anderson v. Rizza Chevrolet, Inc.*, 9 F. Supp. 2d 908, 913 (N.D. Ill. 1998).

15. See *In re Russell*, 72 B.R. 855, 864 (E.D. Pa. 1987).

16. Statutory damages are available even if no actual damages exist—*Baker v. G.C. Servs. Corp.*, 677 F. 2d 775, 781 (9th Cir. 1982), but are limited to $2,000 in transactions secured by real estate and $1,000 for other transactions. 15 U.S.C. 1640(a)(2)(A). Thus, as with actual damages, little financial incentive exists to pursue this remedy.

17. Home Ownership and Equity Protection Act of 1994, subtitle B of Title 1 of the Riegle Community Development and Regulatory Improvement Act, P.L. no. 103-325 (codified as amended to the Truth in Lending Act, at 15 U.S.C. 1601ff. (1994)). Testimony provided during the Senate hearings on HOEPA illustrates the abuses that the Act was intended to cover. For example, in considering HOEPA, the Banking Committee heard from Eva Davis, a 72-year-old home owner contacted at her home by a "home improvement contractor" who advised her of the many problems she purportedly had with her home. The contractor offered to fix the problems and finance the costs of the repairs. By the end of the day, Ms. Davis had agreed to sign a contract to finance $150,000 worth of repairs through a second mortgage and to pay a "prepaid finance charge" of almost $25,000. The monthly payment amount on the loan exceeded Ms. Davis' monthly income. *Hearings Before the Senate Comm. on HOEPA*, Senate Report no. 103–169 (1994), 22.

18. Ibid.; see also 12 C.F.R. 226.32(a)(1).

19. See 12 C.F.R. 226.32(a)(i).

20. 15 U.S.C. 1639(c)–(h).

21. 15 U.S.C. 1639(a)(2).

22. 15 U.S.C. 1639(h).

23. 15 U.S.C. 1602(f).

24. 15 U.S.C. 1640(a).

25. See U.S. Department of Housing and Urban Development and U.S. Department of the Treasury,"Curbing Predatory Home Mortgage Lending," p. 85.

26. See generally Real Estate Settlement Procedures Act, 12 U.S.C. 2601–2617 (2003).

27. 12 U.S.C. 2602(1) (defining "federally related mortgage loan").

28. 12 U.S.C. 2603–2604; 24 C.F.R. 3500.6–3500.7 (2004).

29. 12 U.S.C. 2607.

30. 12 U.S.C. 2605.

31. 12 U.S.C. 2605, 2609.

32. 42 U.S.C. 3601ff. (2003) (FHA); 15 U.S.C. 1691 (2003) (ECOA). See, e.g., *Matthews v. New Century Mortgage Corp.*, 185 F. Supp. 2d 874, 887 (S.D. Ohio 2002); *Eva v. Midwest Nat'l Mortgage Bank*, 143 F. Supp. 2d 862, 880–86 (N.D.

Ohio 2001); *Hargraves v. Capital City Mortgage Corp.*, 140 F. Supp. 2d 7, 20–23 (D.D.C. 2000).

33. 42 U.S.C. 3613(c)(1)–(2) (FHA); 15 U.S.C. 1691e(a)–(d) (ECOA).

34. See 42 U.S.C. 3613(a)(1)(A) (two years to bring civil action); see also 42 U.S.C. 3613(a)(1)(B) (filing of 3610 complaint with HUD tolls two-year limitations period).

35. *Curtis v. Loether*, 415 U.S. 187, 192–195 (1974).

36. Ràckeeteer Influenced and Corrupt Organizations Act, 18 U.S.C. 1961ff. (2004).

37. 18 U.S.C. 1962(c).

38. See, e.g., *Emery v. American Gen. Fin., Inc.*, 71 F. 3d 1343 (7th Cir. 1995); *Eva v. Midwest Nat'l Mortgage Bank*, 143 F. Supp. 2d 862 (N.D. Ohio 2001); *Hargraves*, 140 F. Supp. 2d 7.

39. 18 U.S.C. 1964(c).

40. 18 U.S.C. 1962(d).

41. See Kathleen C. Engel and Patricia A. McCoy, "A Tale of Three Markets: The Law and Economics of Predatory Lending," *Texas Law Review* 80 (2002): 1309 n.199.

42. *Id.; see infra* section III. A.

43. See Engel and McCoy, "A Tale of Three Markets." But see, e.g., *Hargraves*, 140 F. Supp. 2d at 24–26 (holding that plaintiffs properly alleged enterprise made up of mortgage company, its president, and "runners" who identified, targeted, and induced borrowers to sign predatory loan documents).

44. Compare *Religious Tech.Ctr. v. Wollersheim*, 796 F. 2d 1076, 1081–89 (9th Cir. 1986) (holding that injunctive relief is not available under RICO) with *Nat'l. Org. for Women, Inc. v. Scheidler*, 267 F. 3d 687, 695–96 (7th Cir. 2001) (holding that RICO authorizes injunctive relief), *rev'd on other grounds*, 537 U.S. 393 (2003).

45. A second problem lies in the manner in which courts have defined the term "enterprise." Although RICO imposes liability on persons or entities that use an enterprise to conduct a pattern of racketeering activity, the enterprise itself is not liable under the statute. Thus, although a lender may be liable as part of an enterprise, it cannot be held accountable under RICO when it constitutes the enterprise itself.

46. 15 U.S.C. 45 (2004).

47. 15 U.S.C. 45(n).

48. See, e.g., *F.T.C. v. Gill*, 265 F. 3d 944, 950 (9th Cir. 2001); *F.T.C. v. World Travel Vacation Brokers, Inc.*, 861 F. 2d 1020, 1029 (7th Cir. 1988).

49. 15 U.S.C. 45(a)(2).

50. 15 U.S.C. 45(b), 57(b). The FTC Act also authorizes the FTC to enforce its final orders by requesting a federal court to assess a civil penalty up to $10,000 for each violation of a final order. Ibid., 45(l).

51. 15 U.S.C. 45(m)(1)(B).

52. 15 U.S.C. 53(b).

53. See, e.g., *FTC v. Pantron I Corp.*, 33 F. 3d 1088, 1102 (9th Cir. 1994); *FTC v. Elders Grain, Inc.*, 868 F. 2d 901, 907 (7th Cir. 1989).

54. See, e.g., FTC, press release, "Subprime Loan Victims to Receive Additional Redress" (February 2, 2004) ($65 million consumer redress fund obtained in court-approved settlement of action against First Alliance Mortgage Company and its CEO), http://www.ftc.gov/opa/2004/02/first.htm; FTC, press release, "Home Mort-

gage Lender Settles 'Predatory Lending' Charges" (March 21, 2002) (detailing injunctive and monetary relief obtained in settlement of action against First Alliance Mortgage Company and its CEO), http://www.ftc.gov/opa/2002/03/famco.htm; FTC, press release, "Citigroup Settles FTC Charges Against the Associates" (September 19, 2004) (announcing $215 million settlement of FTC claims against Associates First Capital Corporation and Associates Corporation of North America, companies acquired by Citigroup, Inc.), http://www.ftc.gov/opa/2002/09/associates.htm; FTC, press release, "Fairbanks Capital Settles FTC and HUD Charges" (November 12, 2003) (announcing $40 million settlement of FTC claims against Fairbanks Capital Holding Corp. and Fairbanks Capital Corp.), http://www.ftc.gov/opa/2003/11/fairbanks.htm.

55. See "Letter from Fannie Mae to Lenders, Eligibility of Mortgages to Borrowers with Blemished Credit Records" (April 11, 2000), http://www.efanniemae.com/singlefamily/forms_guidelines/lender_letters/db_lender_letters.jhtml#03-00.

56. In addition, Fannie Mae will not purchase loans that are subject to HOEPA requirements applicable to "high-cost" loans. Ibid.

57. See "Industry Letter from Freddie Mac to All Freddie Mac Sellers and Servicers" (December 28, 2000), http://www.freddiemac.com/sell/guide/bulletins/pdf/1228indltr.pdf.

58. In addition to credit life insurance, Freddie Mac's guidelines provide that it will not purchase a mortgage if the borrower obtained a prepaid single-premium credit disability, credit unemployment, or credit property insurance policy in connection with the origination of the mortgage.

59. See Freddie Mac, press release, "Freddie Mac Will No Longer Invest in Subprime Mortgages with Prepayment Penalty Terms Greater Than Three Years" (March 1, 2002), www.freddiemac.com/news/archives2002/subprime_030102.html.

60. See Freddie Mac, press release, "Freddie Mac Promotes Consumer Choice with New Subprime Mortgage Arbitration Policy" (December 4, 2003), www.freddiemac.com/news/archives/afford_housing/2003/consumer_120403.html.

61. See Fannie Mae, "Expanding the American Dream Commitment: Making Homeownership and Rental Housing a Success for Millions of Families at Risk of Losing Their Homes" (2004), www.fanniemae.com/initiatives/pdf/adc/background.pdf; Associated Press, "Fannie Mae Stops Investing in Mortgages That Force Borrowers to Give Up Right to Sue," (February 4, 2004) http://www.predatorylending.org/news_headlines/fanniemae020404.cfm.

62. See, e.g., Fed. R. Civ. P. 9(b); *Hargraves*, 140 F. Supp. 2d at 27.

63. See, e.g., *McCormick on Evidence*, 959–61 (3rd ed. 1984); *Hargraves*, 140 F. Supp. 2d at 27. A common law fraud claim for punitive damages also must be proven by clear and convincing evidence. See 3 American Trial Lawyers' Association, *Litigating Tort Cases* 28:46 (2003).

64. *Restatement (Second) of Torts*, 525–545A (1977); National Consumer Law Center, *Unfair and Deceptive Acts and Practices*, 4.2.12.1 (5th ed. 2001, and supp. 2003). See, e.g., *Banks v. Consumer Home Mortgage, Inc.*, no. 01-CV-8508, 2003 WL 21251584, at *4 (E.D.N.Y. March 28, 2003); *Hargraves*, 140 F. Supp. 2d at 27.

65. See Engel and McCoy, "A Tale of Three Markets," p. 1302.

66. Ibid.

67. See National Consumer Law Center, *Unfair and Deceptive Acts and Practices*, 7.2.

68. Ibid., 10.7.

69. See ibid., 8.6.2.

70. Ibid., 8.4.2.1.

71. Ibid., 8.4.3.1.

72. Ibid., 8.8.1.

73. See ibid., 4.2.3.1.

74. Ibid., 4.2.3–4.2.9, 4.2.12.3, 4.3.3, 4.4.

75. Ibid., 2.2.1.

76. Ibid., 2.2.1.6.

77. Ibid., 2.3.3.6.

78. See, e.g., N.J. Stat. Ann. 46:10B–23 (2003); N.M. Stat. Ann. 58-21A-2 (2003).

79. See generally N.C. Gen. Stat. 24-1.1A ff. (2004).

80. Coalition for Responsible Lending, "Summary of NC Predatory Lending Law" (2002), http://www.responsiblelending.org/pdfs/shortsumm.pdf.

81. N.C. Gen. Stat. 24.1.1E(b)–(c).

82. Compare Roberto G. Quercia, Michael A. Stegman, and Walter R. Davis, *The Impact of North Carolina's Anti–Predatory Lending Law: A Descriptive Assessment* (Chapel Hill: Center for Community Capitalism, University of North Carolina, 2003) with Gregory Elliehausen and Michael Staten, "Regulation of Subprime Mortgage Products: An Analysis of North Carolina's Predatory Lending Law," Credit Research Center Working Paper (Washington, D.C.: Georgetown University, November 2002).

83. Michael S. Greve, "Subprime but Not Half-Bad: Mortgage Regulation as a Case Study in Preemption," *Federalist Outlook* (September 1, 2003), http://www.aei.org/publications/pubID.19271,filter./pub_detail.asp. The experience in North Carolina differs considerably from that of Georgia. In Georgia, the legislature passed a law that allowed for wide-reaching assignee liability, which created an outcry in the lending industry. Freddie Mac announced it would not purchase loans covered by the law, many lenders pulled out of the state, and three major credit agencies stated that they would not rate pools of mortgages that included loans from Georgia. The legislature subsequently amended the law, significantly reducing the potential liability of lenders. See "Georgia Measure Weakens Lending Law," *New York Times*, March 7, 2003, p. C6.

84. See N.J. Stat. Ann. 46:10B-24; N.M. Stat. Ann. 58-21A-3(K)(2).

85. N.J. Stat. Ann. 46:10B-26(e); N.M. Stat. Ann. 58-21A-5(F).

86. See N.J. Stat. Ann. 46:10B-27; N.M. Stat. Ann. 58-21A-11.

87. Ibid.

88. Department of the Treasury, Office of the Comptroller of the Currency, Preemption Determination and Order, 68 *Federal Register* 46,264 (August 5, 2003).

89. See 12 C.F.R. 34.4.

90. Responsible Lending Act, H.R. 833, 104(f)(1), 108th Congress (2003).

91. U.S. Department of Housing and Urban Development and U.S. Department of the Treasury, "Curbing Predatory Home Mortgage Lending," pp. 3–12.

92. Predatory Lending Consumer Protection Act, S. 2438, 107th Congress (2002); H.R. 1051, 107th Congress (2001).

93. Predatory Lending Deterrence Act, S. 2405, 106th Congress (2000).

94. Save Our Homes Act, H.R. 2531, 107th Congress (2001).

95. Responsible Lending Act, H.R. 833, 108th Congress (2003).

96. Predatory Lending Consumer Protection Act, S. 2438, 2(b); see also Predatory Lending Deterrence Act, S. 2405, 5 106th Congress (2000); Save Our Homes Act, H.R. 2531, 3(b)–(c), 107th Congress (2001).

97. See, e.g., Responsible Lending Act, H.R. 833, 104(a).

98. See Save Our Homes Act, H.R. 2531, 3(a) (proposing interest rate threshold of five points above Treasury rate, points and fees threshold of three points or $1,000); Predatory Lending Consumer Protection Act, S. 2438, 2(a) (2002) (proposing interest rate threshold of six points above Treasury rate).

99. See N.J. Stat. Ann. 46:10B-24; N.M. Stat. Ann. 58-21A-3(K); N.C. Gen. Stat. 24-1.1E(a)(5)–(6); see also Save Our Homes Act, H.R. 2531, 3(b); Predatory Lending Consumer Protection Act, S. 2438, 2(b). Several of the cited laws prohibit single-premium credit insurance altogether. See, e.g., N.J. Stat. Ann. 46:10B-25(a); N.M. Stat. Ann. 58-21A-4(a). Given that such insurance virtually always strips equity and could as easily be provided on a month-by-month basis, federal legislation should also include such a prohibition.

100. See Save Our Homes Act, H.R. 2531, 3(a), 107th Cong. (2001).

101. See, e.g., N.C. Gen. Stat. 24-1.1E(c)(3); N.M. Stat. Ann. 58-21A-5(A).

102. See, e.g., Save Our Homes Act, H.R. 2531, 3(a), 107th Cong. (2001); N.C. Gen. Stat. 24.1.1E(c) (1); N.J. Stat. Ann. 46:10B-26(g); N.M. Stat. Ann. 58-21A-5(G).

103. See, e.g., N.C. Gen. Stat. 24-10.2(a).

104. N.C. Gen. Stat. 24-10.2(c). In order to have a record of the circumstances of the loan, lenders would need to document the borrower's reasons for refinancing at the time the loan was made.

105. N.J. Stat. Ann. 46:10B-25(b).

106. See Kurt Eggert, "Held Up in Due Course: Predatory Lending, Securitization, and the Holder in Due Course Doctrine," *Creighton Law Review* 35 (2002): 598–99.

107. See Save Our Homes Act, H.R. 2531, 3(d); Predatory Lending Consumer Protection Act, S. 2438, 4(g).

108. FTC, "Fairbanks Capital Settles FTC and HUD Charges"; FTC "The FTC/HUD Settlement with Fairbanks Capital Corp., Frequently Asked Questions," http://www.ftc.gov/bcp/conline/edcams/fairbanks/faq.pdf. See Order Preliminarily Approving Stipulated Final Judgment and Order as to Fairbanks Capital Corp. and Fairbanks Capital Holding Corp., *United States v. Fairbanks Capital Corp.*, no. 03-12219 (D. Mass., November 21, 2003), http://www.ftc.gov/os/2003/11/0323014order.pdf; Settlement Agreement and Release, *Curry v. Fairbanks Capital Corp.*, no. 03-10895 (D. Mass., November 14, 2003), http://www.ftc.gov/bcp/conline/edcams/fairbanks/classact_agrmt.pdf. See also Kenneth R. Harney, "Mortgage Firm's Clients Tell Many Horror Stories," *Washington Post*, May 3, 2003, p. F1. The settlement agreements received preliminary approval from the court, and final approval was pending at press time.

8

Predatory Lending Goes Global: Consumer Protection in a Deregulation Network Economy

Matthew Lee

If the biggest names in finance—Citigroup, HSBC, General Electric, and AIG—have been engaged in predatory lending in the United States, there's a need for an inquiry into their behavior in less regulated economies internationally.

An inescapable trend in this new millennium is the export of subprime lending models beyond the United States. Citigroup, following its acquisition of Associates First Capital Corporation in late 2000, began offering subprime loans to lower-income consumers in countries from Brazil and Mexico to India and Korea. The Hong Kong Shanghai Banking Corporation (HSBC) bought Household International a month after Household settled predatory lending charges with attorneys general in 42 states for half a billion dollars. In making the deal, HSBC chairman Sir John Bond said that the profits would come from exporting Household's model to the 81 other countries in which HSBC does business;[1] a month later, HSBC announced it would compete in subprime lending with Citigroup in Brazil.

From Australia through North America and back to Eastern Europe, General Electric, through its GE Capital unit, has developed a subprime lending capacity on which the sun never sets. The insurance company AIG has more quietly taken the subprime lending model of American General, which AIG bought in 2001, to the other countries in which AIG does business.

This consensus on high-rate lending in emerging markets by the world's largest bank (Citigroup), insurer (AIG), and corporation (GE) is indicative of the way corporate interests are currently outstripping (or outracing) regulation and the public interest. The lenders and their strategies are global, but the laws are at most national, and in some cases state-, county-, or merely citywide. In the absence of meaningful regulation, lenders like Citigroup and Household view settlement agreements as a cost of doing business. Both have announced unilateral "best practices" commitments that are applicable by their terms only in the United States (or only in the geographic footprint of the consumer organizations with which they make the announcements). In the short term, there is a need to combat this race to the bottom, similar to anti-sweatshop campaigns and environmental advocacy. In the longer term, there is a need for meaningful global regulation, from a consumer and community point of view, of these emerging global lenders.

Related to this inquiry is the view that predatory lending is not *only* a consumer protection and financial soundness issue—it is also a human rights issue. This argument holds that various nations' signing of, for example, the International Covenant on Economic, Social and Cultural Rights (ICESCR) and the International Convention on the Elimination of All Forms of Racial Discrimination (ICERD) require inquiry into and action on the predatory lending that exists in, and is being exported into, their countries. Article 2(1)(d) of the ICERD, for example, requires that "[e]ach state party shall prohibit and bring to an end by all appropriate means, including legislation as required by the circumstances, racial discrimination by any person, group or organization." As explored below, and elsewhere, this may be one avenue to pursue accountability in global high-rate subprime lending.

First, however, it is important to inquire into how—and where, and at what interest rates—global lenders exported predatory lending in the initial years of the twenty-first century.

SUBPRIME GOES GLOBAL

Citigroup has been the leader with this strategy. In acquiring Associates First Capital Corporation in 2000, Citigroup emphasized that the attraction was not only Associates' subprime lending operations in the United States—according to the *Financial Times*, "[t]he other principal attraction for Citigroup is Associates' strong presence in Japan, where it can now go head to head with U.S. competitors such as GE Capital."[2]

Citigroup and its predecessors were engaged in controversial subprime lending well before the acquisition of Associates in 2000. The upper echelon of management at Citigroup—Sandy Weill, Charles Prince, Bob Willumstad, et al.—had all been active with the Baltimore-based subprime lender Commercial Credit, which was challenged for predatory lending in 1997 when it applied to acquire additional subprime business from Bank of America[3] and for a federal savings bank charter.[4] Based on the protests, filed by Inner City Press/Community on the Move (ICP) and the Delaware Community Reinvestment Action Council, the Office of Thrift Supervision agreed to expand its scrutiny of this subprime savings bank nationwide, beyond its Delaware headquarters.[5] After the 1998 merger with Citicorp—

in connection with which, Charles Prince was cross-examined about Commercial Credit's lending practices[6]—Commercial Credit was renamed CitiFinancial; this name was retained and imposed on the controversial Associates business, acquired in late 2000 and then taken global.

By early 2001, it was reported that "Citigroup, the world's largest financial services provider, began its Indian operations with the launch of CitiFinancial Retail Services India Limited. To begin with CitiFinancial will offer easy financing schemes, at retail outlets for the purchase of consumer durable, PC and two wheelers."[7]

As with other things at Citigroup, the global expansion of the subprime CitiFinancial was not piecemeal, but fully strategized and inexorable. Soon after buying the second-largest bank in Mexico, in a transaction that was widely protested,[8] Citigroup formed what it called a Consumer Products Unit For Emerging Markets, saying that "the new unit would accelerate the expansion of non-banking consumer financial services into the emerging markets."[9] This press release indicated how and where CitiFinancial was going, by contrasting the fact that "Citibank has consumer-banking operations in 36 of its 80 emerging market countries" with the fact that "[i]n the Emerging Markets Citigroup today has consumer finance businesses in 8 countries with assets of $2.5 billion." And so, onward!

A major emerging market targeted by CitiFinancial is Brazil. Charging interest rates up to 40 percent, CitiFinancial in early 2003 opened nine offices in Brazil, projecting that it would open 100 more branches over the next five years.[10] Regarding this expansion, CitiFinancial Mortgage Senior Vice President L. Ramesh has been quoted that "[i]n several markets, we are the first ones to give them consumer credit. . . . [We ask:] 'Where do you live? What kind of stuff do you have?' "[11]

Inquiring "what kind of stuff do you have?" is reminiscent of CitiFinancial's inquiries with its U.S. personal loan customers, in order to sell them credit insurance they may not need. ICP documented this practice to the Federal Reserve Board and asked Citigroup CEO Sandy Weill about it at the company's April 2002 annual meeting; the *Wall Street Journal* finally got, and reported, Citigroup's answer:

When it makes a personal loan, CitiFinancial often asks the holders of personal loans to provide collateral. In some cases, according to CitiFinancial documents filed by Inner City Press, that collateral includes fishing lures and tackle boxes, record albums, tents, sleeping bags and lanterns—items that CitiFinancial would almost certainly never bother to collect in the event of a borrower's default. Yet insurance is sold on the collateral in case it is damaged or lost.

"It's predatory: This insurance product has no rationale, because it's not credible that someone would want to have their loan paid with their leaf-blower," said Matthew Lee, executive director of the Fair Finance Watch project at Inner City Press. "Citigroup has not lived up to the subprime lending reforms it announced after acquiring Associates."

Citigroup officials concede seizing such collateral would be more hassle than it's worth. But they say providing such collateral on loans has a purpose—"to make the borrower more responsible for paying the loan back," says Ajay Banga, Citigroup's business head of consumer lending.[12]

Here, Citigroup acknowledged that while it asked its customers "what kind of stuff do you have?" in order to list the items as collateral and sell insurance on them, it has no intention of foreclosing on the collateral. In fact, Inner City Press has been informed by current and former CitiFinancial employees that the property lists are compiled in order to sell insurance.[13]

Outside of the United States, not only can insurance be sold—interest rates of over 25 percent can be commanded. Since acquiring Associates, European American Bank (EAB), and Banamex, CitiFinancial has opened in South Korea, charging interest rates of 30 percent. "Although these rates are higher than the annual 24 percent charged by credit card companies for similar cash advances, CitiFinancial has an edge in that their loans are cheaper than those extended by existing loan sharks. . . . Another reason that people are drawn to the company is because of the renowned brand of its parent group, Citigroup. Customers thus tend to think the company will refrain from excessively aggressive collecting methods."[14]

The trust that Citigroup would eschew excessively aggressive collection practices, particularly overseas, would be misplaced. The *Asian Wall Street Journal,* for example, reported on a Citibank loan in India being collected on with no less than a knife to the throat:

Vikas Dresswala was working in his fabric shop one day in February when three men entered. He says one of them put a knife to his throat and told him: "You give the money now. Otherwise, we'll kidnap you." But this was no robbery. His visitors wanted him to pay his credit-card bills. Mr. Dresswala says he pleaded for time, and the men said they would return in three days, warning that he must pay them then or face the consequences. When they came back, waiting with him were undercover police. "They came in and started threatening," says a police officer, Vanaiak Vast, who says one of the three visitors told the shopkeeper: "I want the money right now or I will kill you."

The police arrested the three and later accused them of extortion and making terrorist threats. The same accusations were filed against the head of the collection agency, known as Quality Consultants. And the credit-card debt? It was owed to Citibank, the leader of India's surging credit-card market, which had hired Quality Consultants to collect the overdue account.[15]

This issue was raised to the U.S. Federal Reserve Board in 2001, when Citigroup in 2001 applied for regulatory approval to acquire EAB and Banamex. The Fed's reaction, in its approval orders, was that "claims about lending activities in India . . . are either outside the jurisdiction of the Board" or "contain no allegations of illegality or action that would affect the safety and soundness of the institutions involved in the proposal, and are outside the limited statutory factors that the Board is authorized to consider when reviewing an application under the [Bank Holding Company] Act."[16]

To jump forward in the inquiry: If the Federal Reserve Board, Citigroup and CitiFinancial's home country supervisor, will not consider CitiFinancial's worldwide compliance practices, who will? The Fed's hands-off approach can be contrasted to the stated jurisdiction of the German regulator, the Bundesanstalt für Finanzdienstleistungsaufsicht, to which ICP and its new internationally minded affiliate, the Fair Finance Watch, directed comments (about GE Capital) in 2003:

In the context of our ownership control following section 2b German Banking Act we have to research not only into GE Capital's business activities in Germany, but also in the USA and worldwide. We consider the information that you delivered on GE Capital's business practices as important. In a first step, we will request from GE Capital a statement on your concern.[17]

U.S. government agencies' unwillingness to consider U.S.-based lenders' practices outside of the United States leads to a major regulatory loophole, at which other lenders are lining up. As argued later in this chapter, with reference to the failure of U.S.-limited subprime lenders The Money Store (which cost Wachovia over $2 billion) and Green Tree (which drove Conseco into bankruptcy), it may well be that subprime lending confined to the United States is a dicey proposition, while taking it overseas to less regulated markets is the industry's future.

This certainly is the business strategy of HSBC, which on November 14, 2002, announced the acquisition of Household International for over $14 billion. A month previously, Household had reached a preliminary settlement of charges of predatory real estate lending and insurance practices with state attorneys general for $484 million. HSBC seemed unconcerned: the *Wall Street Journal* reported that Household "could also be rolled out to other countries, HSBC said. 'This is a business we could take to Japan,' HSBC's Sir John said. 'It's already an international business, but we think we could have opportunities in Brazil and Mexico. We haven't examined all the possibilities, but we think they could be extensive.' "[18]

Over the next four months, ICP Fair Finance Watch filed comments documenting Household's practices, and HSBC's lack of proposed reforms, with regulatory agencies not only in Washington and a dozen U.S. state capitals, but also with regulators in the United Kingdom, Singapore, Poland, and Africa. In terms of global safeguards against predatory lending, to the degree they exist, the responses were instructive.

The U.K. Financial Services Authority said it defers on such matters to

U.S. regulators, primarily the Federal Reserve Board. But HSBC and Household structured their transaction so that no U.S. Fed approval would be needed—even going so far as to sell off one of Household's banks on a "break-even basis" so that no application to the Fed would be required.[19]

ICP Fair Finance Watch commented to Singapore because HSBC was buying an insurance company there; ICP alerted the Monetary Authority of Singapore to HSBC's impending export of Household International and its demonstrably predatory practices into its jurisdiction. HSBC responded that there was no connection between the two proposed transactions.[20]

In Poland this was harder to claim: Kredyt Bank had been preparing to sell its bank charter to a British bank, but then switched the deal to Household International. ICP Fair Finance Watch dug into it, including speaking with Kredyt Bank's spokesman (who said that it would be impossible to explain what had been in Kredyt Bank's chairman's mind in making the switch) and commenting to the Polish regulator.[21] Household's plan in the country was and is to offer high-rate store credit.

Finally, ICP Fair Finance Watch commented to a dozen countries in Africa, when HSBC moved to acquire the 40 percent of Equator Bank which it didn't already own. While the expansion of U.S.-style subprime lending is taking place faster in Eastern Europe, Asia, and Latin markets like Mexico and Brazil, it will be directed to Africa as well. The manager of bank supervision for the Central Bank of Kenya wrote back to ICP:

We appreciate the trouble you took to put the long dossier together and will take full cognizance of your warning about the practice of predatory lending. However we are not aware of any intention by HSBC to buy substantial stakes in any bank in Kenya. Thank you very much for your warning.[22]

This response became the concluding argument in a subsequent *Financial Times* analysis piece, which noted that "the biggest banks in the world by market value, Citigroup and HSBC, have become the biggest players in 'subprime' lending," that "JP Morgan Chase has dipped its toe into the subprime waters by buying a credit card portfolio from Providian Financial," and that "[b]ig-time consumer lending is becoming a small world, after all"—the *Financial Times* notes that there "is a global financial system, but there is no global regulation."[23]

THE LACK OF GLOBAL REGULATION

That *is* the problem: the lack of systemic regulation of this high-rate lending. In the United States, when one jurisdiction passes a law imposing consumer safeguards, many of the lenders adopt a strategy of leaving that jurisdiction for neighboring ones. As recounted elsewhere in this volume, that took place with the Georgia anti-predatory lending law (until, under pressure from the rating agencies and government-sponsored agencies, the Georgia legislature amended the law); the threat of turning off the "spigot of credit" (that's often the imagery used) has been deployed in New York, New Jersey, Kentucky, and elsewhere. It's akin to the race to the bottom of which anti-sweatshop and environmental justice advocates complain: if one nation tries to improve worker protections, for example, the sweatshop contractors simply move to a neighboring (or far away) less-regulated jurisdiction.

The anti-sweatshop/fair labor movement, however, has at least begun to address this problem. It has proposed minimum standards (the specifics of which vary from nation to nation); it has applied pressure leading to global companies like The Gap and Disney having to make global anti-abuse commitments, and submitting to at least some form of outside monitoring.[24] The anti–predatory lending/credit consumer protection movement is years behind, at least in terms of globalizing the movement.

For example, while pressure brought to bear in the United States had led both Citigroup and HSBC's Household to make certain "best practices" commitments in the United States, neither has moved to extend these protections anywhere outside of the United States. Asked about this, at ICP's initiative, "a spokeswoman for HSBC declined to comment" and "Citigroup spokesman Steve Silverman said the company was proud of having 'very good' lending practices throughout the world."[25] But none of Citigroup's U.S. commitments are binding, and the Federal Trade Commission and the class action lawyers in the companion case *Morales v. Citigroup* (San Francisco County Superior Court) failed to impose any injunctive relief in their $240 million settlements with Citigroup. Some such relief would follow in a May 2004 Federal Reserve cease-and-desist order against CitiFinancial.[26] Meanwhile, as sketched above, CitiFinancial was expanding rapidly overseas, with no committed-to safeguards at all.

When American International Group (AIG), the world's largest insurer, applied for regulatory approval to buy American General in 2001, ICP Fair Finance Watch opposed it, noting, among other things, American General's continued use of single-premium credit insurance in connection with its subprime loans. Once ICP raised the issues, AIG's general counsel committed to regulators that single-premium credit insurance would be discontinued.[27] Less than two years later, in reporting its first-quarter 2003 earnings, AIG let drop that its "growing overseas consumer finance business is performing profitably."[28] Needless to say, AIG has not made any "best practices" or consumer protection commitments in connection with its "growing" non-U.S. consumer finance business.

Another U.S.-based lender which engages in high-rate consumer finance overseas with little oversight is Wells Fargo. Its predecessor Norwest was one of the first U.S.-based companies to see the profits possible from a business line targeted overseas and, relatedly, at immigrant groups in the United

States. In 1995, Norwest acquired Puerto Rico-based Island Finance from ITT; in announcing the acquisition, Norwest (and now Wells Fargo) CEO Dick Kovacevich said that it portended further "expansion into other Latin American markets."[29] Along with Island Finance, Norwest acquired branches in Panama, Aruba, the U.S. Virgin Islands, and the Netherlands Antilles. In 1997, Norwest opened a branch of Island Finance at 2866 Third Avenue, in the South Bronx (New York City). ICP/Fair Finance Watch's inquiries found that this branch charged 25 percent interest rates to all customers, without regard to credit history. The office was later closed, and its customers were instructed to travel to a Wells Fargo Financial office in adjacent Queens County to make their payments.

In early 1998, Wells Fargo purchased a consumer finance company in Argentina, Finvercon S.A. Compania Financiera. It also has Island Finance subsidiaries in the Cayman Islands, British West Indies, and Trinidad and Tobago, and operates under the name Financiera el Sol in Panama. While its 2000 SEC Form 10-K listed Wells Fargo Financial offices in Brazil, Hong Kong, and Taiwan, neither in that SEC report nor elsewhere has Wells Fargo made public further information about these stealth, presumably high-rate consumer finance operations.

Wells Fargo is also engaged in controversial high-rate finance in Canada: Its "Trans Canada Credit charges 28.9 per cent interest" in the following ways:

The first thing Labatte did receive appeared to be a credit card statement, showing a limit of $4,150, a billing date of Jan. 23 and a due date of Feb. 23. It stated no minimum payment was owed. Two more monthly statements followed, but Labatte claimed no statements arrived in April or May. He and his spouse both worked and failed to notice the six-month deferment period had expired.

By the time they started making inquiries, a representative of Trans Canada Credit informed them they'd missed the deadline for their "no-interest" offer and now owed approximately $600 in interest payments, dating back to the original date of purchase in November 2002.[30]

This is reminiscent of what is called predatory lending in the United States; Wells Fargo, however, has not included its Canadian or other non-U.S. subsidiaries in what few best practices and/or consumer compliance announcements it has made.

Similarly, while Household signed consent decrees in over 40 U.S. states in December 2002, HSBC has not committed to any safeguards as it exports the Household model overseas. In fact, HSBC's Asia chairman, David Eldon, has been quoted that HSBC has no problem with Household's past practices[31]—something that bodes badly for consumers in HSBC's Asian markets. In Brazil as well: A month after HSBC consummated its acquisition of Household, it announced it was exporting subprime consumer finance to Brazil, aiming at a lower income demographic than CitiFinancial.

Dow Jones newswires captured the tit-for-tat—the accelerating global race to the bottom, so to speak—between HSBC and CitiFinancial:

> [HSBC] is launching its own consumer finance operation targeting low-income clients. This comes just weeks after its larger global rival Citigroup Inc. unveiled a similar plan here. . . . [T]he two global banks are going head to head for the first time in the low-end consumer finance market. . . . [HSBC] looks to conquer 5 % to 10 % of a 10 to 12 billion-real ($1=BRL2.91) market . . . [HSBC] plans to launch its new initiative July 1 with the opening of three outlets in Sao Paulo—Brazil's wealthiest city. Within five years, HSBC plans to raise the total to 120 sites for a brand that doesn't yet have a name. The U.K. bank plans to target customers who earn between BRL400 and BRL1,500 a month. The plan, which has been in the works since last year, is similar to that of CitiFinancial. The U.S. bank is targeting earners of between BRL500 and BRL2,000 and wants to set up 100 sites within five years. . . . Consumers pay up to six times higher for credit than the central bank's current reference lending rate of 26.5 % and consumer groups have accused them of being greedy.[32]

As demonstrated throughout this volume, consumer groups' accusations are more nuanced than "greedy"—the companies do not price according to risk; they strong-arm customers into taking out unnecessary credit insurance of limited value; and so on. But one of the reasons that the new global subprime lenders are focused on non-U.S. markets is due to the underdevelopment to date of consumer protection. For example, GE Capital does retail subprime lending on virtually every continent *but* North America. Beyond GE's acquisition of the U.K. subprime lender First National—a sort of HSBC/Household in reverse—GE, for example, offers high-cost mortgage loans in Australia to "borrowers with court rulings against them,"[33] and has been offering subprime loans in Japan "under the 'Honobono Lake' brand."[34] In subprime consumer finance in the Czech Republic, GE Capital Multiservis is "the largest firm in the field"; its general director, Jioi Pathy, told the *Prague Tribune* that "I don't expect any decrease in demand for consumer loans in the near future, because not all of the types of products that are usual in developed economies have been brought to the market yet, and this type of financing is yet to cover all commodities."[35] In South Korea, GE Capital is offering prime and subprime loans through kiosks:

> GE Consumer Finance-Korea, a unit of GE Capital Korea, said Wednesday it will offer personal loans via "CashVill" kiosks at two downtown subway stations in Seoul as of Thursday. With the "CashVill" offices opening at Uljiro Ipgu and City Hall subway stations, GE Consumer Finance-Korea will provide unsecured personal loans of between 2 million won (U.S.$1,682) and 15 million won (U.S. $12,615). The interest rate of such products will be based on an individual's credit standing, with loan tenures ranging from one to three years to meet different customer

needs. . . . GE Consumer Finance, a unit of General Electric Company, with U.S.$80 billion in assets, provides credit services to consumers, retailers and auto dealers in 36 countries around the world.[36]

If GE Capital is making consumer loans, many of them subprime, in 36 countries, who is watchdogging this lending? No one, apparently. Unlike even CitiFinancial and HSBC's Household, GE has made no "best practices" announcements or commitments. It flies under the radar of the Community Reinvestment Act (CRA) in the United States: The three banks it uses to make its credit card and store card loans are "nonbank banks." In 2003, GE Capital bought home equity loans from Conseco/Greentree, but claimed that the volume of loans was too small to require it to convert from a limited-purpose, credit card bank, with a CRA program limited to the bank's headquarters city, to a broader retail bank. This despite the fact that GE Capital in 2003 began sending out "live checks," personal loan offers with interest rates up to 22 percent.[37]

THE NEED FOR GLOBAL OVERSIGHT

ICP Fair Finance Watch has begun watchdogging this GE activity, and has begun working with advocates in the United Kingdom, where GE Capital is now a leading subprime lender, having bought First National from Abbey National in early 2003. Even prior to GE's purchase, First National was in the news in Britain as a predatory lender:

One borrower who fell behind on repayments on a pounds 1,100 loan saw it balloon to pounds 8,500 once interest was added. Meanwhile, the bank continues to apply contract terms which the Office of Fair Trading described as sucking people into a "vortex of debt." The lender in question is First National . . . the prospect of the bank forcing a sale can be enough to scare people into selling up themselves.

It was in Dave McNevin's case. A former lorry driver, he has had a charging order on his Nottinghamshire semi since 1993. Mr. McNevin borrowed pounds 1,100 for double-glazing in 1991 and later defaulted after he lost his job. Until a few months ago, he had no idea the bank had a claim on his former council house. The legal documents sent to him didn't explain what a charging order was in layman's language. Mr. McNevin said ruefully: "As far as I knew, it was just something to say I'd got to pay money each month or they'd go back to the courthouse."

Now he knows exactly what it does mean he's decided to sell his home to clear the debt. His wife, Joan, says it is breaking her heart. . . . Mr. McNevin can free himself only by selling the home he has lived in for 23 years. "Everything we've been working for has gone down the drain," he says.

He has also suffered from the second of First National's damaging business practices. Once again the bank does something its competitors do not. In the jargon of the credit world it's called "charging interest after judgment." . . . The Office of Fair Trading argued the clause puts borrowers deeper into debt and took the unprecedented step of taking First National to court, claiming the contract term was un-fair and detrimental to consumers.

The case lasted more than two years and ended in the House of Lords last year. First National won. Legally the contract term is not "unfair." But all five Law Lords expressed serious concern about its effects on debtors. Lord Millet said that the consequences of this term "must come as a nasty shock. I think they have a legit-imate grievance." Other Lords called the situation "unacceptable" and "unsatis-factory" . . . the Department of Trade and Industry is looking at the ruling from the OFT court case as part of its review into the Consumer Credit Act.[38]

Cases such as this in the United Kingdom have led to advocacy—and to legislative and regulatory proposals. In early 2003, the U.K. Office of Fair Trading (OFT) proposed revisions to the Consumer Credit Act 1974; OFT's Melanie Johnson, minster for competition, consumers, and markets, said, "This is the biggest shake-up of credit companies for almost 30 years. There is no place for rogue traders, preying on vulnerable consumers, in today's credit market. The current system of credit licensing was designed to deal with a credit sector that was much smaller and less sophisticated than the one we have today. I want to make the licensing rules appropriate for today's competitive marketplace."[39]

The reference to increased entry into, and competition in, the United Kingdom by subprime lenders was timely. As described above, in early 2003 the United Kingdom's largest bank, HSBC, was in the process of acquiring the much-sued U.S.-based subprime lender Household International, which already owned HFC Bank in the United Kingdom. By mid-2003, it was re-ported that "HSBC plans to move into the U.K. sub-prime lending market by referring poorer customers to HFC Bank, acquired as part of the takeover of Household International of the US. HFC's branch network of-fers loans with interest rates as high as 35 percent, using Household's ad-vanced credit-scoring and risk management systems. Barclays is already operating a pilot scheme in the sub-prime market."[40]

Another U.K.-based lender which is exporting subprime lending is Prov-ident Financial, commonly known as the "Provy." In announcing its earn-ings in mid-2003, Provident described the British subprime market as "mature," but reported growth in Eastern Europe ("customer numbers in Poland, the Czech Republic, Hungary and Slovakia grew 34 percent to 1.1 million" pounds); it said it "will launch a home credit service in Mexico later this year."[41] Other U.K. subprime lenders include Shopacheck, Cat-tles, and Caversham Finance's BrightHouse, which is partially owned by the Japanese investment bank Nomura.[42] BrightHouse, "whose annual in-terest rate is nearly 30 per cent compared with the bank base rate of 4 per cent . . . nine out of 10 customers also take out insurance which allows them to return the goods if they cannot maintain payments, boosting in-terest rates to 80 per cent," has given rise in the British press to the following questions: "Why not insist on an interest cap? Why not also enlist the banks' cash and expertise and seconded staff to ensure that a network of viable credit unions exists across Britain?"[43] As surveyed below, these same questions are beginning to be asked not only in North America but also in Southeast Asia and elsewhere, in response to the expansion of high-rate subprime lending.

In Malaysia, outcry about the debt collection practices of loan sharks led to governmental inquiries—which revealed that many of the companies most insistent on repayment are, in fact, licensed lenders. For example, just before Christmas 2002, the *New Straits Times* reported on the case of Lim Seng Choy, who "was assaulted by loan sharks who also carted away his home appliances . . . the loan sharks took his identity card, passport, driving license and his hand phone."[44] By February 2003, stories such as these led to legislative initiatives: "Proposals include banning newspapers from carrying advertisements of money lenders; empowering the police to search premises from which loan sharks operate and seize documents; [and] protecting informers involved in civil or criminal proceedings against loan sharks."[45]

Of the three above-quoted proposals, the first would raise issues under the First Amendment to the U.S. Constitution (although a form of advertising ban has effectively been in place with regard to hard liquor and tobacco products for some years); the last of the three proposals is sorely needed in the United States. In 2002, ICP Fair Finance Watch asked a senior lawyer at the Federal Reserve Board if the Board would take action if CitiFinancial retaliated against a whistle-blowing source; the answer, hardly heartening, was "no."

In Thailand, "[l]oans offered by loan sharks are costing many factory workers . . . a monthly interest rate of 5–20% . . . [W]orkers who turned to such creditors would be asked for their ATM cards and contact addresses. Creditors would call them at work if they failed to pay the debts. Some sent their men or influential figures to intimidate or attack the debtors. Many workers quit work and moved elsewhere. The government should promote cooperative funds to help workers get access to low-interest loans."[46] The methodology for servicing subprime loans, including repeated phone calls to the borrower's work and home, is similar in the United States, Thailand, and elsewhere. If civil society organizations coordinate their efforts, perhaps the loopholes in the U.S. Fair Debt Collection Practices Act can be avoided as subprime consumer finance becomes more prevalent, and more regulated, in Thailand and elsewhere.

In Korea, the legislative initiatives have been directed against domestic and foreign lenders: "As a revision bill on consumer financing passed through the National Assembly on July 31, the Financial Supervisory Service [FSS] has stepped up . . . its efforts to stop usurious practices by local and overseas moneylenders. . . . The FSS has found that most Japanese loan sharks borrowed funds from domestic lenders at an annual interest rate of 14–19 percent and offered the money to South Korean clients in the low-income bracket at an interest rate of 120–150 percent."[47]

The last frontier for the global subprime lenders, however, is clearly mainland China. Citigroup and HSBC are making inroads; AIG has, as it likes to brag, been there since the early 1900s. There are proliferating news reports of consumers and small entrepreneurs in China who have

fallen victim to loan-sharking practices whereby interest payments compounded out of control, loan agreements were exacted by force and threats, and assets ultimately foreclosed. . . . [T]heir plight was taken up in March 2000 by the popular newspaper *Southern Weekend*, published in the relatively liberal southern city of Guangzhou. But Mr. Jin took exception to the term usury and sued for defamation. In a ruling sent to the parties last week, the Xiaoshin Intermediate People's Court upheld the newspaper's case that usury was a reasonable term to describe Mr. Jin's operations, although it said elements of its article were exaggerated. *Southern Weekend*'s economics editor, Feng Qiruo, said the win for the newspaper exposed a failing in China. "Why are the underground banks so rampant?" he said. "Because the state's commercial banks can hardly be relied upon to meet the demand for grassroots finance."[48]

Despite this increasing global proliferation of predatory subprime lending, there is not yet any global bank or lending regulator. The institution that comes closest is the Bank for International Settlement's Basel Committee for Banking Supervision (BCBS). The BCBS's main product is its Capital Accord, on which it had solicited comments from what it describes as "interested parties." Yet when comments were submitted that urged the consideration of predatory lending and the reputational and other harms that can result therefrom, these pleas fell on deaf ears. In the United States, the Federal Reserve in mid-2003 held a series of outreach meetings about the Basel Capital Accords—and invited only bankers. This should be contrasted to, for example, the World Bank's and World Trade Organization's grudging but undeniable outreach to nonprofit civil society groups, and also to large banks' willingness to sign on to global best practices agreements with respect to the environment. In 2003, 10 banks, including Citigroup and HSBC, signed the "Equator Principles," regarding nonfinancial safeguards in their project finance lending to mining, timber, oil, and other extractive industries. That no similar agreements or principles exist regarding the banks' consumer lending, is indicative of the banks' unwillingness to make concessions regarding their direct and lucrative business of high-rate lending to consumers, and of the consumer movement lagging behind environmentalists in terms of global collaboration. It may also be indicative of the continuing need for anti-predatory lending analysis, organizing, and advocacy that look beyond the United States.

NOTES

1. Jonathan Epstein, "HSBC Will Buy Household: Purchase Gives Household a Chance to Escape Reputation," *Wilmington* (Del.) *News-Journal*, November 15, 2002, p. 7B.

2. Andrew Hill, "Associates Attracts Mixed Reception," *Financial Times*, September 7, 2000, p. 31.

3. Heather Timmons, "Calling Travelers 'Predatory,' Group Hits Deal with B of A," *American Banker* (June 13, 1997): 3.

4. Allison Bell, "Travelers Unit's Loan Record Hit," *National Underwriter* (June 23, 1997): 3.

5. Matthew Lee, "OTS Curbs on Travelers' Thrift: a Model for CRA in New Era," *American Banker* (December 10, 1997): 4.

6. Jonathan Epstein, "Travelers Grilled on Buyout Plan," *Wilmington* (Del.) *News-Journal*, June 5, 1998.

7. "Citigroup Unveils Easy Buy Scheme," *India Business Insight* (January 29, 2001).

8. Alice Lipowicz, "Predatory Lending Issues Prey on Citi's Banamex Buy: Consumers Want Careful Review Before Deal with Mexican Bank Gets the OK," *Crain's New York Business* (July 9, 2001): 4.

9. Citigroup, "News Release: Citigroup Forms Consumer Products Unit for Emerging Markets" (New York: Citigroup/*Business Wire*, May 29, 2002).

10. "Branching Out," *Latin Trade* (July 2003).

11. "CitiFinancial Adopts Lending Model to Emerging Markets," *Bank Systems and Technology* (April 21, 2003).

12. Paul Beckett, "Efforts by Citigroup to Reform Subprime Unit Raise Questions," *Wall Street Journal*, July 19, 2002.

13. Laura Mandaro, "Fed Going Extra Mile in Probe of CitiFinancial," *American Banker* (October 11, 2002): 1.

14. "Domestic Banks Forced to Sit By as CitiFinancial Streaks Past," *Korea Herald*, July 30, 2002.

15. Steve Stecklow and Jonathan Karp, "Paid Back: Citibank in India Has Hired Collectors Said to Use Threats," *Asian Wall Street Journal*, May 25, 1999.

16. Federal Reserve Board, "Order Approving Acquisition of a Bank" [Citigroup–EAB], *Federal Reserve Bulletin* 87 (2001): 600 (Fed. Res. Bull. 2001: n.63).

17. Felix Kallmeyer, "Response to Comments from Inner City Press/Fair Finance Watch" (Bonn: Bundesanstalt für Finanzdienstleistungsaufsicht, June 17, 2003), on file with the author.

18. Erik Portanger et al., "HSBC Sets $16 Billion Deal for Household International," *Wall Street Journal*, November 15, 2002.

19. Gary Silverman, "Household Acts to Thwart Block on Bid: HSBC Acquisition Threatened," *Financial Times*, November 20, 2002, p. 24.

20. Sebastian Tong, "HSBC's Keppel Bid Opposed," *Hong Kong Standard*, January 1, 2003.

21. Timothy Sifert, "HSBC Hunting Kredyt Bank," *Warsaw Business Journal* (January 13, 2003).

22. Patrick Ndwiga, "Response to Comments from Inner City Press/Fair Finance

Watch" (Nairobi: Central Bank of Kenya, February 28, 2003), on file with the author.

23. Gary Silverman, "Big Lenders Forced to Bank on 'Untouchables' of the Past," *Financial Times* (London), April 4, 2003, p. 18.

24. Karl Schoenberger, *Levi's Children: Coming to Terms with Human Rights in the Global Marketplace* (New York: Atlantic Monthly Press, 2000).

25. Scott Reckard, "Consumer Group Joins Opposition to Wells Mergers," *Los Angeles Times*, July 30, 2003.

26. http://www.federalreserve.gov/boarddocs/press/enforcement/2004/20040527/default.htm (accessed June 16, 2004).

27. Patrick McGeehan, "Third Insurer to Stop Selling Single-Premium Credit Life Policies," *New York Times*, July 21, 2001, p. C3.

28. American International Group, "News Release: AIG Reports First Quarter 2003 Net Income of $1.95 Billion vs. $1.98 Billion in the First Quarter of 2002" (New York: AIG/*Business Wire*, April 24, 2003).

29. Norwest, "Press Release: Norwest Corporation Completes Purchase of Island Finance Business in the Caribbean" (Minneapolis: Norwest/*PR Newswire*, May 4, 1995).

30. Al MacRury, "Know Your Deferred Contract: Buy Now/Pay Later Plans Can Become Costly," *Hamilton* (Ont.) *Spectator*, June 26, 2003, p. C2.

31. "HSBC Says Hopes to Seal Household Deal as Planned" (Reuters, December 3, 2002).

32. Anthony Dovkants, "Brazil to Become Battleground for Giants Citigroup, HSBC," Dow Jones Newswires, April 20, 2003.

33. John Kavanagh, "Money for Non-conformists," *Business Review Weekly* (Australia) (May 8, 2003): 64.

34. "GE Group to Merge Japanese Consumer Credit and Credit Card Arms," *Japan Economic Newswire*, April 9, 2003.

35. Petr Vykoukal, "Leasing: Diversity, Growth and Change," *Prague Tribune*, June 1, 2003.

36. "GE Consumer Finance Expands in South Korean Market," *Asia Pulse* (July 2, 2003).

37. Kathryn Kranhold, "GE Plans to Move into a Risky Area: World of Unsecured Personal Loans," *Wall Street Journal*, May 9, 2003, p. A3.

38. Lesley Curwen, "Debt: First Principles," *The Guardian* (London), July 20, 2002, p. 2.

39. Hermes Database, "Press Release: Biggest Shake-up of Credit Laws for a Generation" (London: Hermes Database/Department of Trade and Industry, January 30, 2003).

40. "HSBC Moves into Sub-Prime Market," *Bank Marketing International* (June 23, 2003): 2.

41. Andrew Cave, "Provident Makes Hay in Eastern Europe," *Daily Telegraph* (London), July 24, 2003, 31.

42. "BrightHouse to Expand Portfolio with 20 Stores," *Retail Week* (January 31, 2003): 21.

43. Yvonne Roberts, "Need for Credit in the Interest of the Poor," *Community Care* (January 30, 2003): 19.

44. "Loan Sharks Assault Trader and Cart Away His Home Appliances," *New Straits Times*, December 14, 2002, p. 14.

45. Annie Freeda Cruez, "New Rules for Money Lenders," *New Straits Times*, February 3, 2003, p. 8.

46. "Factory Workers at Mercy of Loan Sharks," *Bangkok Post*, December 13, 2002.

47. "FSS to Have Power to Inspect Private Lenders," *Korea Times*, August 24, 2002.

48. Hamish McDonald, "Where the Banks Won't Help, the Moneylenders Flourish," *Sydney Morning Herald*, October 28, 2002, p. 12.

REFERENCES

American International Group. "News Release: AIG Reports First Quarter 2003 Net Income of $1.95 Billion vs. $1.98 Billion in the First Quarter of 2002." New York: AIG/*Business Wire*, April 24, 2003.

Beckett, Paul. "Efforts by Citigroup to Reform Subprime Unit Raise Questions." *Wall Street Journal*, July 19, 2002.

Bell, Allison. "Travelers Unit's Loan Record Hit." *National Underwriter* (June 23, 1997): 3.

"Branching Out." *Latin Trade* (July 2003).

"BrightHouse to Expand Portfolio with 20 Stores." *Retail Week* (January 31, 2003): 21.

Cave, Andrew. "Provident Makes Hay in Eastern Europe." *Daily Telegraph* (London), July 24, 2003, p. 31.

"CitiFinancial Adopts Lending Model to Emerging Markets." *Bank Systems and Technology* (April 21, 2003).

Citigroup. "News Release: Citigroup Forms Consumer Products Unit for Emerging Markets." New York: Citigroup/Business Wire, May 29, 2002.

"Citigroup Unveils Easy Buy Scheme," *India Business Insight* (January 29, 2001).

Cruez, Annie Freeda. "New Rules for Money Lenders," *New Straits Times*, February 3, 2003, 8.

Curwen, Lesley. "Debt: First Principles." *The Guardian* (London), July 20, 2002, p. 2.

"Domestic Banks Forced to Sit By as CitiFinancial Streaks Past." *Korea Herald*, July 30, 2002.

Dovkants, Anthony. "Brazil to Become Battleground for Giants Citigroup, HSBC." Dow Jones Newswires, April 20, 2003.

Epstein, Jonathan. "Travelers Grilled on Buyout Plan," *Wilmington* (Del.) *News-Journal*, June 5, 1998, p. 7B.

Epstein, Jonathan. "HSBC Will Buy Household: Purchase Gives Household a Chance to Escape Reputation." *Wilmington* (Del.) *News-Journal*, November 15, 2002, p. 7B.

"Factory Workers at Mercy of Loan Sharks." *Bangkok Post*, December 13, 2002.

Federal Reserve Board. "Order Approving Acquisition of a Bank" [Citigroup–EAB]. *Federal Reserve Bulletin* 87 (2001): 600.

"FSS to Have Power to Inspect Private Lenders." *Korea Times*, August 24, 2002.

"GE Consumer Finance Expands in South Korean Market." *Asia Pulse* (July 2, 2003).

"GE Group to Merge Japanese Consumer Credit and Credit Card Arms." Japan Economic Newswire, April 9, 2003.

Hermes Database. "Press Release: Biggest Shake-up of Credit Laws for a Generation." London: Hermes Database/Department of Trade and Industry, January 30, 2003.

Hill, Andrew. "Associates Attracts Mixed Reception." *Financial Times*, September 7, 2000, p. 31.

"HSBC Moves into Sub-Prime Market." *Bank Marketing International* (June 23, 2003): 2.

"HSBC Says Hopes to Seal Household Deal as Planned." Reuters, December 3, 2002.

Kallmeyer, Felix. "Response to Comments from Inner City Press/Fair Finance Watch." Bonn: Bundesanstalt für Finanzdienstleistungsaufsicht, June 17, 2003. On file with the author.

Kavanagh, John. "Money for Non-conformists." *Business Review Weekly* (Australia) (May 8, 2003): 64.

Kranhold, Kathryn. "GE Plans to Move into a Risky Area: World of Unsecured Personal Loans." *Wall Street Journal*, May 9, 2003, p. A3.

Lee, Matthew. "OTS Curbs on Travelers' Thrift: A Model for CRA in New Era." *American Banker* (December 10, 1997): 4.

Lipowicz, Alice. "Predatory Lending Issues Prey on Citi's Banamex Buy: Consumers Want Careful Review Before Deal with Mexican Bank Gets the OK." *Crain's New York Business* (July 9, 2001): 4.

"Loan Sharks Assault Trader and Cart Away His Home Appliances." *New Straits Times*, December 14, 2002, p. 14.

MacRury, Al. "Know Your Deferred Contract: Buy Now/Pay Later Plans Can Become Costly." *Hamilton* (Ontario) *Spectator*, June 26, 2003, C2.

Mandaro, Laura. "Fed Going Extra Mile in Probe of CitiFinancial." *American Banker* (October 11, 2002): 1.

McDonald, Hamish. "Where the Banks Won't Help, the Moneylenders Flourish." *Sydney Morning Herald*, October 28, 2002, 12.

McGeehan, Patrick. "Third Insurer to Stop Selling Single-Premium Credit Life Policies." *New York Times*, July 21, 2001, p. C3.

Ndwiga, Patrick. "Response to Comments from Inner City Press/Fair Finance Watch." Nairobi: Central Bank of Kenya, February 28, 2003. On file with the author.

Norwest. "Press Release: Norwest Corporation Completes Purchase of Island Finance Business in the Caribbean." Minneapolis: Norwest/PR *Newswire*, May 4, 1995.

Portanger, Erik et al. "HSBC Sets $16 Billion Deal for Household International." *Wall Street Journal*, November 15, 2002.

Reckard, Scott. "Consumer Group Joins Opposition to Wells Mergers." *Los Angeles Times,* July 30, 2003.

Roberts, Yvonne. "Need for Credit in the Interest of the Poor." *Community Care* (January 30, 2003): 19.

Schoenberger, Karl. *Levi's Children: Coming to Terms with Human Rights in the Global Marketplace.* New York: Atlantic Monthly Press, 2000.

Sifert, Timothy. "HSBC Hunting Kredyt Bank." *Warsaw Business Journal* (January 13, 2003).

Silverman, Gary. "Household Acts to Thwart Block on Bid: HSBC Acquisition Threatened." *Financial Times*, November 20, 2002, 24.

———. "Big Lenders Forced to Bank on 'Untouchables' of the Past." *Financial Times* (London), April 4, 2003, p. 18

Stecklow, Steve, and Jonathan Karp. "Paid Back: Citibank in India Has Hired Collectors Said to Use Threats." *Asian Wall Street Journal*, May 25, 1999, p. 4.

Timmons, Heather. "Calling Travelers 'Predatory,' Group Hits Deal with B of A." *American Banker* (June 13, 1997): 3.

Tong, Sebastian. "HSBC's Keppel Bid Opposed." *Hong Kong Standard*, January 1, 2003, p. 1.

Vykoukal, Petr. "Leasing: Diversity, Growth and Change." *Prague Tribune,* June 1, 2003, p. 38.

9

Predatoriness, and What We Can Do About It

Chester Hartman

While predatory home mortgage lending is a highly disturbing and relatively new phenomenon, no one ought to be surprised at its existence. Ours is a society, a capitalist/market economy, a political system that breeds predatory behavior, particularly against the most vulnerable segments of the population, throughout and consistently. (Just to give the term an additional grim flavor, my dictionary uses these descriptive definitional terms: "plundering," "pillaging," "marauding.") Whether it's the criminal justice system, the health system, the education system, or any other of the society's basics, "the poor pay more" (in David Caplowitz's phrase and title from his 1967 classic), get less, get shafted.[1] And of course, within the housing system, predatory lending is just one piece of the larger picture. Among the other ways the housing system disappoints and preys upon poor, elderly, and minority residents are redlining (mortgage and insurance versions); evictions; discrimination by landlords, lenders, real estate agents, and other gatekeepers; excessive housing cost burdens; poor code enforcement; gentrification pressures; and so on.

Those victimized by predatory lending are primarily persons who already own their homes, although a certain portion of this nefarious activity is foisted upon renters desiring home ownership. And in this regard, we need to question the (bipartisan) push to have everyone attain "the American dream"—a political, advertising, and cultural campaign that unfortunately causes grief for all too many households. While the nation's home ownership rate has been rising, so has the foreclosure rate—primarily, of course, for low-income households. A recent *New York Times* series on New York City residents moving to the Poconos, two states away, as the only place they can afford to buy (and in the process incurring round-trip commutes of five to six hours to their city jobs, as well as severe financial difficulties), reported that "early last year [2003] the foreclosure rate passed 1.1 percent, or roughly 560,000 homes, compared with a rate of 0.86 percent in 1995 when the homeownership campaign began."[2] And we never seem to learn ("that's history" is a common putdown, rather than regarded as a lesson worth heeding): it's as if the Sec. 235 Program of the 1968 Housing Act, which facilitated home ownership by low-income families by providing no downpayment, 1 percent interest rate mortgages, but wound up saddling unsuspecting families with shoddy housing and unexpected and unaffordable costs—all courtesy of predatory real estate agents, appraisers, even FHA officials, as revealed in congressional hearings—as if that experience never happened.[3]

And of course the victims of today's predatory lending are disproportionately minority—folks who are so often and well shut out of the mainstream financial institutions that they desperately grasp at whatever seems possible to secure a decent home.

As often is the case, while we have some data on the problem of predatory lending, we need more and better information. A recent General Accounting Office report noted, "No comprehensive data are available on the extent of these [predatory lending] practices."[4] And so one important recommendation is to establish systems, via regulators (and possibly some more public-regarding private entities and nonprofits), to track and document the extent of the problem, who's being gouged and how, who the perpetrators are, the impact on victims, how effective the measures designed to curb this practice are. And beyond dry but essential data, we need more human interest stories, more popularization and awareness of the problem, who's getting hurt and how they're hurting. That's for the media, both electronic and print, to take on. This stuff is simply outrageous, and popular outrage, thankfully, is still a potent force for change.

While there are variations on the scam, the basic definition Greg Squires offers in Chapter 1, "The New Redlining" (drawn in turn from the National Community Reinvestment Coalition); Patricia McCoy's more succinct definition in Chapter 4, "Predatory Lending Practices: Definition and Behavioral Implications" (followed by her detailed listing of its characteristics); and Squires' catalog of the various practices provide the necessary language and picture.

All this is occurring in an environment of growing economic inequality; as the rich get richer, the poor get poorer (as Squires indicates in his essay). Nowhere is this more virulent and important—and now getting the increased attention it deserves—than with respect to the wealth gap and, within that gap, the place of housing. And of course race is the real dividing line for large segments of the population, independent of income, as documented in Melvin Oliver and Thomas Shapiro's groundbreaking 1995 book, *Black Wealth/White Wealth*,[5] and more recently Shapiro's 2004 book, *The Hidden Cost of Being African American: How Wealth Perpetuates Inequality.*[6] These increasingly obviously housing disparities certainly feed into the complex web of demand for housing ownership, generation of housing-based wealth, and the process of taking advantage of the scenario to plunder, pillage, and maraud.

The broader environment of financial institution restructuring—greased to a considerable degree by hefty campaign contributions to key legislators at the state and federal levels—is a highly relevant contextual element as well. Growing industry concentration, with its accompaniment of decreased supervision and knowledge at the neighborhood level, make it harder for the big banks to be on top of what's happening in the community, even assuming they want to be—but in fact that distancing provides a surely not unwelcome excuse for central executives to claim lack of awareness of abuses. If the major banks backing the mortgage brokers were in touch with the impact of abandoned houses—often the end product of the predatory loan—on the neighborhood (Ira Goldstein, in Chapter 3, "The Economic Consequences of Predatory Lending: A Philadelphia Case Study," cites a Temple University study showing that an abandoned home reduces the value of homes on surrounding blocks by over $6,700), perhaps different and more responsible behavior at the top would ensue.

The profit potential in predatory lending is huge—that's why it has spread so rapidly and widely. But it's not just the front man, the "loan shark in pinstripes," in Clarence Page's nice phrase from the Foreword, who pockets the cash. Keith Ernst and his colleagues, in Chapter 5, "Legal and Economic Inducements to Predatory Practices," nicely lay out all the players who divide the spoils: the lender, the mortgage broker, the secondary market purchaser (Fannie Mae and Freddie Mac come into the act, behind the scenes), the loan servicer, the investor in mortgage-backed securities (Fannie and Freddie again). The mortgage brokers and their employees may be the lead, up-front actors, but behind them stand major financial institutions, financial intermediaries, and other big-time players that supply the funds, trade in investments, and perform all the other paper transactions that make the system work. And the various government regulators, at all levels, do their bit, less by what they do than by what they do not do. The larger political anti-government, anti-regulatory climate must be fought, not least in this area.

Another contextual issue, well described by Matthew Lee in Chapter 8, "Predatory Lending Goes Global: Consumer Protection in a Deregulation Network Economy," is the role that globalization of the nation's and world's economy plays in the predatory lending story. The practice is spreading to other countries, and the increasing country-by-country interpenetration of financial markets means that mortgage money, especially in the form of mortgage-backed securities, is being drawn from an ever larger and more far-flung pool—thereby also increasing the gap between knowledge of/responsibility for/caring about local conditions and the profit-driven motives of investors. Citigroup is the pacesetter, and, as Lee notes regarding General Electric, its Capital unit "has developed a subprime lending capacity on which the sun never sets." Globalization also has an undermining impact on regulation, and international-level regulation is virtually nonexistent. And it is a force for financial institution concentration as well.

Another relatively recent development in the financial world—not at all unrelated to predatory mortgage lending—is the growth of what has been termed the "two-tiered financial system": the web of check-cashing outlets, pawnshops, rent-to-own stores, car title pawns, and cash leasing operations that dot low-income neighborhoods, particularly those occupied by African American, Latino, and recent immigrant households. Cut-and-run behavior by mainstream financial institutions (e.g., closing branch banks), into which vacuum the predatory second-tier lenders crawl, leads to widespread overcharging and other abuses and injustices, setting the scene for mortgage brokers and others to do their work.[7] That a great many borrowers who own their homes free and clear take out loans from the predators (as noted by Patricia McCoy) is likely due to the need to pay off high-interest credit card debt. More research is needed to establish the importance of this link.

The limitations and declining impact and coverage of the Community Reinvestment Act (CRA), as Squires notes in Chapter 1, is a major cause of the problem. CRA has been of enormous benefit to lower-income and minority communities, paving the way for "the investment of more than $1.7 trillion . . . since the law was passed in 1977, nearly half of it in affordable housing and most in the last 10 years."[8] The financial institution consolidation that took place in the 1990s—permitted/abetted by government action—led to entry of new types of lenders not subject to the CRA. And there seems to be little impetus in Congress (see point above regarding campaign contributions) to reform the act to cover all the lenders and lenders' agents/brokers who need to be regulated. And in fact, as of this writing (mid-2004), federal banking officials are seeking to weaken the act by relaxing requirements for smaller lending institutions. Absence of mainstream market lending leads, obviously, to predatory lending.

Behavior issues, as reviewed by Patricia McCoy, present a complex and disturbing picture. She lays out the case that "predatory lenders induce suboptimal decisions by homeowners by exploiting anomalies in consumer behavior through marketing"—perhaps an overly academic and circumlocutory way of expressing the obvious: the marketers are clever ("relentless and fiendishly clever marketing that manipulates cognitive imperfections," in her apt description), and those marketed to are needy and in many cases desperate—and less clever. And while the newish field of behavioral economics can provide some insight into the interplay between predatory lenders and those they prey upon, it is important not to fall into the trap of blaming the victim. "Cognitive biases" there may well be, and "rational actors" can be a useful yardstick. But when people are in real trouble, often desperate—due to issues they cannot control—and the "solutions" (aggressively and manipulatively) proffered them are few and deceptive, expecting fully rational behavior is unreal. "Cognitive anomalies" arise and exist in a context—they are not sui generis; we can change or eliminate these anomalies by altering the context. Poor people play the lottery at far higher rates than do rich people, not because they are less rational (i.e., aware of the infinitesimal probability of winning) but because it's their desperate hope of digging out of the poverty trap (and again contextual, because of the heavy advertising and disproportionate placement of sales outlets in poor and minority neighborhoods). The value of McCoy's approach is to understand better both the behavior and the behavioral constraints of those seeking to borrow when they shouldn't. While the behavior of the predatory lenders is better known and fairly obvious, the more we know about the environmental and personal weaknesses and limits that those in need suffer, the better positioned we are to put remedies in place.

WHAT IS TO BE DONE?

Credit Counseling

Credit counseling is one great need—although some of the authors cast doubt on its effectiveness. But there are serious abuses in the current system, as recent U.S. Senate hearings have revealed. "Some of the nation's nonprofit (i.e., tax-exempt) credit-counseling agencies are engaged in abusive marketing practices that funnel millions of dollars from cash-strapped debtors to the agencies' executives in violation of federal tax and fair trade laws," according to a report by the Senate Permanent Subcommittee on Investigations[9] ("predatory counseling"). The report notes that these agencies are "charging excessive fees, putting marketing before counseling and providing debtors with inadequate educational, counseling and debt management services." Many of these nonprofits (the term obviously is used quite loosely) advertise extensively on television in order to enroll households into debt-management plans—which then "charge exorbitant fees that are siphoned off by affiliated for-profit companies." While this is consumer debt generally, the majority of it related to use of credit cards, such financial hole-digging is of course not unrelated to mortgage debt, usually the largest regular expenditure for most households, particularly at the lower end of the income scale. Problematic debt is epidemic in this country: "Previous reports from consumer groups estimate that 9 million Americans contact credit-counseling agencies annually"![10] Again, somewhat lax oversight by regulatory agencies—in this case, primarily the Internal Revenue Service, is a not insignificant part of the problem. More and better home owner (and potential home owner) education and counseling is clearly needed, which requires funding and sensitive and competent (particularly, in the case of immigrants, culturally and linguistically competent) counselors. Patricia McCoy puts forward the dour view that "In the long run, it is doubtful that sufficient financial resources would ever be devoted to effective nationwide counseling." It would be useful to generate some estimates of the costs of an effective counseling program (one model to draw on—in relation to a somewhat different housing issue—is the counseling provided by the Leadership Council for Metropolitan Open Communities to facilitate Chicago's Gautreaux housing mobility program).[11] I suspect it would by no means be a staggering figure; that it would be offset by eliminating the personal and societal costs that lack of counseling incurs in the predatory lending world; and that effective community and political organizing can bring it about.

Spotlight Mortgage Brokers

Clearly, more oversight is needed on the front persons, principally mortgage brokers, in addition to more research on who they are and how they operate. As Ira Goldstein writes, "Brokers remain a troubling part of the transaction—especially for individuals of more modest means. Interviewees representative of the Title and Appraisal businesses report many more problematic transactions when brokers are involved. . . . Brokers in Pennsylvania have a very low threshold of licensure and have no fiduciary responsibility to the borrower. . . . Although most states have some sort of licensure or registration, most do not require registration of employee originators nor do most have a continuing education requirement." More needs to be done both to regulate this activity and profession (the word is used loosely) and to induce its trade association, the National Association of Mortgage Brokers (www.namb.org), to play a more responsible role, through a code of ethics that is aggressively enforced, in the manner that the National Association of Realtors has taken serious steps to make its members aware of fair housing laws. Patricia McCoy offers a useful model from the world of finance: the "duty of suitability" imposed on securities brokers by the Securities and Exchange Commission, which provides a basis for aggrieved parties to sue for damages. A more general point is the need to foster additional litigation. Though they are costly and time-consuming; have outcomes that are increasingly unpredictable, given the rightward tilt of the judiciary; and lead to uncertain and protracted results even from favorable decisions, well-planned lawsuits are useful tools that create legitimacy, get publicity, and can be the basis for effective organizing.

Disclosure, Disclosure

Improved disclosure is of course the desideratum, given the inherent complexity of the home buying and home financing transaction, and both regulators and Congress (as well as state legislatures) have the power to do this. While, as Patricia McCoy remarks, "It is hard to imagine Congress mandating a disclosure scheme so starkly plain that victims would turn down abusive, irrational loans," we ought not to give up on that route. Maybe not the Congress or national administration in place at the time of this writing (mid-2004); but with more widespread knowledge of—and outrage at—these practices, and more political organizing, there is no reason to accept the proposition that genuine, effective reform cannot occur via legislative and administrative measures. The Securities and Exchange Commission does this quite well, as McCoy points out, with respect to capital markets; what is needed is to spread to our most vulnerable populations the kind of protection that government provides to wealthy (and even average) investors.

But as McCoy points out, even really good disclosure laws and regulations have limits—they do not ensure that nonpredatory loans will be available, and desperate people may be willing to take risks they shouldn't, if no other solution is available. And so the complementary step (which in itself might serve to drive out most predatory lenders) is to introduce programs that provide needed purchase and rehabilitation financing and refinancing geared to the capabilities and needs of borrowers (see below).

Research, Publicity

We need more and better studies of the borrowers and lenders. A good start is provided by John Taylor and his colleagues at the National Community Reinvestment Coalition (NCRC) in Chapter 2, "The Targets of Predatory and Discriminatory Lending: Who Are They and Where Do They Live?" More information about who the lenders are, their links, and their performance (with tools like the NCRC's *America's Best and Worst Lenders*) are highly useful. Such studies and ratings need to be disseminated not only to consumers, consumer groups, and credit counselors, but also to the wider community, in the hope that bad (as well as good) publicity about major financial institutions, intermediaries, and others can influence and change behavior. A particularly useful approach, embodied in NCRC's work, is to look at the issue through a racial lens. That nonprime lending can be shown to be more prevalent in areas where nonwhites predominate generates both public outcry (as with, for example, exposure of the "driving while black" phenomenon) and a possibility of legal action. Gender-related disparities (again documented in NCRC's work) provide yet another handle for effective organizing as well as possible litigation. Age-related data and possible age discrimination legal handles constitute yet another useful approach.

Case studies of individual cities are another useful tool, as illustrated by Ira Goldstein's Chapter 3, on Philadelphia. We need more of these, both to organize for change in specific locales and to document similarities as well as differences in how the predatory lending system operates around the country. Among the important, often neglected issues raised in the Philadelphia study, and alluded to above, is the deleterious impact on the surrounding neighborhood of abandoned buildings, many of which are the end product of the predatory lending process. Mortgage foreclosures themselves (apart from whether the building foreclosed on is temporarily or permanently abandoned) have negative impact on surrounding properties. Goldstein writes that a foreclosure can depress values in surrounding properties by as much as 20 percent.

Organize!

As Maude Hurd and Lisa Bonner's Chapter 6, "Community Organizing and Advocacy: Fighting Predatory Lending and Making a Difference," demonstrates, grassroots community organizing—starting with educating home owners and prospective home owners on the dangers and warning signs of abusive loans, moving to legislative lobbying, and incorporating targeted campaigns against particularly abusive lenders (often accompanied by theatrical direct action tactics like sit-ins and picketing the homes of key officials of abusive lenders—all guaranteed to generate television and newspaper coverage)—can play an effective role in highlighting abuses and bringing about reform. The story of ACORN's Household Finance campaign is impressive and instructive. (See also ACORN's February 2004 study, *Separate: Predatory Lending in America*.) Campaigns of this sort require both time and extraordinary organizing resources. They should be replicated in city after city; it remains to be seen whether ACORN and similar groups have the capacity to mount such efforts as widely as they are needed. Whether confrontational tactics will work or will produce a backlash is an open question. A senior vice president for community development banking at Bank of America Corp., speaking at a recent housing lenders' forum, was quoted as saying, in the spirit of the current administration: "You're either with us or against us. I don't want to hear one more community group tell me something negative and then ask me for $400,000 a week later. That just doesn't work anymore."[12]

Needed—*Federal* Action

As Keith Ernst and his colleagues document in their good treatment of legal and economic inducements to predatory lending (Chapter 5), the extensive deregulation of financial institutions, "an offspring of the troubled economic times of the 1970s and the early 1980s . . . a trend that continues to the present day," is a major piece of the context that provided opportunities—albeit most likely an unintended consequence—to introduce and expand predatory lending entities and practices. This was a big, big change—as they note, "traditionally, credit has been among the most regulated of products." And it was the introduction of (mostly hidden) fees, beyond interest charges, that provided both the real profits to the lenders and their agents, and the soon-to-be-revealed grief to the borrowers.

Congress and the regulatory agencies have acted frequently and powerfully in recent years on lending issues, for good and for bad with respect to the predatory lending issue. But as John Relman and his colleagues rightly assert in Chapter 7, "Designing Federal Legislation That Works: Legal Remedies for Predatory Lending," the current regulatory framework serves no one's interests—neither consumers nor civil rights advocates, not even the lenders: "New, comprehensive federal legislation to combat predatory lending is desperately needed." Their comprehensive review of federal and state laws and regulations makes that point compellingly. And their outline of what is needed by way of comprehensive remedies is right on target, dealing with each and every aspect of current defects: preemption, procedural and servicing issues, mandatory arbitration, flipping, and so on. They correctly point out that state-level reforms, in some cases, have provided useful models, but that "now the time has come for the hard part— meshing the progress that has been made at the local level with the best of the existing federal statutory scheme."

A current, and key, issue is federal preemption of state laws. This is a dicey, and more general, problem, for which there never is a consistent position: those in the civil rights movement certainly and successfully pushed for the feds to override the laws and powers of the southern states that were enforcing an apartheid system. On the other hand, there is real worry that federal preemption can undermine (and is designed to undermine) strong local and state measures. Not too long ago, federal legislation, pushed by the real estate industry and conservative members of Congress, was designed to withhold housing and community development funds from locales with rent control. In that same area, and moving down the government hierarchy a step, progressive housing activists defeated a move by the California legislature to enact a law limiting local rent control ordinances. In mid-2004, the Office of the Comptroller of the Currency (OCC) promulgated an anti–predatory lending standard for national banks that blocks enforcement of stricter state laws.

For those of us who are trying to fight predatory lending, the position is an obvious one: yes, let's have a federal standard strong enough to trump weak and inadequate state laws, but at the same time allow states to have laws and regulations that exceed the federal standard. Virtually the entire real estate industry—Mortgage Bankers Association, American Bankers Association, Consumer Bankers Association, Financial Services Roundtable, America's Community Bankers, Consumer Mortgage Coalition, National Association of Mortgage Brokers, National Home Equity Mortgage Association—supports a uniform national standard, but the one they support is a far cry from what John Relman and his associates, as well as the other contributors to this book, favor; and the reason for such unified (and politically powerful) industry support is largely motivated by an attempt to undercut or head off stronger action by states—North Carolina, New York, and New Jersey, for example—where activists like ACORN have made headway. On the other side, all 50 state attorneys general have signed a letter opposing the OCC move—again, not necessarily because of motives consistent with predatory lending opponents, but because of states' rights principles.[13]

Globalization and Human Rights

Returning to Lee's observations about the relationship of economic globalization to the predatory lending epidemic, he raises the interesting, and potentially effective, point that beyond consumer protection and financial soundness concerns, predatory lending is a human rights issue, and thus amenable to treatment/remedy under one of several international covenants. While this is an innovative and imaginative approach, there are of course limits on what can be done in that arena, in particular in the current environment, given the administration's attitude toward internationalism—somewhere between disregard and contempt. Some organizing and public education work in other arenas—sweatshop labor, for example—does offer a possibly more roseate prospect. One clear need, as Relman et al. point out, is "the continuing need for anti–predatory lending analysis, organizing and advocacy that look beyond the United States."

The Real Solution—Housing Programs

But the real need—to bypass/avoid predatory lending altogether—is better, more socially progressive programs to aid home owners in trouble and avoid foreclosure. While there are some people who merit the all too loosely used term "deadbeats"—that is, those who can pay but simply are trying to avoid their obligations—the overwhelming majority of home owners in trouble are in that situation due to genuine hardship, most often with a cause outside their control: illness or injury, loss of employment, and such. We must ask whether it is in society's interest to allow the normal workings of the free market to displace hundreds of thousands of home owners each year; it certainly is not in the interest of the families themselves, for it leads to massive disruptions in social networks and children's schooling, emotional turmoil, family stress and breakup, and often outright home-lessness—this last result in turn leading to nontrivial costs the society must bear.[14]

There are model programs, for home owners, as well as renters, to prevent eviction and loss of home through mortgage foreclosure. Ira Goldstein cites as examples the Commonwealth of Pennsylvania's Homeowners' Emergency Mortgage Assistance Program (http://www.phfa.org/pro grams/hemap), as well as the City of Philadelphia's two loan products, "designed to make credit available to people with less than perfect credit, in amounts not exceeding need, and at reasonable rates." Additionally, the Home Equity Loan Preservation Program (administered by a housing counseling association, ACORN, and Goldstein's Reinvestment Fund) was created to refinance those people who have fallen victim to abusive lending practices.[15] Such programs require funding (although not in vast amounts) and good counseling services, but the social and human payoff is well worth it.

The Bigger Picture

A multipronged, comprehensive approach clearly is needed if we are to eliminate the scourge of predatory lending. And the quicker we get it, the less suffering for those who are already suffering too much and the better it will be for our communities.

We need to see the phenomenon within and in relation to the broader contexts outlined above. We have to see the issue as part of a broader need to create housing stability for all, home owners and renters alike, the social and personal benefits of which are irrefutable. And moving to a higher level, we need to be working to create a right to housing—beyond the scope of this book, but something we need to think about and work on.[16]

NOTES

1. Imaginative opportunities for predatory behavior emerge constantly. A new wrinkle was brought to my attention in a recent *Washington Post* article: Mary Beth Sheridan, "District Clears Out Illegal Pay Phones," *Washington Post*, April 8, 2004. Companies illegally (i.e., without city permits) install pay phones in neighborhoods populated by low-income and minority, especially immigrant, residents, where cell phones and home-based phones are largely absent. "Many such consumers use phone cards and don't realize the high fees they are charged for using the illegal phones." According to Washington's director of the Downtown Cluster of Congregations, "The phone companies put the [illegal] pay phones in certain areas: around bus stops, near bodegas, wherever immigrants and cash-economy people [congregate]. . . . They're making huge profits."

2. Michael Moss and Andrew Jacobs, "Blue Skies and Green Yards, All Lost to Red Ink," *New York Times*, April 11, 2004. See also Nancy Denton, "Housing as a Means of Asset Accumulation: A Good Strategy for the Poor?" in Thomas M.

Shapiro and Edward N. Wolff, eds., *Assets for the Poor: The Benefits of Spreading Asset Ownership* (New York: Russell Sage Foundation, 2001).

3. Robert Schafer and Charles G. Field, "Section 235 of the National Housing Act: Homeownership for Low-Income Families?" in Jon Pynoos, Robert Schafer, and Chester W. Hartman, eds., *Housing Urban America*, 2nd ed. (Hawthorne, NY: Aldine, 1980).

4. U.S. General Accounting Office, "Consumer Protection: Federal and State Agencies Face Challenges in Combating Predatory Lending," GAO-040412T (Washington, D.C.: GAO, 2004).

5. Melvin L. Oliver and Thomas M. Shapiro, *Black Wealth/White Wealth* (New York: Routledge, 1995).

6. Thomas M. Shapiro, *The Hidden Cost of Being African American: How Wealth Perpetuates Inequality* (New York: Oxford University Press, 2004).

7. Robert Manning, "Poverty, Race and the Two-Tiered Financial System," *Poverty and Race* 8, no. 4 (July/August 1999); Noah Sawyer and Kenneth Temkin, *Analysis of Alternative Financial Service Providers* (Washington, D.C.: The Urban Institute, 2004).

8. "Banking on Local Communities," *New York Times*, April 14, 2004.

9. Caroline E. Mayer, "'Alarming Abuses' in Credit Counseling," *Washington Post*, March 24, 2004, referring to U.S. Senate Permanent Subcommittee on Investigations, "Profiteering in a Non-Profit Industry: Abusive Practices in Credit Counseling."

10. Ibid.

11. Leonard S. Rubinowitz and James E. Rosenbaum, *Crossing the Class and Color Lines: From Public Housing to White Suburbia* (Chicago: University of Chicago Press, 2000).

12. ncrcnews@ncrc.org (February 17, 2004).

13. Dennis Hevesi, "Looser U.S. Lending Rules Are Protested," *New York Times*, April 2, 2004.

14. Chester Hartman and David Robinson, "Evictions: The Hidden Housing Problem," *Housing Policy Debate* 14, no. 4 (Winter 2003); Chester Hartman and Todd Michael Franke, guest eds., "Student Mobility: How Some Children Get Left Behind," *Journal of Negro Education* 72, no. 1 (Winter 2003); Poverty & Race Research Action Council, *Fragmented: Improving Education for Mobile Students* (Washington, D.C.: PRRAC, 2003).

15. For information about similar programs, see Hartman and Robinson, "Evictions."

16. Chester Hartman, "The Case for a Right to Housing in the United States," in Scott Leckie, ed., *National Perspectives on Housing Rights* (The Hague: Martinus Nijhoff, 2003).

Appendix:
Resources on Predatory Lending

The following organizations are involved in research, advocacy, and consumer services pertaining to predatory lending and related economic justice issues.

The American Association of Retired Persons (AARP) is a nonprofit membership organization dedicated to addressing the needs and interests of persons 50 and older. Through information and education, advocacy and service, AARP seeks to enhance the quality of life for all by promoting independence, dignity, and purpose.

AARP
601 East Street, NW, Suite A9
Washington, DC 20049
Phone: 1 (888) 687-2277
E-mail: member@aarp.org
Web site: http://www.aarp.org/

The Association of Community Organizations for Reform Now (ACORN) is the nation's largest community organization of low- and moderate-income families, with over 120,000 member families organized into 600 neighborhood chapters in 45 cities across the country. Since 1970 ACORN has taken action and won victories on issues of concern to its members. Priorities include better housing for first-time home buyers and tenants, living wages for low-wage workers, more investment in our communities from banks and governments, and better public schools. It achieves these goals by building community organizations that have the power to win changes—through direct action, negotiation, legislation, and voter participation.

The Association of Community Organizations for Reform Now (ACORN)
88 3rd Avenue
Brooklyn, NY 11217

Phone: (877) 55ACORN or (718) 246-7900
Fax: 718-246-7939
E-mail: natexdirect@acorn.org
Web site: http://acorn.org/whoisacorn/

The Brookings Institution Metropolitan Policy Program seeks to shape a new generation of urban policies that will help build strong neighborhoods, cities, and metropolitan regions. In partnership with academics, private- and public-sector leaders, and locally elected officials, the Center informs the national debate about the impact of government policies, private-sector actions, and national trends on cities and their metropolitan areas. By connecting expert knowledge and practical experience to the deliberations of state and federal policy makers, the Center aims to help develop integrated approaches and practical solutions to the challenges confronting these communities.

Metropolitan Policy Program
The Brookings Institution
1775 Massachusetts Avenue, NW
Washington, DC 20036
Phone: (202) 797-6139
Fax: (202) 797-2965
E-mail: urbancenter@brookings.edu
Web site: http://www.brookings.org/metro/

The California Reinvestment Committee works to revitalize California's low-income and minority communities by increasing access to credit and deposit services. CRC's approach to stimulate lending and investment began with the negotiation of written commitments from California's major banks. CRC has expanded its programs to include the publishing of reports, research on the financial services industry for public education purposes, the provision of technical assistance to local communities, and participation in the state and federal policy arena.

California Reinvestment Committee
474 Valencia Street Suite 110
San Francisco, CA 94103
Phone: (415) 864-3980
Fax: (415) 864-3981
E-mail: info@calreinvest.org
Web site: http://www.calreinvest.org/index.html

The Center for Community Change (CCC) is committed to reducing poverty and rebuilding low-income communities. To do this, CCC helps people to develop the skills and resources they need to improve their communities as well as change policies and institutions that adversely affect their lives. CCC believes that poor people themselves—through organizations they control—need to lead efforts to eliminate poverty.

Washington, D.C., Office
The Center for Community Change

1000 Wisconsin Avenue, NW
Washington, DC 20007
Phone: (202) 342-0567
Fax: (202) 333-5462
E-mail: info@communitychange.org
Web site: http://www.communitychange.org/default.asp

The Center for Responsible Lending is dedicated to the principles of fair lending, including equitable treatment of all borrowers, fair and reasonable financing terms, accurate loan servicing, and a commitment to building up disadvantaged communities. It was formed in early 1999 and currently includes some 80 organizations with over 3 million members. Individual members include120 CEOs of financial institutions and 200 housing, community development, consumer, and religious leaders. Major organizational members include AARP-NC, NC NAACP, NC Equity, NC Consumers Council, NC Association of Realtors, NC Credit Union League, and 21 local Habitat for Humanity affiliates.

The Center for Responsible Lending
P.O. Box 3619
Durham, NC 27702
Phone: (919) 956-4485
Fax: (919) 956-4605
E-mail: sharon.reuss@responsiblelending.org
Web site: http://www.responsiblelending.org/

CEOs for Cities is a national bipartisan alliance of mayors, corporate executives, university presidents, and nonprofit leaders. Its mission is to advance the economic competitiveness of cities.

CEOs for Cities
One Post Office Square, Suite 1600
Boston, MA 02109
Phone: (617) 451-5747
Fax: (617) 451-0075
E-mail: jziemba@ceosforcities.org
Web site: http://www.ceosforcities.org/

The Community Reinvestment Association of North Carolina (CRA-NC) is a nonprofit agency seeking to build and protect wealth in North Carolina communities. CRA-NC works to improve financial institutions' services to all North Carolina citizens. It is a member of the Coalition for Responsible Lending (CRL), an alliance of financial institutions and other North Carolinians dedicated to the following principles of responsible lending: borrower choice, reasonable fees, disclosure, competition, and enforcement. We encourage other organizations dedicated to these principles to join CRL and help end predatory lending in North Carolina.

CRA-NC
114 W. Parrish Street, 2nd floor
P.O. Box 1929

Durham, NC 27702-1929
Phone: (919) 667-1557
Fax: (919) 667-9987
Web site: http://www.cra-nc.org/default.htm

The Consumer Federation of America (CFA) is an advocacy and education organization working to advance pro-consumer policy on a variety of issues before Congress, the White House, federal and state regulatory agencies, and the courts. Its staff works with public officials to promote beneficial policies, to oppose harmful policies, and to ensure a balanced debate on important issues in which consumers have a stake.

The Consumer Federation of America
1424 16th Street NW, Suite 604
Washington, DC 20036
Phone: (202) 387-6121
E-mail: melhc@consumerfed.org
Web site: http://www.consumerfed.org/backpage/about.html

Consumers Union, publisher of *Consumer Reports,* is an independent, nonprofit testing and information organization serving only consumers. It is a comprehensive source for unbiased advice about products and services, personal finance, health and nutrition, and other consumer concerns.

Washington, D.C., Office
Consumers Union
1666 Connecticut Avenue, NW, Suite 310
Washington, DC 20009-1039
Phone: (202) 462-6262
Fax: (202) 265-9548
E-mail: http://www.consunion.org/contact.htm
Web site: http://www.consumersunion.org/aboutcu/about.htm

The Economic Policy Institute provides high-quality research and education in order to promote a prosperous, fair, and sustainable economy. It stresses real-world analysis and a concern for the living standards of working people, and it makes its findings accessible to the general public, the media, and policy makers.

Economic Policy Institute
1660 L Street, NW, Suite 1200
Washington, DC 20036
Phone: (202) 775-8810
Fax: (202) 775-0819
E-mail: epi@epinet.org
Web site: http://www.epinet.org/

The Fannie Mae Foundation creates affordable home ownership and housing opportunities through innovative partnerships and initiatives that build healthy, vibrant communities across the United States. It is specially committed to improving the quality of life for the people of its hometown, Washington, D.C., and to enhancing the livability of the city's neighborhoods.

Fannie Mae Foundation Headquarters
4000 Wisconsin Avenue, NW, North Tower, Suite One
Washington, DC 20016-2804
Phone: (202) 274-8000
Fax: (202) 274-8100
Web site: http://www.fanniemaefoundation.org/

Ford Foundation Asset Building and Community Development Program helps
strengthen and increase the effectiveness of people and organizations working to
find solutions to problems of poverty and injustice. Sixty-five staff members focus
grant resources on six fields in three program units in New York and abroad.

Ford Foundation Headquarters
320 East 43rd Street
New York, NY 10017
Phone: (212) 573-5000
Fax: (212) 351-3677
E-mail: office-of-communications@fordfound.org
Web site: http://www.fordfound.org/

The Greenlining Institute is dedicated to improving the quality of life for low-
income and minority communities. Among the tools that Greenlining uses to
achieve its mission are leadership development, community organizing, research,
policy analysis, litigation, negotiation, media relations, and traditional civil
rights tactics. In essence, Greenlining is an advocacy oriented think tank that or-
ganizes, educates, and encourages equitable public policies for low-income and
minority communities. The ultimate goal of the institute is to increase low-
income and minority participation in policy-making that results in equitable policies that will improve the quality of life for all communities in California and
nationwide.

The Greenlining Institute
1918 University Avenue, 2nd floor
Berkeley, CA 94704
Phone: (510) 926-4000
Fax: (510) 926-4010
E-mail: questions@greenlining.org
Web site: http://www.greenlining.org/about/index.html

Inner City Press/Community on the Move (ICP) is a nonprofit community, consumers', and civil rights organization headquartered in the South Bronx of New
York City that is engaged in advocacy, reporting, and organizing in the fields of
community reinvestment, fair access to credit, insurance and telecommunications,
environmental justice, and government and corporate accountability.

Inner City Press/Community on the Move and Inner City Public Interest Law
Center
P.O. Box 580188 Mount Carmel Station
Bronx, NY 10458
Phone: (718) 716-3540

Fax: (718) 716-3161
E-mail: info@innercitypress.org
Web site: http://www.innercitypress.org/aboutus.html

Local Initiative Support Corporation (LISC) provides grants, loans, and equity investments to Community Development Corporations (CDCs) for neighborhood redevelopment. When LISC begins a new program, National LISC matches locally raised funds and gives that much more to the community for renovation. The CDC then designates the funds to a variety of projects that will best suit the neighborhood, and the renovation begins.

LISC Headquarters
501 7th Avenue
New York, NY 10018
Phone: (212) 455-9800
Fax: (212) 682-5929
Web site: http://www.lisc.org/

The National Community Reinvestment Coalition (NCRC), a coalition of more than 800 nonprofit organizations, is at the vanguard of a growing community reinvestment movement in which community leaders from across the nation, in urban and rural areas, are becoming educated about, and active in, efforts on how to affect the flow of credit and the provision of banking services in their neighborhoods. NCRC has worked to make community reinvestment activism a common local occurrence and to promote increased community–lender partnerships.

National Community Reinvestment Coalition
733 15th Street, NW, Suite 540
Washington, DC 20005
Phone: (202) 628-8866
Fax: (202) 628-9800
Web site: http://www.ncrc.org/

The National Consumer Law Center (NCLC) is the nation's consumer law expert, helping consumers, their advocates, and public policy makers use powerful and complex consumer laws on behalf of low-income and elderly Americans seeking economic justice. It addresses the financial and legal problems faced daily by low-income families—repossessions, debt collection abuses, electronic benefits transfers, home improvement frauds, usury, bankruptcy, utility terminations, school loans, payday loans, sustainable home ownership, inadequate fuel assistance benefits, and more. In doing so, NCLC helps vulnerable consumers resolve financial crises, gain control over their budgets, and achieve economic independence.

National Consumer Law Center
77 Summer Street, 10th floor
Boston, MA 02110
Phone: (617) 542-8010

Fax: (617) 542-8028
E-mail: nclc@consumerlaw.org
Web site: http://www.consumerlaw.org/about/

The National Fair Housing Alliance (NFHA) is the voice of fair housing. NFHA works to eliminate housing discrimination and to ensure equal housing opportunity for all people through leadership, education and outreach, membership services, public policy initiatives, advocacy, and enforcement.

National Fair Housing Alliance
1212 New York Avenue, Suite 525
Washington, DC 20005
Phone: (202) 898-1661
Fax: (202) 371-9744
E-mail: nfha@nationalfairhousing.org
Web site: http://www.nationalfairhousing.org/Index.htm

National Training and Information Center (NTIC) is a multiethnic, multiracial coalition of community organizations. NTIC's mission is to build grassroots leadership and strengthen neighborhoods through issue-based community organizing. NTIC believes that residents have the ability to identify and resolve the issues in their neighborhoods. What they need are the skills and opportunities to do so. NTIC helps build powerful leadership-driven organizations with the capacity to (a) identify local issues, (b) develop effective strategies to address the root causes of issues, and (c) create opportunities for the organizational leadership to negotiate with decision makers.

National Training and Information Center
810 N. Milwaukee Avenue
Chicago, IL 60622
Phone: (312) 243-3035
Fax: (312) 243-7044
E-mail: NTIC@NTIC-US.ORG
Web site: http://www.ntic-us.org/about/about.htm

The Neighborhood Reinvestment Corporation was created under Title VI of the Housing and Community Development Amendments of 1978, P.L. 95-557, to implement and expand the demonstration activities of the Urban Reinvestment Task Force. The principal purpose of the corporation is "to revitalize older urban neighborhoods by mobilizing public, private, and community resources at the neighborhood level."

The Neighborhood Reinvestment Corporation
1325 G Street, NW, Suite 800
Washington, DC 20005-3100
Phone: (202) 220-2300
Fax: (202) 376-2600
E-mail: nw.org
Web site: http://www.nw.org/network/HomeMAC.asp

The Poverty and Race Research Action Council is a nonpartisan, national, nonprofit organization with a diverse board of directors and staff, and was convened in 1990 by major civil rights, civil liberties, and anti-poverty groups. PRRAC's mission is to generate, gather, and disseminate information regarding the relationship between race and poverty, and to promote the development and implementation of policies and practices that alleviate conditions caused by the interaction of race and poverty.

The Poverty and Race Research Action Council
3000 Connecticut Avenue, NW, Suite 200
Washington, DC 20008
Phone: (202) 387-9887
Fax: (202) 387-0764
E-mail: info@prrac.org
Web site: http://www.prrac.org/abtprrac.htm

The Reinvestment Fund's (TRF) mission is to alleviate poverty by building assets, wealth, and opportunity for low- and moderate-income communities and persons. TRF accomplishes its mission through the strategic use of capital, knowledge, and innovation.

The Reinvestment Fund
718 Arch Street, 300 N
Philadelphia, PA 19106
Phone: (215) 574-5800
Fax: (215) 574-5900
E-mail: contactus@TRFund.com
Web site: http://www.trfund.com/who/index.html

Self-Help is a community development lender that has provided over $2.5 billion in financing to 25,800 home buyers, small businesses, and nonprofits. Self-Help reaches people who are underserved by conventional lenders—particularly minorities, women, rural residents, and low-wealth families—through the support of socially responsible citizens and institutions across the United States.

Self-Help
P.O. Box 3619
Durham, NC 27702
Phone: 1 (800) 476-7428
E-mail: webmaster@self-help.org
Web site: http://www.self-help.org/

The Urban Institute's Center on Metropolitan Housing and Communities focuses on the neighborhoods, cities, and suburbs that make up America's urban regions, investigating forces that affect quality of life in these communities, access to opportunities they offer residents, and impacts of public policies. The center is a primary sponsor of the National Neighborhood Indicators Partnership.

The Urban Institute's Center on Metropolitan Housing and Communities
2100 M Street, NW

Washington, DC 20037
Phone: (202) 833-7200
Fax: (202) 872-9322
E-mail: paffairs@ui.urban.org
Web site: http://www.urban.org/content/PolicyCenters/Housing_Communities/Over
view.htm

U.S. Public Interest Research Group (U.S. PIRG) speaks for the public interest against the special interests, on issues in the news and below the surface. It addresses issues where consumers are victims of private greed, average citizens suffer from the absence of government attention or an excess of government bureaucracy, and the natural environment is threatened. As a public-interest watchdog organization, it uncovers dangers to public health and well-being and fights to end them, using the tools of investigative research, media exposés, grassroots organizing, advocacy, and litigation.

U.S. PIRG
218 D Street, SE
Washington, DC 20003
Phone: (202) 546-9707
Fax: (202) 546-2461
E-mail: uspirg@pirg.org
Web site: http://uspirg.org/uspirg.asp?id2=5729&id3=USPIRG&

The Woodstock Institute is a research and policy advocacy organization that works with community organizations, financial institutions, and regulatory agencies on mortgage and small business lending, community development, and related reinvestment initiatives.

The Woodstock Institute
407 S. Dearborn, Suite 550
Chicago, IL 60605
Phone: (312) 427-8070
Fax: (312) 427-4007
E-mail: woodstock@woodstockinst.org
Web site: http://woodstockinst.org/

Index

About the Editor and Contributors

GREGORY D. SQUIRES is a professor of sociology and chair of the Department of Sociology at George Washington University. Currently he is a member of the board of directors of the Woodstock Institute and the advisory board of the John Marshall Law School Fair Housing Legal Support Center in Chicago. He has served as a consultant and expert witness for fair housing groups and civil rights organizations around the country and as a member of the Consumer Advisory Council of the Federal Reserve Board. He has written for several academic journals and general interest publications including *Social Science Quarterly*, *Urban Affairs Review*, *Journal of Urban Affairs*, the *New York Times*, and the *Washington Post*. His recent books include *Insurance Redlining* (1997), *Color and Money*, with Sally O'Connor (2001), *Urban Sprawl: Causes, Consequences, and Policy Responses* (2002), and *Organizing Access to Capital: Advocacy and the Democratization of Financial Institutions* (2003).

DAVID BERENBAUM serves as the National Community Reinvestment Coalition's senior vice president for policy and director of civil rights. Mr. Berenbaum coordinates NCRC's National Consumer Rescue Fund to refinance problematic mortgages held by victims of predatory lending and NCRC's subprime fair-lending testing compliance initiatives. He has testified before Congress on fair-lending issues and coauthored several NCRC research and resource publications. Mr. Berenbaum has served as the executive director of the Equal Rights Center/Fair Housing Council of Greater Washington and Long Island Housing Services.

LISA DONNER is the director of the ACORN Financial Justice Center, and has managed ACORN's campaign against predatory lending. From 1996 to 2002 she was ACORN's legislative director, and then campaign director. Before joining ACORN she served as an organizer for the Service Employees International Union. She is a graduate of Harvard University.

KEITH ERNST serves as an assistant general counsel to the Self-Help Credit Union and senior policy counsel at the Center for Responsible Lending. He has worked on regulatory compliance issues and provided analytic support to the organization's secondary-market program. Presently, he spends the bulk of his time providing technical assistance to state and federal policy makers and engaging in federal administrative advocacy on financial issues. In addition, he was lead author on the Center for Responsible Lending's 2002 report "North Carolina Subprime Home Loan Market After Predatory Lending Reform," the first study to examine the effect of North Carolina's landmark reform after its implementation.

DEBORAH N. GOLDSTEIN serves as an assistant general counsel to the Self-Help Credit Union and senior policy counsel at the Center for Responsible Lending. She provides technical assistance to policy makers, community groups, and financial institutions on state and federal anti-predatory lending initiatives. In 1999, she was an Emerging Leaders fellow at the Neighborhood Reinvestment Corporation and the Harvard University Joint Center for Housing Studies, where she researched and published a report titled "Predatory Lending: Defining the Problem and Moving Toward Workable Solutions." The report was published as a note in the Winter 2000 issue of the *Harvard Civil Rights–Civil Liberties Law Review*.

IRA GOLDSTEIN is The Reinvestment Fund's (TRF) director of public policy and program assessment. TRF is a regional development finance institution dedicated to building wealth and opportunity for low-wealth communities and low- and moderate-income individuals through the promotion of socially and environmentally responsible development. Prior to joining TRF, Mr. Goldstein was the Mid-Atlantic regional director of Fair Housing and Equal Opportunity for the U.S. Department of Housing and Urban Development. Mr. Goldstein holds a Ph.D. in sociology and has published numerous articles and book chapters primarily related to urban issues. He is a Lecturer at the University of Pennsylvania, where, for more than ten years, he has taught quantitative research methods.

CHESTER HARTMAN is director of research for the Poverty & Race Research Action Council in Washington, D.C. (where he served as founding executive director from 1990 to 2003) and adjunct professor in the Department of Sociology at George Washington University. Prior to taking his present positions, he was a fellow of the Institute for Policy Studies in Washington and of the Transnational Institute in Amsterdam. He has written 17 books; published in a wide variety of social science and law journals, including *The Nation, Journal of the American Planning Association*, and *University of Wisconsin Law Review*; and served or is serving on the editorial boards of several scholarly publications, including *Journal of Urban Affairs, Housing Policy Debate, Urban Affairs Quarterly, Housing Studies*, and *Journal of Negro Education*. He has also served as a board member of the National Low Income Housing Coalition and as a consultant to numerous public and private agencies, including HUD, the U.S. Civil Rights Commission, Stanford Research Institute, Arthur D. Little, California Rural Legal Assistance, the Urban Coalition, the California Department of Housing and Community Development, and the Legal Aid Society of New York.

MAUDE HURD has been the national president of ACORN since 1990, and a member of Boston ACORN's Dorchester United since 1982, serving as its co-chair. In her role as ACORN national president, an elected, nonpaying position, Hurd has both led local and national campaigns to win justice for low-income families, and developed and mentored hundreds of grassroots community leaders. Hurd lives in Dorchester, Massachusetts, where she works as a substance-abuse prevention specialist at the Medical Foundation. Under her leadership, ACORN has become a critical force in campaigns for economic and racial justice across the country, and has grown to over 150,000 member families in 65 cities.

MATTHEW LEE is a community activist and public interest lawyer. He founded Inner City Press/Community on the Move (ICP), a community organization, in the South Bronx of New York City in 1987. ICP's Community Reinvestment Act advocacy has resulted in four new bank branches, and $200 million in new lending commitments, in the South Bronx. ICP's broader CRA challenges have resulted in over $10 billion in new lending and consumer protection commitments. Lee is the author of *Predatory Bender: Toxic Credit in the Global Inner City* (2004); he has written for publications including *U.S. Banker*, the *New York Times*, *Newsday* and the *Amsterdam News*. Since 1997, he has engaged in advocacy against predatory lending, including beyond the United States, using human rights laws, through the Fair Finance Watch project.

PATRICIA A. McCOY is a professor at the University of Connecticut School of Law and a member of the law school's Insurance Law Center. Before entering academe in 1992, she was partner at Mayer, Brown, Rowe & Maw in Washington, D.C., where she specialized in complex securities, banking, and commercial litigation at the trial and appellate levels. A noted authority on federal banking law and mortgage lending, she is author of *Banking Law Manual: Federal Regulation of Financial Holding Companies, Banks and Thrifts* (2nd ed. 2000) and editor of *Financial Modernization After Gramm-Leach-Bliley* (2002). Professor McCoy has served on the Consumer Advisory Council of the Board of Governors of the Federal Reserve, as well as on the board of directors of the Insurance Marketplace Standards Association. In 2001, she was chair of the Section on Financial Institutions and Consumer Financial Services of the Association of American Law Schools.

CLARENCE PAGE has been a columnist and member of the editorial board of the *Chicago Tribune* since 1984. His commentary on social, economic, and political issues is syndicated to over 200 newspapers nationwide. A lifelong journalist and author, he is the author of several books, including *Showing My Color: Impolite Essays on Race and Identity* (1996); he has published articles in *Chicago Magazine*, *Chicago Reader*, *Washington Monthly*, *New Republic*, *Wall Street Journal*, and *New York Newday*; and serves as a panelist/commentator for news programs, including "The McLauglin Group," BET's "Lead Story," ABC's "This Week," and National Public Radio's "Weekend Sunday." A recipient of the 1989 Pulitzer Prize for commentary, he was inducted into the Chicago Journalism Hall of Fame in 1992.

CAMELLIA PHILLIPS is ACORN's assistant director of development. Phillips has worked with ACORN since 2001, helping community organizers around the country raise funds for projects ranging from community-based childhood lead poisoning prevention programs to anti-predatory lending and fair-housing projects. Previously, she worked in various capacities with the National Network for Immigrant and Refugee Rights and the Whatcom County Youth Empowerment Co-op.

JOHN P. RELMAN is the director of Relman & Associates, PLLC, a public interest law firm in Washington, D.C., specializing in civil rights litigation. From 1989 to 1999, he headed the Fair Housing Project at the Washington Lawyers' Committee for Civil Rights. Mr. Relman's better-known cases include *Timus v. William J. Davis, Inc.* ($2.4 million jury verdict for housing discrimination); *Dyson v. Denny's Restaurants* ($17.725 million race discrimination class settlement); *Pugh v. Avis Rent-A-Car* ($5.4 million class settlement); and *Gilliam v. Adam's Mark Hotels* ($2.1 million class settlement). Mr. Relman is the author of *Housing Discrimination Practice Manual*, and teaches public interest law at Georgetown University Law Center. He has written and lectured extensively in the areas of fair-housing and fair-lending law and practice, and has conducted numerous training classes and seminars for plaintiffs' lawyers, fair-housing organizations, the real estate industry, and lending institutions. He received his law degree from the University of Michigan and his undergraduate degree from Harvard University.

CHRISTOPHER A. RICHARDSON is an economist in the Housing and Civil Enforcement Section of the Department of Justice's Civil Rights Division. He contributed to this book while he was a senior research fellow at the Center for Responsible Lending, the nonprofit affiliate of the Self-Help Credit Union, a community development lender that has provided more than $2.5 billion in financing to over 25,000 home buyers, small businesses, and nonprofit organizations. Previously, Richardson was a staff economist in the Federal Deposit Insurance Corporation's Division of Research and Statistics (now the Division of Insurance and Research). Richardson has published research on predatory lending and the Community Reinvestment Act in *Housing Policy Debate* and *Fordham Urban Law Journal*.

FRED RIVERA is a partner at the Seattle-based law firm Perkins Coie, where he specializes in civil litigation concerning consumer financial services, equal housing and employment opportunity, complex construction disputes, and other commercial litigation. Mr. Rivera represents lenders in litigation concerning consumer compliance and protection laws and government investigations, in addition to advising lenders on a broad range of fair-lending issues. Before joining Perkins Coie, he was a senior trial attorney in the Civil Rights Division of the U.S. Department of Justice. In 1997 he received the Attorney General's Special Achievement Award for his litigation work on *United States v. Chevy Chase FSB* (redlining) and *United States v. First National Bank of Donna Anna County* (underwriting discrimination). Mr. Rivera has been a speaker at a number of conferences concerning fair-housing and fair-lending issues. He is the current president of the Washington Hispanic Bar Association and is on the board of directors of the Fair Housing Center of South Puget Sound.

SHILPA S. SATOSKAR is an attorney at Relman & Associates, PLLC. Prior to joining Relman & Associates, Ms. Satoskar practiced in the civil rights and class actions group at Gessler Hughes Socol Piers Resnick & Dym in Chicago, and at the Washington, D.C., office of Jenner and Block. She received her law degree from Harvard Law School, where she served as an articles editor for the *Harvard Civil Rights–Civil Liberties Law Review*, and received her undergraduate degree from the University of Michigan.

JOSH SILVER is vice president of research and policy of the National Community Reinvestment Coalition. He develops NCRC's policy positions, writes congressional testimony, and produces research studies on community reinvestment and the role of financial institutions. Major NCRC reports coauthored by Mr. Silver are "The Broken Credit System: Discrimination and Unequal Access to Affordable Loans by Race and Age," "The Performance of GSEs at the Metropolitan Level," "America's Best and Worst Lender's," and "CRA Commitments." In his technical advisory role, Mr. Silver helps community organizations devise neighborhood reinvestment strategies and interpret HMDA and CRA data on lending activity. He was a policy analyst at the Urban Institute for five years before coming to NCRC. He has 14 years of experience in the housing and community development field.

JOHN TAYLOR is president and chief executive officer of the National Community Reinvestment Coalition. Raised in the housing projects of Boston and trained as an attorney, he has dedicated his life to economic justice. In over 25 years in the field, he has received numerous local, state, and national awards, including the Martin Luther King Jr. Peace Award; a U.S. congressional citation (twice); the State of Massachusetts Award for community economic development; and a presidential appointment to the CDFI Fund. Taylor has served on numerous national boards, including the Consumer Advisory Council of the Federal Reserve Board, the Fannie Mae Housing Impact Division, and the Freddie Mac Housing Advisory Board. He has appeared on ABC's "Nightline," CBS, Fox news, CNN, CSPAN, in the *New York Times*, *Washington Post*, and *Chicago Tribune*; and hundreds of other print, television, and radio media.

MEERA TREHAN is an attorney at Relman & Associates, PLLC. Prior to joining Relman & Associates, Ms. Trehan was an attorney at Altshuler, Berzon, Nussbaum, Rubin & Demain in San Francisco. She received her law degree from Stanford Law School, where she served as an article editor for the *Stanford Law Review*, and her undergraduate degree from the University of Virginia.